# Dissociative Disorders

# Dissociative Disorders: A Clinical Review

Edited by David Spiegel, M.D.

The Sidran Press
2328 West Joppa Road
Suite 15
Lutherville, MD 21093
(410) 825-8888

Permission was granted by American Psychiatric Press, Inc. to reprint this material from *Review of Psychiatry, Volume 10, 1991,* edited by Allan Tasman, M.D. and Stephen M. Goldfinger, M.D.

International Standard Book Number: 0-9629164-1-2
Library of Congress Card Catalogue Number: 92-082037
Printed in the United States of America

Dissociative disorders : a clinical review / edited by David Spiegel.
p. cm.
Preassigned LCCN: 92-082037.
ISBN 0-9629164-1-2

1. Dissociation (Psychology)    I. Spiegel, David, 1945-

RC553.D5D57 1993                616.852'3
                                QBI93-20019

Dissociative
Disorders:
A Clinical
Review

# Contents

# *Dissociative Disorders*
# Introduction

This state-of-the-art review of the field of dissociative disorders was published in 1991 as part of the American Psychiatric Press' annual *Review of Psychiatry (Volume 10)*. American Psychiatric concurred with our assessment of the need to make this vital information available to a broader audience, and generously granted permission for Sidran to reprint this section of the *Review* in an inexpensive paperback edition. We are most grateful.

Because this collection of articles was prepared by psychiatric professionals for psychiatric professionals, the language is understandably specialized. That having been said, the information included here is simultaneously basic and inclusive, encompassing: definitions of terms, epidemiology (studies of incidence and distribution), etiology (studies of cause), the courses of the disorders, and treatment approaches. The contributors are stellar practitioners and researchers with extensive experience in the specialty of dissociation.

By making this concise review more easily available to lay readers as well as to non-specialist therapy and service providers, we hope to foster understanding and help demystify dissociative disorders.

Esther Giller
The Sidran Foundation

# Dissociative Disorders
# Preface

*by David Spiegel, M.D., Editor*

Unity of consciousness is an achievement, not a given. From this point of view, dissociative phenomena are not an oddity but rather a central problem in the study of psychopathology. The issue is no longer why dissociative symptoms occur; it becomes rather why they do not occur more often. The continuity of experience, memory, and identity is an accomplishment. The complexity of mental processing requires that most of it occur out of consciousness, making it possible if not probable that certain perceptions and memories may seem dis-integrated.

The phenomena of dissociation have themselves been dissociated from the mainstream of psychiatry and psychiatric theory despite origins at the heart of early psychiatric and psychological thought. William James, Boris Sidis, Morton Prince, Joseph Breuer, Sigmund Freud, and Pierre Janet based their diverse but influential theories of psychological functioning in large measure on their observations of dissociation and its effects. Despite this history, the phenomenon has been viewed as something of an oddity in psychiatry, causing many to doubt the validity of the disorders.

Dissociation is here to stay. The chapters that follow indicate that there is a growing body of clinical observation and research documenting the prevalence, phenomenology, psychophysiology, and treatment of dissociation. Dr. Putnam reviews the phenomenology of dissociation, underscoring the fact that dissociation is a normal as well as a pathological phenomenon. Dr. Kluft skillfully reviews the rapidly growing literature on multiple personality disorder, distilling what is known about the etiology of this rare and intriguing disorder in summarizing the principles of treatment, with an emphasis on using various techniques to access and integrate these dissociated mental states in the context of working through traumatic memories. Dr. Loewenstein systematically reviews the literature on psychogenic fugue and amnesia, examining the combination of memory loss for specific episodes with evidence of availability of such memories that is at the heart of the dissociative process. A dissociated memory is not simply forgotten or unavailable; it is not available to consciousness and yet makes itself manifest. Dr. Steinberg provides a review of new work in the systematic assessment of depersonalization. This disorder is somewhat atypical for the dissociative disorders in that it can occur in a large variety of settings and has comorbidity with most other major psychiatric disorders, such as anxiety and depression. Dr. Nemiah demonstrates the important role of dissociation in conversion symptoms. Patients with dissociative symptoms have unusual abilities to alter somatic process to reflect psychological state, a theme illustrated by Dr. Putnam and Dr. Kluft as well. Dr. Nemiah argues that the dichotomy in the recent nosology between the dissociative symptoms on the one hand and somatoform symptoms do not do justice to the fundamental dissociative nature underlying many conversion symptoms. Finally, I review the literature suggesting that most dissociative disorders are in fact posttraumatic stress disorders. Trauma seems to be a common thread in the etiology of most of the dissociative disorders. Indeed, what is new in the field in the last decade is the recognition that dissociation is a response to trauma, both as it is occurring and then in the subsequent posttraumatic symptomatology. Many of the symptoms of posttraumatic stress disorder, the sudden reliving of trauma as though it were recurring, the numbing or loss of responsiveness, and the exaggerated startle response, are reminiscent of dissociative reliving of traumatic experiences and the related phenomenon of hypnotic age regression. All of the chapters in this section make heavy reference to the high prevalence of traumatic experience in the histories of patients with dissociative disorders, and to the importance of working through traumatic memories in treatment.

Work by these authors and others had led to recommendations for changes in the dissociative disorders section in DSM-IV. The following are the major proposed alterations.

*Psychogenic amnesia* can be diagnosed even in the absence of sudden onset, but its usual occurrence in the wake of trauma should be noted.

*Psychogenic fugue* may occur without the development of a new identity. The loss of usual identity should be the requirement, with the assumption of a new identity optional.

*Multiple personality disorder* can be diagnosed when more than one personality or personality state takes control of the person. The requirement for *full* control should be deleted, since intrusions by one personality state when another is in control are not uncommon in the syndrome. The requirement for amnesia as part of the diagnosis should be reinstituted. It is often extremely helpful in making the diagnosis to obtain a history of "losing time" or being unaware of having done things others commented on. This would also tighten the diagnostic criteria for the disorder.

*Brief reactive dissociative disorder* is being proposed as a new diagnostic entity. It is an acute dissociative response occurring during or within one month of a traumatic episode. It may involve stupor, depersonalization, amnesia, derealization, or other disconnection from the trauma that leads to dysfunction, for example failure to obtain necessary medical or legal assistance. There is no place in the current psychiatric nosology to describe an extreme, acute reaction to physical trauma.

Dissociation is a fascinating phenomenon. It presents us with dramatic shifts in cognition and affect, unusual changes in the boundary between conscious and unconscious experience, and is an effective means of coping with extreme discontinuities in physical experience. This section will provide you with an opportunity to integrate dissociation with our understanding of the response to trauma, differential diagnosis, and the range of psychiatric treatments.

# Chapter 1

# Dissociative Phenomena

## by Frank W. Putnam, M.D.

Dissociation is a process that produces a discernible alteration in a person's thoughts, feelings, or actions so that for a period of time certain information is not associated or integrated with other information as it normally or logically would be (West 1967). This process, which is manifest along a continuum of severity, produces a range of clinical and behavioral phenomena involving alterations in memory and identity that play important roles in normal and pathologic mental processes. In extreme cases, it gives rise to a set of psychiatric syndromes known as the dissociative disorders.

The last decade has brought a renewed interest in the clinical and scientific implications of dissociation. The psychophysiologic phenomena associated with dissociative states of consciousness were, however, the first mental processes to receive scientific scrutiny and have had a profound impact on the development of modern psychiatry (Ellenberger 1970). Much of what we know about "dynamic unconscious" mental mechanisms is, in fact, based on dissociative models, which continue to play a central role in modern models of the mind (Bowers and Meichenbaum 1984; Hilgard 1986; Kihlstrom 1987).

There are two major domains of knowledge about dissociation. The first involves clinical work with patients suffering from dissociative disorders and related conditions. The second comes from laboratory studies of hypnosis. Although the connections between clinical dissociation and hypnosis were evident to Janet and other early researchers, little systematic attention has been given to the relationship between these two bodies of knowledge. Current work would suggest that hypnosis and clinical dissociation are overlapping processes that share a set of common phenomena but also diverge in important ways (Carlson and Putnam 1989). At present the degree of similarity and separateness between hypnosis and clinical dissociation is difficult to assess because the instruments and experiments used to study each sample are from different realms of experience and behavior. The focus of this chapter is on dissociation as it is manifest in a clinical context. Relevant data from research on hypnosis will be included, however, because it illuminates our understanding of the dissociative process.

## HISTORY OF DISSOCIATION

The earliest work in this area resulted from discoveries made by Franz Anton Mesmer (1734–1815). Although modern practitioners would disavow his theories of animal magnetism, they are the recipients of a body of knowledge stemming from these first clinical explorations of dissociation (Crabtree 1988). Mesmer's theories were discredited in his lifetime by two royal commissions convened in 1784 to examine his claims, but a host of disciples and physicians in France and England continued to pursue Mesmerism enthusiastically because of its pragmatic utility with some patients (Crabtree 1988).

The foundation for current research and theory in the dissociative disorders was laid, however, by the exacting investigations of Pierre Janet (1859–1947). Trained as a philosopher, psychologist, and psychiatrist, Janet spent his life studying the mental phenomena manifest in patients with hysteria, a broadly defined 19th century diagnosis that would encompass the current diagnoses of dissociative, conversion, somatization, borderline personality, and posttraumatic stress disorders (van der Hart and Friedman 1989). He identified a set of principles that form the basis of modern work on dissociative psychopathology, including the linkage of dissociation to traumatic antecedents, recognition of the role of state-dependent memory phenomena in dissociative amnesias, and the role of altered states of consciousness in the disturbances of identity characteristic of the dissociative disorders (Putnam 1989b). Janet also pioneered abreactive and hypnotherapy techniques for the recovery and reintegration of dissociated traumatic material. His clinical insights and careful work were disrupted by two world wars and subsequently ignored or dismissed by adherents to early Freudian psychoanalytic theory. It is only recently that his neglected legacy has been rediscovered (van der Hart and Friedman 1989).

Interest in dissociative disorders declined during the 1920s as Freudian theory, with its rejection of hypnosis and child sexual abuse and its substitution of repression for dissociation in clinical formulations, gained disciples. In addition, experimental studies by Messerschmidt (1927–1928) cast doubt on the validity of the concept of dissociation at the same time that the introduction of the diagnosis of schizophrenia led to a decline of clinical interest in the dissociative disorders and the misdiagnosis of many of these cases (Rosenbaum 1980). The introduction of criterion-based diagnostic systems, most notably the DSM-III (American Psychiatric Association 1980), resulted in an increasing recognition of these patients and heralded the current resurgence of clinical attention to the dissociative disorders. Recent laboratory investigations of dramatic hypnotic phenomena, such as the hidden observer, have also contributed to a renewed appreciation of the role of dissociation in normal and pathologic mental processes (Hilgard 1986).

## PRINCIPLES OF DISSOCIATION

### The Dissociative Continuum

It has long been recognized that dissociation is a continuum process spanning a range from minor or normative forms to major or pathologic forms (Bernstein and Putnam 1986; Shor et al. 1962; Spiegel 1963; Tellegen and Atkinson 1974). Evidence for the continuum nature of dissociation comes from studies of the distribution of hypnotizability in normal and psychiatric populations and studies of the distribution of dissociative phenomena using the Dissociative Experiences Scale (DES) (Bernstein and Putnam 1986). The DES is a 28-item, self-report questionnaire that inquires about dissociative experiences such as amnesia, depersonalization, derealization, identity disturbances, and absorption or enthrallment experiences. The DES has good reliability and validity and has been widely adopted to assess dissociative phenomena in normal and clinical populations (Bernstein and Putnam 1986; Ross et al. 1988; Sanders et al. 1989).

Recently, Ross et al. (in press) used the DES to study dissociative phenomena in the general population. Figure 1-1 shows the distribution of DES scores for a stratified random sample of adults in Winnipeg, Canada. These data indicate that minor dissociative experiences are rather common in the general population. In normal individuals, the majority of these micro-dissociative experiences involve transient episodes of "spacing out" or inattention during conversations or driving, intense absorption while reading or watching television, and infrequent episodes of depersonalization. DES scores can range from 0 to 100, with normal individuals having a median score of about 7. About 5% of this large general sample have DES scores of 30 or greater, an empirical threshold often associated with the development of significant dissociative psychopathology (Bernstein and Putnam 1986; Ross et al. 1988; Ross et al. 1989a). These data indicate that dissociative phenomena exist along a continuum, with a subset of the general population at risk for the development of major dissociative psychopathology.

## Factors Affecting the Degree of Dissociativity

Defining *dissociativity* as the tendency for an individual to dissociate spontaneously in naturally occurring situations, one can look for factors that influence this tendency. Studies of clinical dissociation and hypnosis both indicate that age appears to affect an individual's capacity for dissociation significantly. A number of studies have found that there is a significant negative correlation between age and DES scores (Bernstein and Putnam 1986; Ross et al., in press). Figure 1-2 shows cross-sectional data from the Ross et al. study of dissociation in a general population sample age 18 years or greater. Hypnotizability, as assessed by standardized

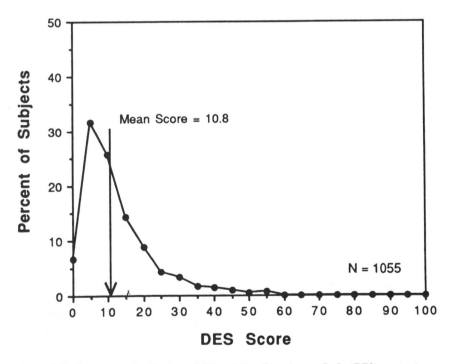

*Figure 1-1.* Frequency distribution of Dissociative Experiences Scale (DES) scores in a randomized sample of the general population. Data from Ross et al. (in press).

measures, also demonstrates a similar gradual decline with age, as illustrated in Figure 1-3 (Berg and Melin 1975; Morgan and Hilgard 1973; Spiegel and Spiegel (1978).

At present, there is no validated measure of clinical dissociation in children, although several instruments are under development. Standardized measurements of hypnotizability in children suggest that there is a modest curvilinear relationship with age (Gardner and Olness 1981). Figure 1-3 shows scores on the Stanford Hypnotic Susceptibility Scale, Form A (SHSS) by age of subjects (Morgan and Hilgard 1973). These cross-sectional data show that hypnotizability peaks at about age 9–10 years and declines after that. Some investigators believe that the apparent curvilinear relationship of hypnotizability with age during childhood is an artifact of the measurement process and that preschool children and even infants are highly hypnotizable but that the current measures that require a degree of understanding and cooperation from the child are unable to document this (Gardner and Olness 1981).

There does not appear to be a relationship between gender and capacity to dissociate. Males and females have similar DES scores in nonpsychiatric samples, as illustrated in Figure 1-2, and in psychiatric samples (Bernstein and Putnam 1986; Ross et al., in press; Sanders et al. 1989). Likewise, there is no evidence that overall hypnotizability differs between the males and females (Gardner and Olness 1981; Hilgard 1965; Spiegel and Spiegel 1978). Although some cohorts of patients with dissociative disorder have skewed male to female ratios—for example, female

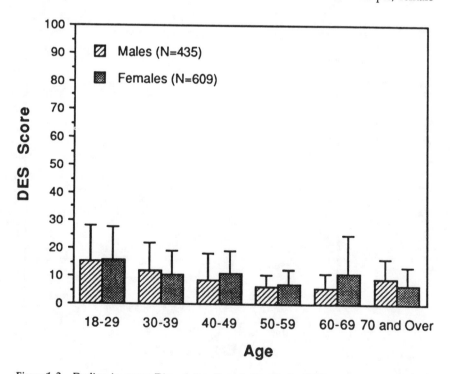

*Figure 1-2.* Decline in mean Dissociative Experiences Scale (DES) scores with age in a randomized sample of the general population. Data from Ross et al. (in press).

patients with multiple personality disorder (MPD) outnumber male cases by as much as 9 to 1 in two large samples (Putnam et al. 1986; Ross et al. 1989c)—it is thought that this is the result of case-selection biases and other social factors (e.g., females being at greater risk for sexual abuse) rather than an intrinsic, gender-linked difference in capacity or propensity to dissociate (Putnam 1985; Putnam 1989a).

It does appear as if certain rather specific developmental experiences may increase dissociativity in adult life. Although Janet clearly identified the role of traumatic antecedents in the development of dissociative symptoms, it has taken the century following his seminal observations to incorporate this fact into clinical practice (Putnam 1989b). Current data illustrating the linkage between dissociation and trauma are summarized by Spiegel (Chapter 6, this volume).

Evidence that childhood trauma enhances dissociativity comes from the clinical literature (Putnam 1985) and from recent studies of adults victimized in childhood. Chu and Dill (1990) demonstrated that there is a significant relationship between early childhood trauma, particularly sexual abuse, and elevated DES scores in psychiatric inpatients. Sanders et al. (1989) found a similar relationship between childhood stress and DES scores in college students. Using standard measures, Nash et al. (1984) found that subjects who had been physically abused in childhood had significantly higher hypnotizability scores compared to nonabused subjects. These preliminary studies must be replicated and extended, but taken together with evidence that innate dissociative capacity appears to peak during childhood, these findings have suggested to several investigators that childhood trauma acts to enhance or preserve into adulthood the child's normatively elevated dissociativity (Frischholz 1985; Putnam 1985; Spiegel 1984).

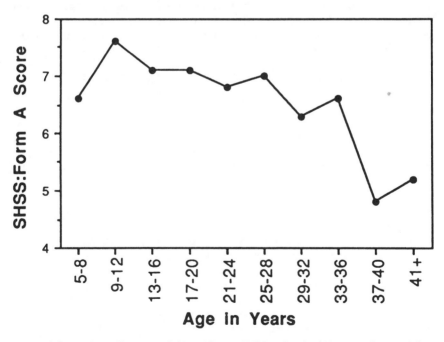

*Figure 1-3.* Decline of hypnotizability with age. SHSS = Stanford Hypnotic Susceptibility Scale. Data from Morgan and Hilgard (1973).

It is recognized that dissociation serves as a protective response in the face of trauma and that it is perhaps even neurologically related to the freezing and sham-death reflexes evoked by predators in the young of many species (Ludwig 1983). Ludwig summarized the adaptive functions of dissociation as including 1) the automatization of behaviors, 2) the resolution of irreconcilable conflicts, 3) the isolation of catastrophic experiences, 4) the cathartic discharge of feelings, and 5) escape from the constraints of reality. He argued that "the widespread prevalence of dissociative reactions and their many forms and guises argues for their serving important functions for man and their possessing great survival value" (p. 95).

The repeated use of dissociative defenses by a child, perhaps in response to a repetitive trauma such as incest, is thought to lead to a generalization of dissociative defenses to other stresses and possibly the development of a chronic dissociative disorder such as MPD. What begins as an adaptive, often lifesaving, process may evolve into a maladaptive condition as the child grows into an adult faced with social, occupational, and family situations that demand continuity of memory, behavior, and sense of self.

## PATHOLOGIC DISSOCIATION

The recognition of a continuum of dissociative phenomena ranging from the minor dissociations of everyday life to major disorders forces clinicians to draw a line where normative experiences stop and psychopathology begins. Any such division is a culture-bound process as the degree of culturally sanctioned dissociation varies greatly from societies that promote dissociation as part of religion, ritual, healing, and magic to those that discourage or suppress dissociative behavior (Bourguignon 1968). The DSM-III-R (American Psychiatric Association 1987) emphasizes that the essential feature of the dissociative disorders is a disturbance or alteration in the normally integrative functions of identity, memory, or consciousness.

### Dissociative Symptoms

In individuals with high dissociativity, frequent or prolonged episodes of dissociation generate a complex clinical picture with a core set of dissociative symptoms and a set of secondary symptoms. The amnesias and identity disturbances can be thought of as direct results of the dissociative process; other symptoms, such as depression, anxiety, and hyperarousal, probably result from nondissociative processes activated by the traumatic antecedents or as reactive responses to the distress generated by profound dissociative experiences. Clinical experience indicates that unless the dissociative process is directly addressed in therapy, secondary and reactive symptoms such as depression and anxiety are largely refractory to treatment (Putnam 1989a).

Psychogenic amnesias are among the most prominent symptoms found in dissociative disorders. Classically, the individual experiences amnesia for self-referential information, often personal identity, while the person's general fund of knowledge remains largely intact. This is in contradistinction to organic amnesias where general information is usually seriously degraded before self-referential knowledge begins to deteriorate. In MPD, individuals experience frequent episodes of "time loss" or blackouts where they have no memory of performing complex behaviors. MPD patients also have extensive amnesias for childhood memories (Putnam 1989a; Schacter et al. 1989).

Surprisingly, most patients experiencing these frequent and often profound amnesias do not complain about them directly or seek medical attention. They usually report that they have had these experiences for years and did not recognize that they were unusual until adolescence or adulthood, at which point they attempted to hide them from others. The amnesias appear to be an extreme form of state-dependent memory retrieval, and in many cases the missing information either returns "spontaneously" or can be retrieved in an altered state of consciousness (e.g., hypnotic or barbiturate-facilitated interviews).

These amnesias play a crucial role in the disturbances and alterations of identity characteristic of dissociative disorders. The suppression of personal information and autobiographical memory, often obliterating the individual's primary sense of identity, permits the expression of alternate identities. This may take the form of alter personalities, such as occurs in MPD and some cases of psychogenic fugue. In cases where no alter identity emerges, the individual may suffer a total loss of identity, such as the John and Jane Does brought to emergency rooms by the police. In instances where there is a less than total suppression of personal information, the individual may report a sense of depersonalization in which their past history is recalled as if it happened to someone else.

Closely related to the alter identities of MPD and psychogenic fugue are the embodiment phenomena of shamanism and spirit possession. Demonic, spirit, and trance possession states are extraordinarily widespread, occurring in the vast majority of societies around the world, and are common within certain subcultures of the United States (Bourguignon 1968; Noll 1989). Bourguignon extensively documented the dissociative nature of possession states, although some authorities dispute his requirement that amnesia must always be present for events occurring during possession experiences (Noll 1989).

Phenomenologically, possessed individuals closely resemble cases of MPD, with similar switching behaviors, personality changes, and amnesias (Krippner 1987; Ravenscroft 1965). Possession may either be somnambulic, in which the person loses consciousness of self and speaks with the "I" of the intruder, or lucid, in which the individual remains aware of self but feels invaded by another spirit (Ellenberger 1970). In lucid possession, the individual may feel compelled by the invading spirit to behave in ways that are against his or her wishes, judgment, or values. Similar "influence" experiences, once considered to be pathognomonic for schizophrenia, are very common in MPD (Kluft 1987; Ross et al. 1989a).

Depersonalization is another dissociative disturbance of self. It occurs both in normal individuals and is very common in psychiatric patients. Depersonalization can also be induced by a wide range of psychoactive substances (Good 1989; Putnam 1985). Transient experiences of depersonalization are common in adolescents and decline with age in normal individuals (Putnam 1985). Closely allied with traumatically induced experiences of depersonalization are out-of-body experiences and near-death experiences. Although there is a well-established literature, research in this area is descriptive and dependent on anecdotal accounts or questionnaire surveys. Out-of-body experiences have been related to autoscopy, the hallucination or psychic experience of seeing oneself, but are distinguished by a sense of having left the body behind (Roberts and Owen 1988). Often the individual experiencing an out-of-body experience describes seeing his or her own body as if viewed from above and reports a sense of sharpened but detached mental processes.

Like depersonalization, out-of-body experiences may occur spontaneously in normal individuals, but are more frequently associated with severe stress or near-death events (Greyson 1985; Roberts and Owens 1988). Out-of-body and near-death experiences have been described throughout history and across a wide range of cultures but investigators are divided as to the degree of similarity in reports of these events (Roberts and Owen 1988). Out-of-body experiences are commonly reported by patients with MPD and are part of a set of paranormal experiences described by patients with dissociative disorders (Ross et al. 1989a).

One of the most dramatic symptoms or behaviors associated with MPD is the "switching" between alter personalities. These transition events appear to be similar to other types of rapid shifts in state of consciousness such as observed in bipolar illness, panic attacks, abreactions, and catatonia (Putnam 1988). Alter personality switches, onset of possession states, psychogenic amnesia and fugue states, and conversion symptoms are typically rapid processes that occur within seconds to a few minutes (Coons et al. 1988; Putnam 1988). Typically alter personality and possession state switches are accompanied by changes in facies, speech (pitch, rate, accent, and language usage), motor activity, cognitive processes, affect, behavioral repertoire memory retrieval, and sense of self (Krippner 1987; Pattison and Wintrob 1981; Putnam 1988, 1989a; Ravenscroft 1965).

There are physiologic parallels between switches and the changes in behavioral states occurring in the normal infant, and it is hypothesized that these switches reflect a basic neurobiologic mechanism underlying modulation of states of consciousness (Putnam 1988). Psychophysiologically, switches typically take place within seconds to a few minutes and are often associated with a hypnotic-like upward eye roll. During the transition period, there appears to be a momentary dysregulation of ongoing biological rhythmic activities—such as heart rate, respiration, brain electrical activity—which then restabilize into new patterns with the emergence of a different alter personality state (Putnam 1988). Often unrecognized, switches among alter personality states are responsible for the lability of affect, behavior, and cognition that result in the misdiagnosis of MPD patients as having borderline personality or bipolar affective disorders.

Dissociative disorder patients, particularly those with MPD, often report very specific types of hallucinations. Auditory and visual hallucinations are common in these disorders (Coons et al. 1988; Putnam et al. 1986; Ross et al. 1989c). Classically, the auditory hallucinations are experienced as occurring within the head and are distinct voices with specific attributes (e.g., "a hateful old woman's gravelly voice," "sounds like a small child crying for her mother") as opposed to the indistinct voices of schizophrenia, which often emanate from outside of the head (Coons 1984; Putnam 1989a). The voices may argue with each other, comment on the person's behavior, urge harmful acts, or provide support and consolation. Visual hallucinations are typically vivid and involve complex scenes. Like auditory hallucinations, they may be persecutory or they may involve "flashbacks" of prior trauma.

## THE PSYCHOPHYSIOLOGY OF DISSOCIATION

### State-Dependent Learning and Dissociative Amnesias

State-dependent learning refers to a set of findings in which behaviors or information is learned or stored in one state; defined in behavioral, pharmacologic, neurochemical, or other terms; and later tested or retrieved in either the same or a disparate state (Weingartner 1978). Typically, retrieval of information learned in one state is impaired when the subject's state is changed compared to retrieval in the same state in which it was acquired. Ribot is credited with first proposing in 1891 that effects similar to state-dependent learning were responsible for dissociative amnesias, stressing that bodily sensations, physiologic states, and other cues were necessary to access certain memories in an individual (Putnam 1986). Several studies support the hypothesis that state-dependent learning contributes to dissociative amnesias and impairment of memory transfer across alter personality states (Ludwig et al. 1972; Nissen et al. 1988; Silberman et al. 1985).

All of the studies have shown that certain types of learned information is compartmentalized within specific alter personality states, a finding that is in agreement with clinical observations. The studies demonstrate, however, that the amnesic barriers between different personality states are not impermeable, and leakage of information does occur even between alter personalities that subjectively report no awareness of each other. Summarizing the results of an intensive case study, Nissen et al. (1988) noted that

> the degree of compartmentalization of knowledge in this patient appears to depend on the extent to which that knowledge is interpreted in ways that are unique to a personality as well as the extent to which processes operating at the time of retrieval are strongly personality-dependent. (p 131)

Silberman et al. (1985) concluded that the alter personality states of the MPD patients served as powerful state-dependent learning markers and contexts for the encoding and retrieval of information, which were not duplicated by simulating control subjects.

Research currently in progress on the implicit and explicit memory functions within and across the alter personality states of MPD patients indicates that implicit or knowledge base memory retrieval is profoundly affected across alter personality states but shows normal within personality state savings on test-retest trials. Explicit memory retrieval appears to be intact within and across alter personality states, although alter personalities tested on explicit material learned by other alter personalities often report that they have never seen this material before. Nonetheless, they perform essentially normally (C. Szostak, unpublished data). Additional studies of state-dependent learning and cognitive functions in MPD are in progress at a number of laboratories and promise to shed light on functional amnesias as well as the storage and retrieval mechanisms of memory in general (Schacter and Kihlstrom 1989).

## The Neurophysiology of Dissociation

Dissociation was the first mental process to be subject to scientific investigation (Putnam 1986). Psychophysiologic studies of dissociation have focused on three broad areas: 1) the possible connection between dissociative symptoms and forms of epilepsy, such as complex partial seizures or other "temporal lobe" dysfunction; 2) possible alterations in cerebral dominance as a mechanism underlying alter personality state differences; and 3) physiologic correlates of alter personalities and hypnotic, mystical, and altered states of consciousness.

Charcot and others linked MPD to epilepsy at the end of the 19th century, a hypothesis that continues to be advanced by some modern investigators

(Loewenstein and Putnam 1988). Clinicians have long noted that epilepsy in general and temporal lobe epilepsy in particular share an overlapping set of symptoms with the dissociative disorders: blackouts and amnesias; fugues; depersonalization; déjà vu and derealization experiences; unusual somatic sensations; and auditory, visual, and olfactory hallucinations (Devinsky et al. 1989). A review of case reports and data from three studies indicate that although MPD and epilepsy may coincide in some individuals, an epileptic process per se is not the primary pathophysiologic mechanism for developing dissociative symptoms (Devinsky et al. 1989; Loewenstein and Putnam 1988; Ross et al. 1989b).

The search for differences in cerebral hemispheric dominance in the dissociative disorders is even older, dating back to Benjamin Rush's hypothesis that MPD resulted from a disconnection of the two cerebral hemispheres (Carlson 1981). Galin (1974) creatively expanded this hypothesis, proposing that hemispheric specialization of cognitive functions (e.g., language, spatial relations, and musical capacity) leads to shifts in cognitive style, depending on which hemisphere is dominant. He noted that there are parallels between aspects of right hemisphere functioning and primary process thinking and that hemispheric differences in coping strategies and affective reactions may underlie psychological defense mechanisms, such as denial and repression, as well as explain "dissociations of experience" (i.e., incongruities between verbal and visual-spatial modes of processing information).

Despite a compelling subjective sense of unity, which Galin (1974) suggested is to some extent an illusion, most individuals have two (or more) separate streams of consciousness that attend to information in different ways. Complete or partial functional disconnection of the cerebral hemispheres (e.g., by inhibition of neural transmission across the cerebral commissures) may produce different constellations of cognitive, affective, and physiologic variables as well as a cleavage in the sense of unity of self. This hypothesis suggests that the alter personalities represent discrete patterns of selective inhibition of certain hemispheric functions.

There is mixed evidence in favor of this hypothesis. Approximately one-third of MPD patients show differences in dominant handedness across alter personalities (Putnam et al. 1986). In addition, several single case studies appear to demonstrate personality state-specific left-right asymmetries in autonomic nervous system activity (Brende 1984; Gott et al. 1984). However, the only controlled study of autonomic nervous system activity in MPD failed to find any evidence for personality state-specific shifts in lateralization of activity (Putnam et al. 1990). In addition, Sidis (1986) argued that a review of the psychological testing of patients with commissurotomies for intractable epilepsy fails to demonstrate any evidence of an MPD-like syndrome in "split-brain" patients, making it unlikely that a functional hemispheric disconnection accounts for dissociative symptoms. If anything, the striking lack of observable changes found in split-brain patients is evidence of a strong drive toward a unified functional state.

Until recently, the search for psychophysiologic correlates of clinical dissociation and MPD was dominated by single case reports. Intriguing as they are, uncontrolled case reports do not constitute an acceptable standard of scientific evidence. Research is this area has never been well supported and is often burdened by the perceived need to "prove" the existence of the disorder (Putnam 1986). Recently, a number of more rigorous and controlled studies that document degrees of difference across alter personality states that are not matched by control groups have begun to appear. Hopefully, as the quality of scientific investigation in this area improves, it will be matched by increased support from academic institutions and funding agencies. MPD and dissociative phenomena such as conversion and somatoform symptoms have a great deal to teach us about "mind-body" interfaces.

Attempts to study alter personality differences have primarily concentrated on alterations in central nervous system activity, although a few investigators have studied autonomic nervous system correlates. Electroencephalogram (EEG) studies of MPD patients, like those of hypnosis, have been varied and contradictory, with some investigators reporting significant differences and others finding only artifact or nonspecific changes (Coons 1988). Recent studies of spontaneous EEG and visual evoked potentials indicate that there are significant differences in brain electrical activity across the alter personalities of MPD patients (Putnam, unpublished data). These differences primarily involve the higher frequency bands of the EEG and probably include significant myogenic components. These differences are group statistical effects and do not represent an EEG "signature" for MPD. They are not, however, duplicated by matched, simulating control subjects and suggest that the shifts in alter personality states of MPD subjects are accompanied by psychophysiologic changes, although the mechanism(s) responsible remains to be identified.

There are no undisputed EEG correlates of the hypnotic state, although a number of studies suggest that hypnosis may be associated with increases in theta or alpha activity (Tebecis et al. 1975). There is stronger evidence that both somatosensory and visual-evoked-potential amplitude components can be altered by using hypnotically induced hallucinations to enhance or block sensory input (Spiegel et al. 1985, 1989). These studies suggest that hypnosis and clinical dissociative states may alter the neurophysiology of sensory systems, resulting in alterations of perception of external stimuli. This mechanism may be responsible for the sensory and motor variability and aberrations that frequently occur in dissociative disorders.

Miller's (1989) study of optical differences across the alter personalities of MPD subjects compared to simulating controls is an example of the increased range of variability of experimental measures found in the dissociative disorders. He found that MPD subjects had significantly more differences in measures of visual acuity, visual fields, manifest refraction, and eye muscle balance than did his role-playing controls. It is this finding of increased variability rather than any specific marker that seems to characterize the psychophysiologic shifts seen in MPD.

## The Neurochemistry of Dissociation

Little is actually known about the neurochemical systems mediating dissociation, although several promising lines of evidence suggest that dysregulation of central serotonergic function and the endogenous opiate system may play important roles (Demitrack et al. 1990). While infusion of serotonin receptor agonists such as metachlorophenylpiperazine appears to elicit dissociative states, a large number of other psychoactive substances affecting cholinergic, beta-adrenergic, dopaminergic, and other neurotransmitter systems are also capable of producing at least a subset of dissociative symptoms (e.g., amnesias or depersonalization) in some patients (Good 1989; Zohar et al. 1987).

Intriguing work by van der Kolk, Pitman, and others examining alterations in pain threshold produced by stimuli reminiscent of traumatic experiences in patients with posttraumatic stress disorder implicates the endogenous opiate system in the analgesias often associated with dissociative states (van der Kolk et al., in press).

The endorphin system has also been a recent focus of investigation in possession trance states (Prince 1982). However, naloxone, a narcotic antagonist that blocks and reverses the effects of opiates, does not reverse hypnotically induced analgesia or modify the depth of hypnotic trance (Spiegel and Albert 1983; Spruiell et al. 1983). Although the specificity of any given neurochemical system for dissociative processes has yet to be demonstrated, a number of potential pharmacologic and animal models of dissociation remain to be investigated (Good 1989; Putnam 1989b).

## MODELS OF THE DISSOCIATIVE DISORDERS

There are three broad classes of theoretical models of clinical dissociation: 1) the autohypnotic and discrete states-of-consciousness model; 2) neurologic models; and 3) role-playing or malingering models. Each of these models originated during the last century and has been periodically revised to account for newer information.

The autohypnotic model, currently championed by Bliss (1986) and often invoked by others, builds on the long-recognized connection between dissociation and hypnosis and conceptualizes clinical dissociation as self-hypnosis gone awry. Central to this model is the observation that patients with dissociative symptoms uniformly score in the highly hypnotizable range on standard hypnotic tests (Bliss 1986; Carlson and Putnam 1989; Frischholz 1985). Many of the symptoms characteristic of dissociative disorders (e.g., amnesias, hallucinations, and conversion-like disruptions of sensory and motor function) can be produced with hypnosis in some highly hypnotizable subjects. Psychological divisions of identity, such as the "hidden observer" and age-regression produced in a subset of highly hypnotizable individuals, have been likened to the alter personalities of MPD, although important distinctions between these phenomena and alter personalities exist (Hilgard 1984).

The states-of-consciousness model is an extension of the autohypnotic model that differs in its emphasis on the general properties of discrete states of consciousness, irrespective of the type of state, as important mechanistic processes responsible for cardinal features of the dissociative disorders (Putnam 1988, 1989b). While recognizing that dissociative states of consciousness possess unique "hypnotic" properties that account for many symptoms, this model proposes that the core phenomena of the dissociative disorders, such as the amnesias and disturbances of sense of self, arise out of traumatically induced disruptions in capacities for modulation of states of consciousness and integration of self across highly discrete states of consciousness.

This model would suggest that the dissociative disorders share a set of basic behavioral and cognitive phenomena with other disorders characterized by rapid changes in state of consciousness, although the intensity of these symptoms may differ as function of the frequency, duration, and instability of state perturbations. Indeed, powerful state-dependent psychological, physiologic, and memory retrieval effects are noted in affective disorders, panic attacks, catatonic reactions, abreactions, premenstrual tension syndrome, and other disorders characterized by abrupt shifts in mood and behavior (Putnam 1988; Weingartner 1978).

Neurologic theories of dissociation, primarily the epileptic and hemispheric disconnection models, have historically played an important role in stimulating research. Although conceptually tantalizing, currently there are few data to support either model. Galin's (1974) hypothesis of varying degrees of functional disconnection of the cerebral hemispheres could provide a neurophysiologic substrate for the expression of alter personality states. Further research in this area is warranted.

The strategic role enactment model promulgated by Spanos (1986) is the latest of a long line of arguments that contend that hypnosis and MPD are produced, wittingly or unwittingly, by social role demands imposed by the hypnotist or therapist on the subject or patient. Similar charges have been leveled over the last century at notables such as Morton Prince who investigated the dissociative disorders (Putnam 1989a). According to Spanos (1986), hypnosis and MPD differ from other social roles only in that the "actors convey the impression that their enactments are non-self guided happenings" (p. 49). The data advanced to support this argument are circular in that they involve an experiment in which college students were instructed to role play an accused murderer being questioned by an experimenter role playing a psychiatrist using a script from a nationally televised sensational murder case involving a disputed case of MPD. Not too surprisingly, the role-playing students produced "symptoms" of MPD, typically manifest by the adoption of a different name. They did not produce, however, documentable amnesias, enduring disturbances of identity, somatoform symptoms, discernible switches, or any of the many other symptoms and behaviors routinely observed in dissociative patients.

Implicit in this model are the following assumptions. First, that MPD is considered a desirable social role, with significant secondary gain for any given patient. Second, that therapists and others working with MPD patients actively reinforce this social role. Third, that both patients and therapist have a clear and explicit consensus of what MPD is and how MPD patients act. Fourth, that all the symptoms and behaviors exhibited by MPD patients are under volitional control. Finally, that an undergraduate student role playing a psychiatric disorder, such as MPD or schizophrenia, is functionally equivalent to a patient suffering from that disorder. Although provocative, this model falls far short of the clinical and experimental facts observed in MPD and the other dissociative disorders. Several research studies using stimulating control subjects have found that role playing does not produce the same degree of psychological or physiologic variability manifest by MPD patients (Miller 1989; Putnam et al. 1990; Silberman et al. 1985).

## SUMMARY

Dissociation, as manifest in the dissociative disorders and hypnosis, has had a profound historical influence on the conceptualizations of "dynamic unconscious processes" employed by modern psychiatry and psychology. While existing on a continuum from normative to pathologic forms, the degree of dissociativity in a given individual is influenced by age and early developmental experiences, particularly episodes of trauma and stress. In the context of severe trauma, dissociation may serve as an effective defense insulating the individual from overwhelming experiences and affects. In some cases, however, it appears to generalize to lesser stresses and becomes a chronic maladaptive process.

Pathologic dissociation is characterized by disruptions in memory retrieval, usually expressed as amnesias, and by profound disturbances in sense of identity. Chronic pathologic dissociation produces a complex clinical picture characterized by primary dissociative symptoms and associated secondary or reactive symptoms. The range of psychophysiologic phenomena associated with the dissociative disorders touch on many of the salient issues in psychiatry and provide a unique experimental window into mind-body interactions. A number of explanatory models exist and provide a framework for experimental and clinical research.

## REFERENCES

American Psychiatric Association: Diagnostic and Statistical Manual of Mental Disorders, 3rd Edition. Washington, DC, American Psychiatric Association, 1980

American Psychiatric Association: Diagnostic and Statistical Manual of Mental Disorders, 3rd Edition, Revised. Washington, DC, American Psychiatric Association, 1987

Berg S, Melin E: Hypnotic susceptibility in old age: some data from residential homes for old people. Int J Clin Exp Hypn 23:184–189, 1975

Bernstein E, Putnam FW: Development, reliability and validity of a dissociation scale. J Nerv Ment Dis 174:727–735, 1986

Bliss EL: Multiple Personality Allied Disorders and Hypnosis. New York, Oxford University Press, 1986

Bourguignon E: World distribution and patterns of possession states, in Trance and Possession States. Edited by Prince R. Montreal, Bucke Memorial Society, 1968, pp 3–34

Bowers KS, Meichenbaum D (eds): The Unconscious Reconsidered. New York, John Wiley, 1984

Brende JO: The psychophysiologic manifestations of dissociation. Psychiatr Clin North Am 7:41–50, 1984

Carlson ET: The history of multiple personality in the United States, I: the beginnings. Am J Psychiatry 138:666–668, 1981

Carlson EB, Putnam FW: Integrating research on dissociation and hypnotizability: are there two pathways to hypnotizability? Dissociation 2:32–38, 1989

Chu JA, Dill DL: Dissociative symptoms in relation to childhood physical and sexual abuse. Am J Psychiatry 147:887–892, 1990

Coons PM: The differential diagnosis of multiple personality: a comprehensive review. Psychiatr Clin North Am 7:51–65, 1984

Coons PM: Psychophysiologic aspects of multiple personality disorder: a review. Dissociation 1:47–53, 1988

Coons PM, Bowman ES, Milstein V: Multiple personality disorder: a clinical investigation of 50 cases. J Nerv Ment Dis 176:519–527, 1988

Crabtree A: Animal Magnetism, Early Hypnotism and Psychical Research, 1766–1925. White Plains, NY, Kraus International Publications, 1988

Demitrack MA, Putnam FW, Brewerton TD, et al: Relation of clinical variables to dissociative phenomena in eating disorders. Am J Psychiatry 147:1184–1188, 1990

Devinsky O, Putnam FW, Grafman J, et al: Dissociative states and epilepsy. Neurology 39:835–840, 1989

Ellenberger HF: The Discovery of the Unconscious: The History and Evolution of Dynamic Psychiatry. New York, Basic Books, 1970

Frischholz MA: The relationship among dissociation, hypnosis, and child abuse in the development of multiple personality disorder, in Childhood Antecedents of Multiple Personality. Edited by Kluft RP. Washington, DC, American Psychiatric Press, 1985, pp 99–126

Galin D: Implications for psychiatry of left and right cerebral specialization. Arch Gen Psychiatry, 31:572–583, 1974

Gardner GG, Olness K: Hypnosis and Hypnotherapy with Children. Orlando, FL, Grune & Stratton, 1981

Good MI: Substance-induced dissociative disorders and psychiatric nosology. J Clin Psychopharmacol 9:88–93, 1989

Gott PS, Everett CH, Whipple K: Voluntary control of two lateralized conscious states: validation by electrical and behavioral studies. Neurophysiologia 22:65–72, 1984

Greyson B: A typology of near-death experiences. Am J Psychiatry 142:967–969, 1985

Hilgard ER: Hypnotic Susceptibility. New York, Harcourt Brace Jovanovich, 1965

Hilgard ER: The hidden observer and multiple personality. Int J Clin Exp Hypn 32:248–253, 1984

Hilgard ER: Divided Consciousness: Multiple Controls in Human Thought and Action, Revised Edition. New York, John Wiley, 1986

Kihlstrom JF: The cognitive unconscious. Science 237:1445–1452, 1987

Kluft RP: First-rank symptoms as a diagnostic clue to multiple personality disorder. Am J Psychiatry 144:293–298, 1987

Krippner S: Cross-cultural approaches to multiple personality disorder: practices of Brazilian spiritism. Ethos 15:273–295, 1987

Loewenstein RJ, Putnam FW: A comparison study of dissociative symptoms in patients with partial complex seizures, MPD, and posttraumatic stress disorder. Dissociation 1:17–32, 1988

Ludwig AM: The psychobiological functions of dissociation. Am J Clin Hypn 26:93–99, 1983

Ludwig AM, Brandsma JM, Wilbur CB, et al: The objective study of a multiple personality. Arch Gen Psychiatry 26:298–310, 1972

Messerschmidt R: A quantitative investigation of the alleged independent operation of conscious and subconcious processes. Journal of Abnormal and Social Psychology 22:325–340, 1927–1928

Miller SD: Optical differences in cases of multiple personality disorder. J Nerv Ment Dis 177:480–486, 1989

Morgan AH, Hilgard ER: Age differences in susceptibility to hypnosis. Int J Clin Exp Hypn 21:78–85, 1973

Nash MR, Lynn SJ, Givens DL: Adult hypnotic susceptibility, childhood punishment, and child abuse: a brief communication. Int J Clin Exp Hypn 32:6–11, 1984

Nissen MJ, Ross JL, Willingham DB, et al: Memory and awareness in a patient with multiple personality disorder. Brain Cogn 8:117–134, 1988

Noll R: What has really been learned about Shamanism? Journal of Psychoactive Drugs 21:47–50, 1989

Pattison EM, Wintrob RM: Possession and exorcism in contemporary America. Journal of Operational Psychiatry 12:13–20, 1981

Prince R: Shamans and endorphins. Ethos 10:409–423, 1982

Putnam FW Jr: Dissociation as a response to extreme trauma, in Childhood Antecedents of Multiple Personality. Edited by Kluft RP. Washington, DC, American Psychiatric Press, 1985, pp 65–97

Putnam FW: The scientific investigation of multiple personality, in Split Minds Split Brains. Edited by Quen JM. New York, New York University Press, 1986, pp 109–126

Putnam FW: The switch process in multiple personality disorder and other state-change disorders. Dissociation 1:24–32, 1988

Putnam FW: Diagnosis and Treatment of Multiple Personality Disorder. New York, Guilford, 1989a

Putnam FW: Pierre Janet and modern views of dissociation. Journal of Traumatic Stress 2:413–429, 1989b

Putnam FW, Guroff JJ, Silberman EK, et al: The clinical phenomenology of multiple personality disorder: review of 100 recent cases. J Clin Psychiatry 47:285–293, 1986

Putnam FW, Zahn TP, Post RM: Differential autonomic nervous system activity in multiple personality disorder. Psychiatry Res 31:251–260, 1990

Ravenscroft K: Voodoo possession: a natural experiment in hypnosis. Int J Clin Exp Hypn 13:157–182, 1965

Roberts G, Owens J: The near-death experience. Br J Psychiatry 153:607–617, 1988

Rosenbaum M: The role of the term schizophrenia in the decline of multiple personality. Arch Gen Psychiatry 37:1383–1385, 1980

Ross CA, Norton GR, Anderson G: The dissociative experiences scale: a replication study. Dissociation 1:21–22, 1988

Ross CA, Heber S, Norton GR, et al: Differences between multiple personality disorder and other diagnostic groups on structured interview. J Nerv Ment Dis 177:487–491, 1989a

Ross C, Heber S, Anderson G, et al: Differentiating multiple personality disorder and complex partial seizures. Gen Hosp Psychiatry 11:54–58, 1989b

Ross CA, Norton GR, Wozney K: Multiple personality disorder: an analysis of 239 cases. Can J Psychiatry 34:413–418, 1989c

Ross CA, Joshi S, Currie R: Dissociative experiences in the general population. Am J Psychiatry (in press)

Sanders B, McRoberts G, Tollefson C: Childhood stress and dissociation in a college population. Dissociation 2:17–23, 1989

Schacter DL, Kihlstrom JF: Functional amnesia, in Handbook of Neuropsychology. Edited by Boller F, Grafman J. New York, Elsevier, 1989, pp 209–231

Schacter DL, Kihlstrom JF, Kihlstrom LC, et al: Autobiographical memory in a case of multiple personality disorder. J Abnorm Psychol 98:1–7, 1989

Shor RE, Orne MT, O'Connell DN: Validation and cross-validation of a scale of self-reported personal experiences which predicts hypnotizability. J Psychol 53:55–75, 1962

Sidis JJ: Can neurological disconnection account for psychiatric dissociation?, in Split Minds Split Brains. Edited by Quen JM. New York, New York University Press, 1986, pp 127–148

Silberman EK, Putnam FW, Weingartner H, et al: Dissociative states in multiple personality disorder: a quantitative study. Psychiatry Res 15:253–260, 1985

Spanos NP: Hypnosis, nonvolutional responding, and multiple personality: a social psychological perspective. Progress in Experimental Personality Research 14:1–62, 1986

Spiegel D: Multiple personality disorder as a post-traumatic stress disorder. Psychiatr Clin North Am 7:101–110, 1984

Spiegel D, Albert LH: Naloxone fails to reverse hypnotic alleviation of chronic pain. Psychopharmacology (Berlin) 81:140–143, 1983

Spiegel D, Cutcomb S, Ren C, et al: Hypnotic hallucination alters evoked potentials. J Abnorm Psychol 94:249–255, 1985

Spiegel D, Bierre P, Rootenberg J: Hypnotic aleration of somatosensory perception. Am J Psychiatry 146:749–754, 1989

Spiegel H: The dissociation-association continuum. J Nerv Ment Dis 136:374–378, 1963

Spiegel H, Spiegel D: Trance and Treatment. New York, Basic Books, 1978

Spruiell G, Steck C, Lippincott CK, et al: Failure of naloxone to modify the depth of hypnotic trance experientia. 39:763–764, 1983

Tebecis AK, Provins KA, Farnbach RW, et al: Hypnosis and the EEG: a quantitative investigation. J Nerv Ment Dis 161:1–17, 1975

Tellegen A, Atkinson G: Openness to absorbing and self-altering experiences ("absorption"), a trait related to hypnotic susceptibility. J Abnorm Psychol 83:268–277, 1974

van der Hart O, Friedman B: A reader's guide to Pierre Janet on dissociation: a neglected intellectual heritage. Dissociation 2:3–16, 1989

van der Kolk BA, Greenberg MS, Orr PS, et al: Pain perception and endogenous opioids in post-traumatic stress disorder. Psychopharmacol Bull (in press)

Weingartner H: Human state dependent learning, in Drug Discrimination and State Dependent Learning. Edited by Ho BT, Richards DW, Chute DC. New York, Academic, 1978, pp 361–382

West L: Dissociative reaction, in Comprehensive Textbook of Psychiatry. Edited by Freedman AM, Kaplan HI. Baltimore, MD, Williams & Wilkins, 1967, pp 885–898

Zohar J, Mueller EA, Insel TR, et al: Serotonergic responsivity in obsessive-compulsive disorder: comparison of patients and healthy controls. Arch Gen Psychiatry 44:946–951, 1987

# Chapter 2

# Multiple Personality Disorder

*by Richard P. Kluft, M.D.*

Multiple personality disorder (MPD) is a complex, chronic, dissociative psychopathology (Kluft 1987e) characterized by disturbances of memory and identity (Nemiah 1980). It is distinguished from other mental disorders by the ongoing coexistence of relatively consistent but alternating subjectively separate identities and recurrent episodes of memory distortion, frank amnesia, or both. It is increasingly understood to be a posttraumatic condition that almost invariably emerges as the sequela of overwhelming childhood experiences (Putnam et al. 1986; Spiegel 1984). After providing a brief review of the history of MPD, I will discuss its phenomenology, etiology, epidemiology, differential diagnosis, comorbidity with other conditions, and treatment.

## A HISTORICAL AND CROSS-CULTURAL PERSPECTIVE

The majority of studied societies and cultures have conditions in which another entity is understood to have taken over the body of an afflicted individual (i.e., possession states). Their common core is that

> An individual suddenly seems to lose his identity to become another person. His physiognomy changes and shows a striking resemblance to the individual of whom he is, supposedly, the incarnation. With an altered voice, he pronounces words corresponding to the personality of the new individual. (Ellenberger 1970, p 13)

Until the end of the 18th century, many individuals in Western society demonstrated such phenomena. They were understood, within the explanatory paradigms of their eras, to be afflicted with the various Judeo-Christian forms of possession, and were treated with culturally endorsed forms of exorcism. When theological explanations of mental disease gave way to the first dynamic psychiatry, a process chronicled by Ellenberger (1970), the psychological constructs that underlay the possession states and the mental conflicts they expressed did not abruptly cease to exist. Instead, what is now called MPD (and allied conditions) began to enter the literature. MPD provides a secular expression of many of the same mental structures found in possession syndromes. In those societies in which indigenous possession states remain powerful and sanctioned idioms for expressing subjective experiences and conflicts, the psychopathologic "niche" that MPD occupies elsewhere is already filled, and MPD will be quite uncommon (e.g., Adityanjee et al. 1989)

Although Bliss (1986) attributed a case description to Paracelsus, Petetain published the first descriptions of MPD phenomena in 1787. The first attempt to delineate a specific syndrome or disorder consisting of these phenomena—*umgetauschte Personlichkeit* (exchanged personality)—is that of Eberhardt Gmelin in

1791. Benjamin Rush described such patients early in the 19th century (Carlson 1981). Numerous authorities thereafter made substantial contributions to the study of MPD, most of whom are nearly forgotten by history. For example, the three Despines together saw more than 40 cases; Antoine Despine, Sr., is credited with the first psychotherapeutic cure of MPD, in 1836 (see Fine 1988b). Under Charcot and Janet, many such patients were identified and treated at the Salpêtrière; Janet's contributions remain fresh and relevant. In the United States, Morton Prince drew attention to the disorder and made observations of lasting importance.

The study of MPD and dissociation flourished briefly and then waned. Appropriate doubt was cast on many of Charcot's demonstrations. Janet left few followers; his influence was further eroded by his conflicts with the Freudians. Although Freud began with a close affinity to the study of dissociation and MPD (Anna O. suffered this condition), he distanced himself from them as he developed his own models of the mind and repudiated the seduction theory. Bleuler included MPD under the rubric of schizophrenia; as the diagnosis of schizophrenia rose in acceptance, the use of the diagnosis of MPD dropped off precipitously (Rosenbaum 1980). Dismissed as a subject of importance by the rising tides of psychoanalysis, descriptive and organicist psychiatry, and behaviorism, the study of dissociation and MPD declined to near extinction within a generation.

The current rise of interest in MPD reflects the convergence of many influences. DSM-III (American Psychiatric Association 1980) recognized MPD as a free-standing condition and provided landmark clinical descriptions. Feminism made a most powerful impact. It sensitized the mental health professions to the hitherto unacknowledged high incidence of child abuse, incest, and the exploitation of women. Increasingly clinicians are listening to their adult patients' accounts of childhood abuse without discounting them in advance as fantasies. MPD is primarily a disorder of sexually abused women; in this atmosphere, its recognition has soared.

Also, there has been an explosion of interest in posttraumatic stress disorder (PTSD), which, like MPD, occurs consequent to trauma and has many dissociative features (Spiegel et al. 1988; Stutman and Bliss 1985). Many have noted the similarity of the two conditions, bringing credibility to MPD, an appreciation of the dissociative aspects of PTSD, and an application of the treatment approaches useful for PTSD to MPD, and vice versa.

Advances in psychopharmacology have encouraged greater diagnostic precision and closer scrutiny of treatment failures, a group that includes many unrecognized MPD patients (Kluft 1987e). A renaissance of interest in hypnosis is underway, and with it increased interest in dissociation. Lay attention in celebrated cases of MPD and its fictional representation in the media have played a role. Schreiber's book *Sybil*, describing Cornelia B. Wilbur's work with an MPD patient, was particularly influential. Excitement was generated by studies on the psychophysiologic aspects of MPD (Putnam 1984), discussed elsewhere (Putnam, Chapter 1, this volume). A final influence has been the dedicated teaching efforts of many of the pioneers in the field.

Between 1980 and 1984 a vigorous modern literature developed; until then it was more likely that a clinician's information about MPD came from lay rather than from professional sources. Annual international conferences on MPD began in 1984. A specialized journal, *Dissociation*, commenced in 1988. MPD had entered the mainstream of contemporary psychiatry.

# PHENOMENOLOGY

## *Diagnostic Criteria*

As psychiatry moves to achieve accurate and reliable diagnostic criteria, MPD has been redefined twice within a decade; a third revision is underway. DSM-III proposed three criteria:

A. The existence within the individual of two or more distinct personalities, each of which is dominant at a particular time.
B. The personality that is dominant at any particular time determines the individual's behavior.
C. Each individual personality is complex and integrated with its own unique behavior patterns and social relationships (American Psychiatric Association 1980, p. 259).

These criteria were written as a number of new and important findings were emerging. In retrospect, they reflect the phenomenology of several classic cases that were intelligent, creative, and female; had relatively few personalities; and were not typical in all respects. They implicitly endorse a classic but superceded model of dissociation (Frischholz 1985). With regard to criterion A, the term *dominant* is misleading because it implies that the relationship among the personalities is an incessant power struggle that is won completely for the moment. In fact, personalities may determine behavior from behind the scenes without emerging, and may share or contend for control. Emitted behavior often is the combined vector of numerous influences, functioning as a system. Personalities commonly try to pass for one another. The same concerns apply to criterion B. Also, recent findings indicate that contemporary cases average 13 to 15 alters (Kluft 1984d; Putnam et al. 1986; Ross et al. 1989c; Schultz et al. 1989). Kluft (1985) found that only about half a dozen or fewer of these personalities spend significant periods of time in executive control, that alters demonstrate a wide range of distinctness and complexity, and that their importance, dominance, and elaborateness may vary over time. Therefore, criterion C required revision. DSM-III-R (American Psychiatric Association 1987) criteria are more flexible, less reified, and reflect clinical findings in the broader range of MPD patients:

A. The existence within the person of two or more distinct personalities or personality states (each with its own relatively enduring pattern of perceiving, relating to, and thinking about the environment and self).
B. At least two of these personalities or personality states recurrently take full control of the person's behavior. (p. 272)

Just as DSM-III drew criticism as skewed toward false negative diagnoses, DSM-III-R, despite its consistency with the natural history of MPD (Kluft 1985), has been seen as making the diagnosis too easy to achieve and encouraging false positives. This fear has been disproven (Ross 1989). A greater awareness of MPD, rising rapidly at the time DSM-III-R was published, accounts for most of the accelerated reporting of such cases. Nonetheless, although these criteria accurately reflect a condition that can have a wide spectrum of manifestations, they have confused and distressed some who prefer a crisper delineation of the margins of clinical disorders.

There has always been considerable pressure toward including an amnesia criterion (Braun 1986; Coons 1984; Putnam 1984). Occasionally patients are encountered who have classic personalities but are without classic amnesia. MPD patients frequently have periods during which their amnestic barrier become more permeable than usual. Many dissociative distortions of memory do not involve formal amnesia (Kluft et al. 1988). Excluding patients without amnesia from the MPD diagnosis would eliminate only 5% of MPD patients, but it might delay the making of the diagnosis in as many as one-third of them, because amnesia is not endorsed at first interview by this percentage of MPD patients (Putnam et al. 1986; Ross 1989; Ross et al. 1989c). DSM-IV seems prepared to endorse as a third criterion: "C. The inability to recall important personal information that is too extensive to be explained by ordinary forgetfulness" (unpublished observations). Disagreement over its merit must await resolution in further studies. DSM-IV will also eliminate the word *full* in criterion B, more accurately reflecting the function of a system of alters over time (Kluft 1985; Putnam 1989).

## What Is a Personality?

In the context of general psychiatry personality is taken to mean "The characteristic way in which a person thinks, feels, and behaves; the ingrained pattern of behavior that each person evolves, both *consciously* and *unconsciously*, as the style or way of being in adapting to the environment" (Talbott et al. 1988, p. 1261). In MPD:

> Personality is here defined as a relatively enduring pattern of perceiving, relating to, and thinking about the environment and one's self that is exhibited in a wide range of important social and personal contexts. Personality states differ only in that the pattern is not exhibited in as wide a range of contexts. (American Psychiatric Association 1987, p. 269).
> Alter personalities are psychological structures, not separate people.

Several approaches to the issue of personality are current. Coons (1984), Kluft (1984b), and Putnam (1989) agree that the sum total of all the personalities and their interactions constitute the MPD patient's personality in the more general sense. Braun (1986) attempted to distinguish quantitatively between personalities as defined in the above quotation and less elaborated entities he termed fragments.

Putnam (1989) "conceptualize[d] the alters as highly discrete states of consciousness organized around a prevailing affect, sense of self (including body image) with a limited repertoire of behaviors and a set of state dependent memories" (p. 103). I have stated elsewhere (Kluft 1988b): "A dissaggregate self state (i.e., personality) is the mental address of a relatively stable and enduring particular pattern of selective mobilization of mental contents and functions, which may be behaviorally enacted with noteworthy role-taking and role-playing dimensions and sensitive to intrapsychic, interpersonal, and environmental stimuli. . . . It has a sense of its own identity and ideation, and a capacity for initiating thought processes and actions." (p. 51) Putnam and I described reconfigurations rather than reified divisions, emphasizing the personalities should be understood as ways the mind may be organized rather than "pieces of a pie." From this flows an appreciation that the number of personalities can be quite large because they constitute configurations, rather than portions of a unity. Many speculate that "we are all multiple personalities"; that is, that an individual manifests many states of mind and/or facets. Since the unity of the self is more a subjective illusion rather than an actuality (Hilgard 1986), this stance has a kernel of truth. However, clinical MPD is distinguished from normative aspects of human experience in several ways. First, the normal individual in a wide range of situations and roles experiences no change of identity and retains a sense of continuity as to who and what one is. Second, there is no change in self-representation. If one feels younger, for example, one does not experience one's self as an actual child with a physical appearance different from one's own. Third, notwithstanding the state- and mood-dependent memory (Bower 1981), there are few major barriers in self-referential memory for the normal individual who experiences him- or herself differently in various moods or situations. Fourth, unlike in MPD, there is no loss of the sense of ownership of what goes on or is done. For better or for worse, one's behavior (experientially) remains one's own. Therefore, the statement "we are all multiple personalities" is misleadingly reductionistic.

## Phenomenology of the Personalities

Several recent studies (Bliss 1980; Coons and Milstein 1986; Coons et al. 1988; Putnam et al. 1986; Ross et al. 1989c) are largely consistent in terms of the general trends that they demonstrate. At the time of diagnosis (prior to exploration), approximately 2 to 4 personalities are in evidence. In the course of treatment, an average of 13 to 15 are encountered, but this figure is deceptive. The mode in virtually all series is 3, and the median number of alters ranges from 8 to 10. Complex cases, with 26 or more alters (described in Kluft 1988d), occurring in 15% to 25% of such series, unduly inflate the mean.

The personalities' overt differences and disparate self-concepts may be striking. They may experience and represent themselves as being different ages, genders, races, religions, and sexual orientations; they may experience themselves as having different appearances and hold discrepant values and belief systems. Their awareness of one another may range from complete to nil. Directionality of knowledge is quite common, such that alter A knows of the doings of alter B, but B is unaware of the activities of A. It is not uncommon for some alters to have symptoms that others do not suffer. Psychophysiologic differences (see Putnam, Chapter 1, this volume) have been documented. Differences in handwriting and handedness, voice and vocabulary, accents and speech patterns, and even preferred languages are encountered. Their facial expressions and movement characteristics, both when neutral and affectively engaged, may show impressive and rather consistent differences (Kluft et al. 1986). When the personalities have acquired separate wardrobes, followed different interests, pursued different forms of creative expression, their differences may be marked.

Investigators have attempted to describe types of personalities (Coons et al. 1988; Putnam et al. 1986; Ross et al. 1989c). Unfortunately, their classification systems are not readily reconcilable. It appears that the picture of MPD as the ongoing clash of polarized personality types (e.g., good girl/bad girl, upright citizen/sociopath) is hard to sustain, although such clashes, when they occur, arrest attention and at times become a concern of the forensic psychiatrist. Most patients have personalities that are named, but there may be those who are nameless or whose appellations are not proper names (e.g., "the slut," "rage"). Child personalities, those who retain long periods of continuous awareness, those who claim to know about all of the others, and depressed personalities are the most frequent types enumerated (Putnam et al. 1986).

The classic host personality, which usually (more than half of the time) presents for treatment, nearly always bears the legal name and is depressed, anxious, somewhat neurasthenic, compulsively good, masochistic, conscience-stricken, and constricted hedonically, and suffers both psychophysiologic symptoms and time loss or distortion. Although no personality types are invariably present, many are encountered quite frequently: childlike personalities (fearful, recalling traumata, or love-seeking), protectors, helpers-advisors, inner self helpers (serene, rational, and objective helpers and advisors first described by Allison in 1974), personalities with distinct affective states, guardians of memories and secrets (and of family boundaries), memory traces (holding continuity of memory), inner persecutors (often based on identification with the aggressor), anesthetic personalities (created to block out pain), expressors of forbidden impulses (pleasurable and otherwise, such as defiant, aggressive, or antisocial), avengers (which express anger over abuses endured and may wish to redress their grievances), defenders or apologists for the abusers, those based on lost love objects and other introjections and identifications, specialized encapsulators of traumatic experiences and powerful affects, very specialized personalities, and those (often youthful) that preserve the idealized potential for happiness, growth, and the healthy expression of feelings (distorted by traumata) in others (Kluft 1984b).

The often dramatic differences among the personalities are more an arresting epiphenomenon than the core of the condition. Characterological factors, cultural influences, imagination, intelligence, and creativity make powerful contributions to the form taken by the personalities. Most MPD patients are rather muted compared to those cases incorrectly assumed to epitomize the condition (Kluft 1985). The personalities enact adaptational patterns and strategies that developed in the service of defense and survival. Once this pattern, which disposes of upsetting material and pressures rapidly and efficiently, is established, it may be repeated again and again to cope with both further overwhelming experiences and more mundane developmental and adaptational issues. Once the MPD that developed to cope with intolerable childhood circumstances has achieved some degree of secondary autonomy, it becomes increasingly maladaptive.

Less compelling but far more crucial than their overt manifestations are their inner belief systems, cognitive processes, and complex interrelationships. The personalities may have considerable investment in their own separateness and express a pseudo-delusional degree of conviction about their being separate and autonomous (Kluft 1984b). Although not formally psychotic, they may behave with the conviction that the actions that they take against the body or the other personalities will not affect them. Because the various alters have different memories, the information that they use to inform their behaviors is not uniform, nor are their modes of thinking identical. Hence, the several alters live in discrepant assumptive worlds, fail to function by uniform cognitive rules and processes, and manage identical data quite differently (Fine 1988a). The personalities may have quite a complex and subjectively compelling inner world, in which they have alliances, relationships, and civil wars among themselves.

## Psychophysiologic Aspects of MPD

It is intriguing indeed to encounter personalities with different handedness, different allergic responses (Braun 1983), and different responses to the same medication (Kluft 1984a), requiring different eyeglass prescriptions and differing on objective ophthalmologic measures (Miller 1989), and demonstrating measurably different patterns of response to a given stimulus (Putnam 1984). Coons (1988) reviewed the massive but primarily anecdotal literature in this area. Although there have been those who see such differences as proof of the "reality of MPD," many thoughtful students of the field, preeminently Putnam (1984), caution against such inferences. The reader is referred to his discussion of these issues elsewhere in this volume (Chapter 7). In sum, the phenomena that attract a perhaps undue attention when they occur in the context of MPD are actually expressions of more basic structures of the mind and processes in the brain; their exploration has implications far beyond the study of MPD (Putnam et al., in press; Spiegel et al. 1989).

## The Natural History of MPD

The longitudinal study of more than 200 MPD patients has clarified the natural history of MPD and shown that MPD does not undergo spontaneous remission and rarely resolves in a treatment that fails to address it directly (Kluft 1985). MPD has been demonstrated in children as young as 3 years old (Riley and Mead 1988), but many children demonstrate rather vague dissociative features that gradually coalesce into precursors of MPD (Braun and Sachs 1985; Fagan and McMahon 1984) and progress into a fully structured MPD condition (Kluft 1984c, 1985) that may become overt or may remain clandestine. Although often there appears to be a clear relationship between the form taken by the MPD and the developmental phases in which traumata occur, in others the dissociative response to trauma seems to stand aside from such considerations. Most children with MPD or its precursors show many trance-like behaviors; fluctuations in abilities, age appropriateness, and moods; intermittent depression; amnesia; hallucinated voices; passive influence experiences; disavowed polarized behaviors; and disavowed witnessed behaviors (Kluft 1984c). They may appear to be liars, show muted and attenuated signs of MPD, have inconsistencies in school behavior, and appear to have other possible diagnoses. In addition, they may show suicidal or self-injurious behaviors, have imaginary companion phenomena when over 5 years of age, and show fluctuating physical symptoms (Putnam in Kluft 1984c). Children with MPD or its precursors infrequently are invested in remaining divided; many can be treated rather rapidly (Kluft 1986b).

In adolescence, the structure of MPD usually becomes more complex and diverse, and the personalities more invested in retaining their autonomy. Often the process of personality formation becomes a general way of coping with nontraumatic material as well, and specialized alters are formed in connection with new academic, social, and psychosexual challenges. Several patterns are noted. One group of adolescent females appeared quite chaotic. Promiscuity, drug use, somatoform complaints, and self-injury were not uncommon. Three-quarters of them switched alters quite floridly, but denied this. They usually were diagnosed as impulsive, histrionic, ictal, schizophrenic, borderline, or a combination. More recently such patients have been considered as having rapid-cycling bipolar disorder. Many of them owed their confusing manifest appearance to the rapid switching of alters and to constant inner bombardment (passive influence) of the personality ostensibly in control by the other alters. Another group of the female adolescents had a more withdrawn presentation. They had either a residual childlike form of MPD, or were evolving toward the classic adult presentation of a depressed and neurasthenic host with amnesias, headaches, and disremembered out-of-character behaviors. They usually were diagnosed with affective disorders, somatoform complaints, and anxiety disorders.

The group of adolescent males includes subgroups whose confrontation with the law or school authorities were due to the actions of aggressive alters, a depressed subgroup not unlike the second subgroup of females, and a small number of individuals whose homosexual concerns dominated their presentations. The aggressive subgroup often received psychotic diagnoses on the basis of their disorganized behaviors and hallucinations, which often had a command quality.

Older adults with MPD sometimes retain a rather classic presentation and simply had never been diagnosed earlier in life. Others, however, demonstrate the increased dominance of one alter over time, the others making their presence known by passive influence intrusions. Also, in many patients, the amnestic barriers begin to fray. Many have been thought to have involutional disorders, because as the barriers across the alters became more porous with age, unpleasant memories, dysphoric affects, and the overheard voices of other alters flooded the presenting personality (Kluft 1985).

Although approximately 20% of MPD patients manifest classic phenomena over a sustained period of time, and 20% are so expert at dissimulation, so infrequent in their switching, or so covert that they rarely show diagnosable signs of MPD, the remaining 60% have periods in which their psychopathology is intrusive or symptomatic and periods (sometimes a year or more) in which it is quiescent, suppressed, or readily disavowed. Hence, 80% of a series of patients known to have DSM-III MPD had only certain "windows of diagnosability" during which their circumstances could be recognized with ease by an alert clinician (Kluft 1985, 1987b). At other times, it would have been necessary to suspect or infer their diagnosis from history, or to pursue their diagnosis with intrusive inquiries.

Overtness and the elaboration of the personalities' individual ways of behaving are not the basic phenomena of MPD. These are epiphenomena of the personalities'

modes of interaction, manner of influencing one another, type of internal hierarchy, battles for control, narcissistic investments in separateness, differential responses to intercurrent life stressors, and occasionally to secondary gain. When the personalities cooperate, collude to pass as one, have inner dialogues, or conversely, succeed in suppressing one another, little may be seen. When there is a mixture of contention and collaboration, pictures of incomplete dominance may emerge, leaving the patient polysymptomatic, but with little overt MPD. If the personalities are invested in separateness, specialized in their roles, but cooperative, an overt but smoothly functioning picture may emerge. . . . If separateness is valued, differentness is marked, and contention is high, the patient will show the "classical" picture of major abrupt dramatic shifts of personality dominance in response to psychosocial stressors and inner battles, yielding a florid clinical presentation. (Kluft 1988a, pp. 574–575)

Only approximately 10% of MPD patients (6% of adults and a small minority of adolescents) are exhibitionistic about their condition; in general, MPD is, in Gutheil's words, "a pathology of hiddenness" (Kluft 1985). MPD patients may show a degree of impairment that ranges from minimal to profound. Their degree of impairment may appear to fluctuate widely.

## ETIOLOGY

The etiology of MPD and models for its understanding have been studied (Braun 1984c; Braun and Sachs 1985; Kluft 1984d; Putnam 1989; Stern 1984). The four-factor theory (Kluft 1984d) encompasses most of the observations in the literature. It holds that the person who will develop MPD will have 1) the capacity to dissociate, which becomes mobilized for defensive purposes in the face of 2) life experiences that traumatically overwhelm the nondissociative defenses and adaptational capacities of the child's ego. Furthermore, 3) shaping influences and available substrates will determine the form taken by the dissociative defenses in the process of alter formation. Although the conjunction of these three factors is quite common, and many overwhelmed children have dissociative episodes or briefly show dissociative signs, those who will develop MPD also experience 4) the inadequate provision of stimulus barriers, soothing, and restorative experiences by significant others. The dissociative defenses continue to serve a purpose, and the person must fall back on aspects of him- or herself to provide necessary functions and relationships.

Factor 1, dissociation potential, is the biological rather than the compliance-suggestibility component of hypnotizability (Spiegel and Spiegel 1978). MPD patients, when stable and cooperative enough for such testing, are highly hypnotizable on standard instruments; it has been reported that abused populations score more highly than control subjects on measurements of hypnotizability and/or dissociation. High hypnotizability is present in 8% to 12% of the population; hypnotizability in general is highest in late childhood (discussion in Kluft 1986b).

Overwhelming experiences, factor 2, are reported in two major surveys (Putnam et al. 1986; Schultz et al. 1989); 97% of North American MPD patients alleged histories of child abuse. The majority alleged sexual abuse, usually incestuous. Child abuse is all too common, and sexual abuse may affect more than one-third of American women. Other common factors in dissociation are related to the death or loss of significant others in childhood, witnessing deaths or the deliberate destruction of a significant other, and exposure to dead bodies (especially being forced to touch or kiss them). Exposure to the deaths of others in the course of war, accidents, and various disasters may prove overwhelming, as may be severe threats to one's survival or bodily integrity, such as in severe sustained pain, debilitating illness, or a near-death experience. Cultural dislocation, brainwashing by embattled parents, being treated as if one were a different gender, and excessive exposure to family chaos may prove decisive. Some factors seem to lower the child's defenses and render subsequent events more traumatic. These include illness and pain, unintentional physical trauma, fatigue, separation-individuation complications, and having congenital anomalies and narcissistic hurts or body ego disturbances.

MPD patients often give unsettling histories of severe and bizarre abuse experiences. The vagaries of memory are well known. Although it often is possible to document allegations, and Coons and Milstein (1986) were able to do so for 85% of a series of 20 MPD patients, often there is likely to be no surviving record or cooperative witness. Few abusers indict themselves by confession. Herman and Schatzow (1987) found that 74% of their 53 non-MPD subjects were able to get confirmation of their memories of incest, 9% got suggestive but not definitive information, and most of the remainder actually did not pursue the inquires. It is of note that those whose abuse was most violent were most likely to have had amnesia for it prior to treatment. It appears likely that the MPD patient who alleges abuse was indeed abused but that the precise details of the recollection are subject to the vicissitudes of memory (see Kluft 1984d, p. 14).

Factor 3, shaping influences, notes that there are many unique configurations of intrapsychic structures and dynamics and environmental influences that may converge to give rise to the phenomenologic expression of MPD. There are many naturally occurring phenomena that may serve as the substrates for alter formation and many environmental factors that play a role as well. These include inherent mechanisms and potentials for dividedness that may be enlisted in the presence of factors 1 and 2: dissociation per se; autohypnosis; the existence and operations of multiple systems of cognition and memory (e.g., the hidden-observer phenomenon described by Hilgard 1986); ego state phenomena (Watkins and Watkins 1979); state- and mood-dependent memory (Bower 1981); the many developmental lines described in the psychoanalytic literature; imaginary companionship; the processes of introjection, internalization, and identification; state phenomena; protoaffect structures; and others.

Extrinsic influences play roles as well, especially those of one's culture. Those developing MPD today often have alters based on television characters, an event unthinkable 50 years ago. Factors of interest in childhood may be the encouragement of role playing and acting by parents, contradictory parental demands and reinforcement systems, numerous caretakers, and identification with an MPD parent, among others. Certainly representations in the media and the techniques of the therapist may influence the patient's phenomenology somewhat.

The absence of soothing and restorative experiences, factor 4, relates to observations that many children with MPD or incipient dissociative features (Fagan and McMahon 1984) simply stop manifesting them when they are protected from further traumatization. If children are not subjected to conditions under which their nascent MPD remains adaptive, in a substantial minority of cases there is a spontaneous remission; in the others there usually is a rapid response to treatment (Kluft 1986b).

The four-factor theory is consistent with clinical experience but is less than satisfactory in addressing the issues raised by the psychophysiologic differences across the alters (see Putnam 1989).

It has long been held that the etiology of MPD is iatrogenic, especially likely to be caused by the use of hypnosis and the interviewing styles of those interested in MPD, but there is no evidence to sustain this venerable stance (Braun 1984a; Gruenewald 1984; Kluft 1982, 1989; Ross 1989). Furthermore, Ross and Norton (1989) demonstrated that MPD patients who had been hypnotized both before and after treatment did not differ substantially from those who had not experienced hypnosis. Ross et al. (1989b) showed that the phenomena in groups of MPD patients reported by those with an avowed interest in MPD and those without such interest are the same. Schultz et al. (1989) found the only dimension on which clinicians interested in MPD differed from a control group was in the frequency with which they inquired about histories of child abuse. In sum, although many phenomena of MPD are very easy to suggest or to feign, and there is no reason to suspect that this has not occurred, the iatrogenic creation of a full and sustained clinical picture of MPD has yet to be demonstrated and reported (Kluft 1987e).

## EPIDEMIOLOGY

Although Coons (1984) and Worrall (unpublished data) both estimated the prevalence of MPD at 1 per 10,000 population by comparing known cases to the population base from which they were drawn, these are considered underestimates. Bliss and Jeppsen (1985) screened their practices (a skewed sample) and calculated that 10% or more of patients might suffer MPD. From new cases discovered in sequential admissions to a general hospital psychiatric unit, I estimated 0.5% to 2% of the admissions suffered MPD. Recently, Anderson et al. (unpublished data) studied sequential general psychiatric patients (excluding only known MPD and patients with organicity). Those with high scores on the Dissociative Experiences Scale (Bernstein and Putnam 1986), a screening instrument, were administered a structured interview, the Dissociative Disorders Interview Schedule (Ross 1989; Ross et al. 1989a); 6% suffered previously undiagnosed MPD.

Systematic studies undertaken to assess its prevalence in clinical populations routinely demonstrate that previously undiagnosed MPD patients can be identified with relative ease. Therefore, although its incidence and prevalence remain unknown, MPD is far from rare.

In studies completed to date, the majority of the identified patients are females: 100% (Bliss 1980), 92% (Coons et al. 1988; Putnam et al. 1986), 90% (Schultz et al. 1989), 87.7% (Ross et al. 1989c). Their average age at diagnosis is over 30. There is widespread belief that many males with MPD enter the legal rather than the psychiatric system and therefore go unrecognized. Kluft (1985) found that the majority of male adolescents with MPD encounter difficulties with the authorities. Bliss (1986) found a high incidence of dissociative disorders among convicted sex offenders. Also, the majority of childhood MPD cases reported to date are male. Taken as a whole, these findings suggest that as males with MPD mature, certain aspects of their behavior may lead to their evading clinical detection. The nearly 9 to 1 female-to-male ratio or lower indices of clinical suspicion noted above probably misrepresents the true gender distribution of MPD.

## DIFFERENTIAL DIAGNOSIS

### Diagnosis

The diagnosis of MPD has been the subject of several studies (Coons 1984; Kluft 1987b, 1988a; Solomon and Solomon 1982). Putnam et al. (1986), Ross et al. (1989c), and Coons et al. (1988) found that series of MPD patients averaged 6.8, 7.1, and 7.0 years, respectively, between their entry into the mental health system and their receiving the MPD diagnosis. They usually have had more than three prior psychiatric diagnoses.

MPD or dissociative disorder not otherwise specified (DDNOS) with the structure of MPD should be suspected whenever both alternating separate identities and episodes of amnesia or time distortion are present. Further exploration will indicate whether the condition is MPD or DDNOS and which concomitant diagnoses ought to be rendered. Because a plethora of symptoms and signs may be found in the current mental status, the history, and previous records, the psychiatrist may be perplexed by what appear to be findings suggesting coexistence of the stigmata of several conditions. The superordinate diagnosis concept noted above is useful.

Apart from a patient's manifesting the classic features of MPD, there are a number of findings that suggest a patient merits careful scrutiny for this condition: 1) prior treatment failure; 2) three or more prior diagnoses; 3) concurrent psychiatric and somatic symptoms; 4) fluctuating symptoms and levels of function; 5) severe headaches and/or other pain syndromes; 6) time distortion, time lapses, or frank amnesia; 7) being told of disremembered behaviors; 8) others noting observable changes; 9) the discovery of objects, productions, or handwriting in one's possession that one cannot account for or recognize; 10) the hearing of voices (80% experienced as within the head) that are experienced as separate, urging the patient toward some activity; 11) the patient's use of "we" in a collective sense and/or making self-referential statements in the third person; 12) the eliciting of other entities through hypnosis or a drug-facilitated interview; 13) a history of child abuse; and 14) an inability to recall childhood events from the years 6 to 11.

Concerning item 12, it is quite important to realize that there are many phenomena that may be elicited in the course of hypnosis and drug-facilitated interviews and overendorsed as MPD (Kluft 1982) (e.g., the ego states that may be mobilized in the course of the ego state therapy paradigm of Watkins and Watkins [1979–1980] and the "hidden-observer" cognitive systems described by Hilgard [1986]). Concerning item 14, failure to recall the events of early childhood is a nearly universal experience and quite normative. However, many MPD patients have large amnestic gaps with regard to their grade school and preadolescent years.

The interview of the MPD patient may provide many subtle signs of the condition (Franklin 1988), such as brief switch-like phenomena; fluctuations of behavior, facies, and personal style; and micro-amnestic episodes within the session. Loewenstein et al. (1988) reasoned that if the modal MPD patient demonstrates 1) indications of the MPD process at work (e.g., differences in behavior, linguistic indications, switching), 2) signs of the patient's high hypnotic potential (e.g., enthrallment, trance logic, out-of-body experiences), 3) amnesia, 4) somatoform symptoms, 5) PTSD symptoms, and 6) affective symptoms, the patient who shows symptoms and signs in all of these areas in a first interview is highly likely to have MPD. That an apparently bewildering welter of manifestations may itself constitute a coherent and recognizable presentation is a useful insight.

That MPD patients endorse a number of first-rank symptoms, once considered pathognomonic for schizophrenia in the absence of organicity, makes them useful diagnostic signs for MPD. These include feelings, impulses, and volitional acts experienced as imposed on one from some other source and not as being one's own (the "made" phenomenon); voices arguing in one's head; influences playing on the body; experiencing thoughts ascribed to others; thought withdrawal; and voices commenting on one's actions. The average MPD patient endorses 3.6 of these symptoms in initial interviews and more as treatment goes on (Kluft 1987a; Ross and Norton 1988). Since most MPD patients but few schizophrenic patients score highly on the Hypnotic Induction Profile (HIP), a test of hypnotizability (Spiegel and Spiegel 1978), this may prove a useful differential diagnostic measure.

The overt signs of MPD may not become manifest within one or more diagnostic encounters. On occasion, only a tentative diagnosis is possible, based on history, ancillary data, and clinical judgment. Many clinicians assign patients the task of keeping a journal for 20 to 30 minutes a day, because other personalities may make entries. The author's experience is that when an MPD process is active, an extended interview is often helpful. Spontaneous dissociation is often witnessed after a period of 2.5 to 3 hours (Kluft 1987b, 1987d).

Experienced diagnosticians frequently focus on making detailed inquiries about perplexing events, amnestic periods, and the onset of symptomatic behaviors. Often this precipitates the spontaneous emergence of alters associated with them. When information suggestive of MPD is available, but an alter has not emerged spontaneously, asking to meet an alter directly is an increasingly accepted intervention (Putnam 1989). This is usually done in connection with a puzzling or out-of-character event that the patient is known to have had, but for which the patient lacks recall (e.g., "I would like to talk to that part of you that purchased several dresses last Thursday"). Initial attempts of this nature may not be successful; the denial, resistance, and apprehension may prove insurmountable. The response to such a request may be the emergence of an alter, but, more frequently, there will be signs of visible discomfort, and the pursuit of the discomfort that is experienced will lead to more highly suggestive data, and finally to the emergence of an alter. In some instances, the use of hypnosis or of drug-facilitated interviewing may prove a useful adjunct, with the caveats noted above.

Patients suspected of having MPD may be assessed with the Dissociative Experiences Scale, mentioned earlier. This brief self-administered instrument is for screening purposes only. False negatives are encountered in known MPD patients, but most will have high scores in a range rarely endorsed by adult patients from other diagnostic groups.

Two structured interviews for the diagnosis of MPD have been devised. The Dissociative Disorders Interview Schedule, also mentioned earlier, is a 131-question instrument that thus far has demonstrated a 90% sensitivity and a specificity of 100%. It invites the patient to endorse or not to endorse a series of symptoms keyed to various DSM-III diagnostic criteria. The Structured Clinical Interview for Dissociative Disorders (Steinberg et al. 1990) is a more elaborate interview currently undergoing field trials. It is extremely comprehensive and sensitive and has shown the capacity to pick up previously unsuspected cases of dissociative disorders.

If the diagnostic criteria for MPD are fulfilled, and there is no reason to suspect malingering, MPD is present. The issue then becomes which concomitant diagnoses ought be rendered (Kluft 1987b, 1988a).

## Differential Diagnosis

Psychogenic fugue and psychogenic amnesia usually occur as single discrete and brief episodes. Such patients infrequently have the wide range of symptoms encounted in MPD, except for the episode at hand. Psychotic disorders may be confused with MPD because such patients complain of being influenced or possessed and hearing or talking with other voices; their pseudo-delusional self-concepts and the distorted interpretations of the circumstances that flow from them may also confuse. Incoherence and true looseness of associations, and items 3, 4, 5, 6, and 8 of DSM-III-R schizophrenia criterion D,[1] which focus on negative

---

[1] "(3) markedly peculiar behavior (e.g., collecting garbage, talking to self in public, hoarding food); (4) marked impairment in personal hygiene and grooming; (5) blunted or inappropriate

symptoms and deteriorated behavior, are unusual in MPD patients unless they have been institutionalized. Almost two-thirds of MPD patients suffer auditory hallucinations, and about 80% of those who do experience them as emanating from within their heads. They are overhearing the thought processes of the other alters or experiencing their memories, wishes, emotions, and reactions. The flashbacks of traumata and the conflicts and interactions among the alters give rise to a large number of quasi-psychotic features, all of which can be induced with hypnosis: hallucinations in all spheres (including hearing voices arguing and commenting on one's actions), reliving of past events with misperception of the present for the past, catatonia as alters in conflict render the body immobile, thought withdrawal, thought insertion, influences playing on the body, and "made" feelings, impulses, and volitional acts (Kluft 1987a). The use of the HIP and the response of MPD patients' "psychotic" symptoms to hypnosis may be a useful clue.

Rapid-cycling affective disorders have become a common misdiagnosis of MPD; the conditions are distinguished by the mercurial nature of the MPD patient's mood shifts, which can occur within seconds or minutes, and the discovery of the alters associated with the moods in question. Most MPD patients manifest borderline phenomenology, but do so on the basis of the chaos occasioned by the switching and contention of the alters rather than on the basis of ego weaknesses and primitive defenses (Solomon and Solomon 1982). The diagnoses of MPD and borderline personality disorder (BPD) are not mutually exclusive. I find it useful to withhold the BPD diagnosis unless its criteria are encountered within the several personalities rather than as an epiphenomenon of their interaction.

Many behaviors of malingerers overlap with the natural phenomenology of MPD (Kluft 1987d). The data provided by ancillary data sources may prove crucial, but cannot automatically be regarded as more reliable than the patient's (e.g., interviewing a father alleged to be an incest perpetrator and eliciting a denial). Most (but not all) malingerers base their rendition of MPD on lay sources, enact primarily good-bad personalities, are less complex and less consistent than genuine cases, and are less competent in enacting MPD behaviors in subject areas remote from their forensic concerns. They rarely endorse the plethora of physical and mental complaints that afflict genuine cases. True MPD patients in difficult straits may augment or dissimulate their condition to serve the needs of the moment. True MPD patients usually will demonstrate their dissociation potential on a convenient measure of hypnotizability, such as the HIP. However, false negatives are encountered.

Partial complex seizures usually are brief (30 seconds to 5 minutes), rarely chronic or longer. Therefore, it is easy to confuse the switch process in MPD with brief ictal events, but more difficult to confuse the sustained appearance of complex out-of-character behavior by an alter with a seizure event. Often either hypnosis, drug-facilitated interviews, or newer combined telemetric and observational techniques can resolve the issue (Kluft 1988a).

In forensic circumstances, it is critical for the psychiatrist to abstain from blurring the roles of evaluator and therapist. The scrupulous assessment of ancillary data is essential, and, if the evaluation may go on to employ hypnosis or a drug-facilitated interview, guidelines appropriate for the use of such intrusive measures should be followed.

---

affect; (6) digressive, vague, overelaborate, or circumstantial speech, or poverty of speech, or poverty of content of speech; . . . (8) unusual perceptual experiences (e.g., recurrent illusions, sensing the presence of a force or person not actually present" (DSM-III-R, p. 195).

# COMORBIDITY

MPD is usually a polysymptomatic and pleiomorphic condition, varying widely over its clinical course even within a single patient. Putnam et al. (1984) suggested that MPD is best understood as a superordinate diagnosis, under which a vast array of symptomatology suggestive of other diagnostic entities may be subsumed. Several investigators have described the concomitant psychopathology (Bliss 1980, 1986; Coons et al. 1988; Horevitz and Braun 1984; Putnam et al. 1986; Ross et al. 1989c). Unfortunately, their protocols and definitions were not uniform. Therefore, although it is possible to discuss the association of certain symptoms with MPD, it is far more difficult to make statements concerning actual comorbidity.

Combining data from the above sources, MPD patients demonstrate anxiety symptoms (psychophysiologic, $\approx 100\%$; phobic, $\approx 60\%$; panic attacks, $\approx 55\%$; obsessive-compulsive, $\approx 35\%$); affective symptoms (depressive, $\approx 90\%$; "highs," 15–73%); allied dissociative symptoms (amnesias, 57–100%; fugues, 48–60%; depersonalization, $\approx 38\%$); somatoform symptoms (all, $\approx 90\%$; conversion, $\approx 60\%$); sexual dysfunctions (60–84%); suicide attempts (60–68%); self-mutilation (34%); psychoactive substance abuse ($\approx 40$–45%); eating disorders (16–40%); sleep disturbance ($\approx 65\%$); symptoms suggestive of schizophrenia (depending on symptoms, 35–73%); symptoms of PTSD (70–85%); and the stigmata of BPD (70%).

Symptoms of PTSD often occur in MPD. The conditions have similar etiologies; it is arguable that MPD is a PTSD variant. Many phenomena are shared by MPD and schizophrenia, as noted above. The coexistence of MPD and schizophrenia has not yet been reported in the modern era.

The phenomena of BPD commonly co-occur with MPD. MPD has been considered a BPD variant, but many MPD patients are without signs of BPD. Horevitz and Braun (1984) and Schultz et al. (unpublished data) both found that 70% of MPD patients satisfied DSM-III criteria for BPD. Horevitz and Braun (1984) found that MPD and BPD were separate conditions. Those who satisfied criteria for both disorders had a far lower level of function and were more distressed. The MPD-BPD interface is quite complex. First, BPD patients are a highly abused population; many could have a posttraumatic condition. Second, Solomon and Solomon (1982) demonstrated that the core phenomena of MPD lead to the appearance of BPD rather than to an identical condition; that is, MPD generates a phenocopy of BPD rather than coexists with true BPD in many instances. Third, Schultz et al. (unpublished data) found that coexistent BPD features did not alter the frequency with which MPD patients achieved and sustained integration, which is the opposite of what we would expect if true BPD were present. Fourth, Kluft (unpublished data) found that of treatment adherent patients who appear to have both MPD and BPD, one-third rapidly ceased to show BPD features once they settled into treatment, one-third lost their apparent BPD as their MPD resolved, and one-third retained BPD features even after integration. He concluded that MPD generates a phenocopy of BPD and that only a minority of MPD patients have true BPD.

# TREATMENT

## Modalities

Many therapeutic approaches to MPD have been described (reviewed in Kluft

1984a, 1984d, 1986a), but individual psychotherapy, psychodynamic in orientation and supportive-expressive in stance, augmented when necessary with hypnosis or drug-facilitated interviews, has been used in the vast majority of reported successful treatments. Other modalities may play valuable ancillary roles (Kluft 1984a; Putnam 1989; Sachs 1986). Although the need for the treatment of MPD phenomena has been challenged, such approaches have resulted in the substantial betterment of many MPD patients who had not responded to numerous prior therapies. Follow-up studies of those who decline treatment or whose MPD is untreated remain MPD indicate that they retain their MPD (Kluft 1984d, 1985, 1986a, unpublished data). In the absence of controlled studies, the weight of clinical experience indicates that intense individual psychotherapy facilitated when necessary by hypnosis or other measures is the treatment of choice for MPD and that the prognosis for motivated patients working with therapists experienced with is quite good.

## Today's Therapeutic Pluralism

Four main approaches to MPD appear to be emerging. The first, integrationalism, sets as its goal the integration of the individual in the course of the resolution of problematic symptoms and difficulties in living. The second, personality-focused, is less inclined to see dividedness itself as problematic, and focuses on a problem-solving inner diplomacy or group or family therapy among a family of selves, which are encouraged to collaborate more harmoniously without necessarily ceding their separateness. A more functional and facile arrangement among the elements of the mind is the major objective. The third, adaptationalism, focuses primarily on managing here-and-now difficulties and maximizing function. A fourth, which might be called minimalism, actively discourages work with the MPD per se. The latter has not been demonstrated to be effective, and will not be discussed further.

## Goals of Treatment

The unification of the MPD patient is only one aspect of the treatment of a suffering individual. . . . The tasks of the therapy are the same as those of any reasonably intense change-oriented approach. However, these tasks are pursued in an individual who lacks a unified personality (and hence observing ego). The several personalities may have different perceptions, memories, problems, priorities, goals, and different degrees of involvement with and commitment to the treatment and to one another. It usually becomes essential to replace dividedness with unity, at least of purpose and motivation, for any treatment to succeed. Work toward this goal and possible integration of all personalities distinguishes the treatment of MPD. (Kluft 1984d, p. 11)

Authorities differ as to whether integration should be pursued. Putnam (1989) observed that it is the patient's right to remain multiple (just as it is the right of any patient to interrupt any treatment at any point). Nonetheless, the vast majority of experienced therapists value integration and find that patients who continue as "well MPDs" remain differentially vulnerable due to their ongoing dissociation, which is ego weakening. In Kluft's (1984d) follow-up of patients who elected resolution rather than integration, most either moved toward unification or relapsed into dysfunctional MPD. What follow are the author's experience-based observations as to treatment goals.

With children with MPD, integration is universally desirable if the patient can be protected against further abuse, but treatment should remain supportive until this is achieved. For MPD adolescents, many of their developmental tasks and priorities are at odds with treatment toward integration, and many of them decline or combat therapy. Often all one can do is to attempt to protect the potential trajectory of their lives and to build a foundation for later treatment. For the person who is or who may become a parent, integration is preferable. Studies of MPD mothers (Kluft 1987c) show that while 38% are good or exceptional parents, for the remainder, their self-report as good parents may be at odds with reality. A minority are frankly abusive, but the majority are compromised in their parental function by the amnesias and inconsistencies of the alters. Also, identification with an MPD parent is hardly the basis for strong personality development. For those without such concerns, an outcome that will stabilize their lives is optimal, and perhaps resolution can effect that. For older or medically infirm MPD patients, quality of life issues are paramount. Treatment toward integration may prove too unsettling for them to endure, although methods exist to attenuate the impact of the therapy.

## Principles of Successful Therapy With MPD

Bowers et al. (1971) first enunciated the guiding principles of treating MPD, in essence, the respectful treatment of the personalities and their difficulties while discouraging their irresponsible autonomy and always indicating that they are parts or aspects of a single human being. What follows is the author's attempt to crystallize his reading and clinical experience into a series of precepts that characterize the successful treatment of MPD, and are violated in many therapies that fail to prosper.

1. MPD is a condition that was created by broken boundaries. Therefore, a successful treatment will have a secure treatment frame and firm, consistent boundaries.
2. MPD is a condition of subjective dyscontrol and passively endured assaults and changes. Therefore, there must be a focus on mastery and the patient's active participation in the treatment process.
3. MPD is a condition of involuntariness. Its sufferers did not elect to be traumatized and find their symptoms are often beyond their control. Therefore, the therapy must be based on a strong therapeutic alliance, and efforts to establish this must be undertaken throughout the process.
4. MPD is a condition of buried traumata and sequestered affect. Therefore, what has been hidden away must be uncovered, and what feeling has been buried must be abreacted.
5. MPD is a condition of perceived separateness and conflict among the alters. Therefore, the therapy must emphasize their collaboration, cooperation, empathy, and identification with one another so that their separateness becomes redundant and their conflicts are muted.
6. MPD is a condition of hypnotic alternate realities. Therefore, the therapist's communications must be clear and straight. There is no room for confusing communication.
7. MPD is a condition related to the inconsistency of important others. Therefore, the therapist must be evenhanded to all the alters, avoiding "playing favorites" or dramatically altering his or her own behavior toward the different personalities. The therapist's consistency across all of the alters is one of the most powerful assaults on the patient's dissociative defenses.

8. MPD is a condition of shattered security, self-esteem, and future orientation. Therefore, the therapy must make efforts to restore morale and inculcate realistic hope.

9. MPD is a condition stemming from overwhelming experiences. Therefore, the pacing of the therapy is essential. Most treatment failures occur when the pace of the therapy outstrips the patient's capacity to tolerate the material under discussion. It is wise to adhere to the author's "rule of thirds" (unpublished): if one cannot get into the difficult material one planned to address in the first third of the session, to work on it in the second, and process it and restabilize the patient in the third not approaching the material, lest the patient leave the session in an overwhelmed state. Abreaction cannot be allowed to become retraumatization.

10. MPD is a condition that often results from the irresponsibility of others. Therefore, the therapist must be very responsible, and hold the patient to a high standard of responsibility once the therapist is confident that the patient, across alters, actually grasps what reasonable responsibility entails.

11. MPD is a condition that often results because people who could have protected a child did nothing. The therapist can anticipate that technical neutrality will be interpreted as uncaring and rejecting and is best served by taking a warmer stance that allows for a latitude of affective expression.

12. MPD is a condition in which the patient has developed many cognitive errors. The therapy must address and correct them on an ongoing basis.

## The Stages of Therapy

Both Braun (1986) and Putnam (1989) have attempted to outline the stages or phases in therapy. Many of these stages are overlapping and/or ongoing. What follows is a synthesis of their work and the author's.

1. *Establishing the psychotherapy* involves the creation of an atmosphere of safety in which the diagnosis can be made, the security of the treatment frame can be assured, the patient begins to understand the concept of the treatment alliance in a preliminary way, the nature of the treatment is introduced to the patient, and sufficient hope and confidence is established so that the patient feels prepared to begin what may be a long and difficult process.

2. *Preliminary interventions* involve gaining access to the more readily reached personalities; establishing agreements or contracts with the alters against terminating treatment abruptly, self-harm, suicide, and as many other dysfunctional behaviors as the patient is able to agree to curtail; fostering communication and cooperation among the alters (a process that is the core of the treatment from here on); expanding the therapeutic alliance by achieving the patient's acceptance of the diagnosis across increasing numbers of the personalities (some will deny it to the end); and offering what symptomatic relief is possible. Hypnosis may play an invaluable role in facilitating these measures.

3. *History gathering and mapping* refers to learning more about the personalities, their origins, and their relationships with one another. The MPD patient may be regarded as a system with its own rules of interaction. Here one learns the who, when, why, where, what, and how of the alters (Braun 1986): their names (if any); age of onset and self-perceived age; the reasons for their creation and persistence; where they fit in the patient's overall history and in their relationships within

"the world of the personalities"; and their particular problems, functions, and concerns. On this basis, one begins to work with their individual and interactional issues and presses for still more cooperation and collaboration.

4. *Metabolism of the trauma* refers to the often strenuous efforts needed to access and process the overwhelming events associated with the origins of the MPD. Such work should not be undertaken until one has some idea of the "lay of the land" in terms of the patient's system of personalities and at least some intellectual insight into what material is likely to be encountered. Negative therapeutic reactions are not uncommon. Precipitous or premature entry into this stage before stages 1 through 3 are achieved is a frequent cause of unnecessary crises and interruptions of therapy.

5. *Moving toward integration-resolution* involves the working through of recovered materials across the alters and facilitating still further cooperation, communication, and mutual awareness with enhanced mutual identification and empathy. Communication is increased, many internal conflicts become muted or resolved, and the alters begin to show some blurring of their once more discrete characteristics. Some experience identity diffusion (e.g., "for a moment I wasn't sure who I was"; "I guess I am both Sally and Joanie").

6. *Integration-resolution* consists of the patient's coming to a new and more solid stance toward his or her self and the world. A smooth collaboration among the alters will constitute a resolution; their blending into a unity is an integration (see below).

7. *Learning new coping skills* is quite important. The patient may have to face for the first time perspectives on his or her life that were not appreciable before, and be helped to negotiate the circumstances that once were handled in a dissociative manner in more constructive ways. Many important life decisions and relationships may require renegotiation.

8. *Solidification of gains and working through* may require as much therapy as reaching integration or resolution. The MPD patient has to relearn how to live in the world. Often working through in the transference what has been learned about the past is invaluable. Characterological issues that were inaccessible before or hidden behind a welter of symptoms must be addressed. Often extensive coaching on the management of relationships and intercurrent traumata is necessary.

9. *Follow-up* is advisable on several grounds. The stability of the outcome should be assessed, especially for those who opt for resolution rather than integration. Also, layers of personalities that had not entered the prior treatment may be encountered, and some apparent good results are flights into health.

## Pragmatic Aspects of the Treatment

The major vehicle of treatment is intense individual psychotherapy. It can be an arduous, prolonged, and painful experience for the patient, who may be dealing with difficult material for years on end. Although some highly functioning, some mildly afflicted, and some MPD patients seen supportively or with an adaptationalist emphasis do well in a single session a week, most therapists agree that two or more sessions, or at least a session of double length, is preferable. Putnam (1989) advocates sessions of 90 minutes, others emphasize more the structure and support offered by several contacts. The author's experience is that more rapid and satisfactory results with fewer crises and hospitalizations are encountered in a treatment of greater intensity; that for many patients seen less frequently, the therapy is never sufficiently intense and structuring to offer them a safe environment to do the work that has to be done. Although many uncomplicated patients treated intensively recover in months, the treatment of more complex cases may take many years (Kluft 1984d, 1986a, 1988b).

Because the MPD patient is inherently crisis prone, and the treatment is demanding and may prove destabilizing, emergencies and telephone calls between sessions are commonplace. The therapist who is accessible, but who insists on his or her accessibility being respected and not abused, usually creates an atmosphere in which such occasions diminish. Very commonly resolutions of crises among alters in conflict can be negotiated over the telephone quite rapidly, with a resolution that the matter be addressed in the next session.

Typical patterns of countertransference responses to MPD patients may be expected. Initial fascination and overinvestment usually yield to feelings of bewilderment, exasperation, and a sense of being drained by the patient. Therapists may feel angry or fatigued (Coons 1986; Kluft 1984a). Most react with one or more of the following four countertransferences at various times: 1) Withdrawal from empathic involvement to a detached, skeptical, and detective-like stance in which the patient's credibility is overtly or covertly doubted or tested; 2) The decision that this individual has been so badly harmed that nothing but tangible redress can cure them—the boundaries of therapy are abrogated in the attempt to love the patient into health; 3) It seems clear that action, not therapy, is in order, and the therapist becomes an advocate for the patient; and 4) The transient trial identification of empathy is breached and full counteridentification occurs. The therapist develops a variant of secondary posttraumatic stress and becomes devastated by work with the patient's pain. If such reactions become fixed rather than transient, supervision and/or therapy of the therapist may be in order.

## Integration

Personalities integrate or can be integrated when their reason for being is ablated, but in some instances a narcissistic investment in separateness outlives the alters' function. Integration is often used as an all-encompassing concept, and as a synonym for fusion, but within the MPD field, integration refers to an ongoing process of undoing all aspects of dissociative dividedness that begins long before there is any reduction in the number or distinctness of the personalities, persists through their fusion, and continues at a deeper level even after the personalities have blended into one. An alter believed to have ceased being separate is considered "apparently fused" (Kluft 1982, 1984d) as of that moment. Any patient's system of personalities should not be considered actually to have fused until there have been three stable months of 1) continuity of contemporary memory, 2) absence of overt behavioral signs of MPD, 3) subjective sense of unity, 4) absence of alters (or the particular alter) on reexploration (preferably involving hypnosis), 5) modification of the transference phenomena consistent with the bringing together of the personalities, and 6) clinical evidence that the unified patient's self-representation includes acknowledgment of attitudes and awarenesses that were previously segregated in separate personalities (Kluft 1982, 1987e).

In sum, integration and fusion, often used as synonyms, differ in that integration refers to an ongoing process whereas fusion refers to the moment in time at which alters can be considered to have ceded separateness. A final integration of the patient usually occurs only after the failure of some preliminary attempts and the working through of whatever issues led to them (including the discovery of other alters). Many fusions occur abruptly and spontaneously after critical work is completed, others occur slowly and gradually as alters approximate or negotiate their differences, and others are facilitated by hypnosis.

In a series of 91 integrated MPD patients, Kluft (1988c) identified seven recurrent areas of concern. First, coping with psychophysiologic changes due to integration is often difficult. Some patients have periods of exquisite sensory acuity and exhilarating hyperalertness, others have easy fatigability or somnolence, and some have both experiences. Symptoms may vanish or resolved ones may transiently reappear. Responses and tolerances to medicines, foods, and customary activities may fluctuate before achieving a new stability. Second, coping with psychological changes may be trying. What was disavowed and intolerable no longer can be cordoned off; displeasing subjective experiences must be endured. The experience of strong affects and ambivalence, the complexity of life, and the confusion occasioned by its many gray areas, all may be troublesome for a person accustomed to evading the problematic and seeing the world in black and white terms. Third, much more working through will be necessary by a patient who usually has overdramatized the importance of integration and hoped that the pain of therapy was in the past. Much has been lost; much must be grieved. Fourth, the patient will need help with abandoning autohypnotic evasions. Fifth, modification of the patient's adaptive style and coping strategies will be essential. One major issue is the need for some reeducation concerning power and morality. Most MPD patients have come to identify strength with evil and weakness with good. It is often hard for them to be assertive and deal with issues of activity and passivity. Sixth, interpersonal adjustments may be painful and complex. Such patients may require extensive reeducation about the nature of relationships. It is often painful for them to decide what to do about abusers with whom they, long amnestic for the abuse, have had ongoing relationships. Finally, major life changes may have to be considered.

## Special Application of Hypnosis in the Treatment of MPD

As noted above, all treatments of MPD involve hypnosis, whether it is introduced deliberately or not. The therapeutic use of hypnosis for MPD has been the subject of several authors (e.g., Braun 1984b; Kluft 1982; Putnam 1989). Supportive uses include hypnosis to help the patients understand and begin to master the nature of dissociation by restructuring their understanding, so that they begin to see that it is possible to master the process that they experience as so out of control. Also, its use in anxiety and symptom relief, ego strengthening, and providing useful deep trance experiences can be helpful. Often the collaborative effort of patient and therapist in working toward trance facilitates the therapeutic alliance in general. Hypnosis can also be used in a variety of ways that attenuate the impact of powerful events and affects and that allow the patient some surcease of the pressures of the treatment by placing memories and feelings "on hold."

Exploratory uses involve the use of ideomotor signaling to allow the questioning of alters without their full emergence; accessing alters; or gaining historical information by direct inquiry, by age regression, by affect bridge, or by other evocative techniques. Hypnosis is often used, in connection with some exploratory uses, to facilitate the abreaction of traumatic events. Often it is possible to exert some control over the process of abreactions that are hypnotically induced. Hypnotically suggested time distortion may give the patient a subjective experience of a prolonged abreaction when the procedure has in fact been done rather rapidly.

Hypnosis has many roles to play in facilitating integration (Kluft 1982). A suggestion can be made that several or all alters listen during instructions or particular pieces of therapeutic work. The author's most common hypnotic instruction is to request "Everybody listen." One can talk through or over the alter currently in ostensible control to many at once. Alters can be instructed to converse in internal dialog and to spend time close together, and can be called out simultaneously. When alters approaching integration experience themselves as being different ages, and this subjective experience does not change spontaneously, age progression can be suggested. Finally, and most dramatically, hypnosis can be used to offer rituals of integration, which usually consist of vivid images of joining with which the alters identify. Hypnosis is also quite useful for making periodic rechecks of the personalities and their progress in short order.

## Ancillary Therapeutic Modalities

Although intensive individual psychotherapy is the mainstay of the treatment of MPD, many other modalities may be of use. MPD patients often fare poorly in heterogeneous verbal group therapies, both proving disruptive to and disrupted by such approaches (Kluft 1984a). Homogenous MPD groups have proven a valuable adjunct (Caul et al. 1986; Coons and Bradley 1985). An exception may occur if the MPD patient can remain without overt switching in the group, or if the MPD patient has much in common with those in a specialized group, such as Alcoholics Anonymous or an incest survivors' group. MPD patients often do well in the more structured formats of art, movement, music, and occupational therapy. Family therapy with MPD patients' families of origin is rarely productive, and usually counterproductive, but supportive family work with their current significant others can be very helpful (Kluft et al. 1984). The marital treatment of MPD patients and their partners is often necessary and desirable (Sachs et al. 1988). Not only are their relationships often troubled or dysfunctional, but their partners may need considerable education and support. Cognitive and behavioral techniques may be quite valuable, but rarely as the core of the treatment (Fine 1988a).

Many clinicians have used videotape technology and advocated its use in providing both confrontation and feedback to the patient (first described by Caul 1984). The technology itself is without curative powers; providing such experiences to a patient may prove disruptive rather than healing. Certain therapists and patients have found the carefully timed and monitored review of such material helpful, but many have not.

## Psychopharmacology

No medication has yet demonstrated a specific impact on dissociative psychopathology. The available reviews (Barkin et al. 1986; Kluft 1984a; Putnam 1989) concur that medications with such patients are employed to treat coexisting conditions, to palliate intense dysphoria, and to approach particular target symptoms, many of which are of a posttraumatic variety. As a group, MPD patients are characterized by a higher than average degree of complaints about side effects, a tendency to deceptive brief placebo responses, and occasional instances of differential drug responses across personalities. Anxiolytics and sedatives are useful palliatives, but rarely offer complete relief and are prone to misuse by the overwrought patient. Antidepressants are often effective for a coexisting or symptomatic depression if it is experienced across the several personalities. Their effects on so-called depressed personalities is usually equivocal. No role for major tranquilizers, mood stabilizers, or anticonvulsants has been established.

Loewenstein et al. (1988) demonstrated that clonazepam was quite useful in alleviating posttraumatic symptoms in the majority of MPD patients in a small open trial. Anecdotally, propranolol is considered useful in many MPD patients, especially those that appear quite chaotic and to be switching rapidly (Braun, personal communication, 1988). The author has used a combination of these two medications in several MPD patients with considerable relief of their subjective distress. Until controlled studies are available, it is useful to be circumspect:

> Neither automatically denying nor readily acceding to the patient's requests for relief is reasonable. Several questions must be raised: 1) Is the distress part of a medication-responsive syndrome? 2) If the answer to 1) is yes, is it of sufficient clinical importance to outweigh possible adverse impacts of prescription. If the answer to 1) is no, whom would the drug treat (the physician's need to "do something," an anxious third party, etc.)? 3) Is there a non-pharmacological intervention which might prove effective instead? 4) Does the overall management require an intervention which the psychiatrist realizes is non-specific, but feels is essential? 5) What is the patient's "track record" in response to interventions similar to the one which is planned? 6) Weighing all considerations, do the potential benefits outweigh the potential risk? (Kluft 1984a, p. 53)

## The Hospital Treatment of MPD

The indications for hospitalization for MPD are the same as for other disorders, with the additional caveat that at times the clinician can anticipate that work with particular types of material may prove so taxing that the structure of a hospital setting will be a useful "prosthetic environment" and/or protection against a negative therapeutic reaction. Brief hospitalizations may be indicated, for example, to weather situational crises that trigger self-destructive urges or outward-directed hostility, minor regressions in the face of unsettling material, and psychotic-like symptoms reflecting acute conflicts among alters. Hospitalizations of moderate length may be necessary to deal with severe regressions, refractory pressures toward self-harm or outward-directed aggression, and decompensations of the personality system such that the patient is too chaotic by virtue of amnesias and switches to function or that the alters are so conflicted or decompensated that they cannot easily reestablish a functional modus vivendi. Prolonged hospitalizations may be required for profound decompensations, particularly refractory pressures to hurt self or others, or when the abuse the patient has suffered has continued into the present.

The literature on the hospital care of MPD is small and not in total accord. It is useful to place the patient in a private room when possible, and to inform the staff about the diagnosis, the goals of the admission, and any proposed therapeutic interventions that are novel to the unit in question. Opinions differ as to whether the patient (outside of therapy sessions) should be addressed by the name the patient gives at a given moment in time or by the legal name, but there is agreement that the patient must agree to respond to the legal name for administrative purposes and for most interactions. Addressing alters by name is mostly the province of dyadic interactions, not of the patient's general commerce with all staff and the community. The staff need not assume the responsibility of recognizing the alters; the alters must identify themselves. Alters based on children or alters that would be extremely disruptive to the milieu in other ways should be encouraged to restrict their emergences to therapy sessions and the privacy of their own rooms. Ward rules should be explained by the therapist, requesting all alters to listen. Reasonable compliance must be enforced; when amnestic barriers or the conflicts of alters result in rule breaking, a firm but kindly and nonpunitive stance is useful. Likely crises should be anticipated with the staff, and tangible management plans set in place. The patient should be excused from those therapeutic activities that are counterproductive for MPD, such as many of the heterogeneous group therapies, unless the patient can contract to attend them in a single alter. The MPD patient must be encouraged to address him- or herself to the main tasks of the admission and discouraged from prolonged fretfulness over minor mishaps in the milieu.

Specialized treatment facilities for the management of MPD patients have emerged. It is likely that the fruits of their experience will contribute much to the understanding of the management of MPD patients in other settings as well.

## EMERGING TRENDS AND FUTURE DIRECTIONS

The study of MPD is expanding with such vigor and rapidity that it is difficult to anticipate the growth of the field. Advances in work with MPD children and adolescents are highly desirable, because it is clear that the treatment of children has the potential to be much more rapid than that of adults, and because, in all candor, the treatment of adolescents with MPD is in its infancy, with many authorities agreeing that this is the population with which they have the least success. Therefore, it will be essential either to learn how to approach the adolescents with more facility, or to become more effective in identifying and treating childhood MPD and its precursors. Current research holds the promise of accelerating the recognition of MPD in adults. Hopefully, future studies will allow psychiatrists to treat this condition more rapidly and effectively and make possible the better allocation of available resources. The study of the psychophysiology of MPD may prove to be a valuable window into the mind-body interface.

## REFERENCES

Allison RB: A new treatment approach for multiple personalities. Am J Clin Hypn 17:15–32, 1974

American Psychiatric Association: Diagnostic and Statistical Manual of Mental Disorders, 3rd Edition. Washington, DC, American Psychiatric Association, 1980

American Psychiatric Association: Diagnostic and Statistical Manual of Mental Disorders, 3rd Edition, Revised. Washington, DC, American Psychiatric Association, 1987

Adityanjee, Raju GSP, Khandelwal SK: Current status of multiple personality disorder in India. Am J Psychiatry 146:1607–1610, 1989

Barkin R, Braun BG, Kluft RP: The dilemma of drug therapy for multiple personality disorder, in Treatment of Multiple Personality Disorder. Edited by Braun BG. Washington, DC, American Psychiatric Press, 1986, pp 107–132

Bernstein EM, Putnam FW: Development, reliability, and validity of a dissociation scale. J Nerv Ment Dis 174:727–734, 1986

Bliss EL: Multiple personalities: a report of 14 cases with implications for schizophrenia and hysteria. Arch Gen Psychiatry 37:1388–1397, 1980

Bliss EL: Multiple Personality, Allied Disorders and Hypnosis. New York, Oxford University Press, 1986

Bliss EL, Jeppsen EA: Prevalence of multiple personality among inpatients and outpatients. Am J Psychiatry 142:250–251, 1985

Bower GH: Mood and memory. Am Psychol 36:129–148, 1981

Bowers MK, Brecher-Marer S, Newton B, et al: Therapy of multiple personality. Int J Clin Exp Hypn 19:57–65, 1971

Braun BG: Psychophysiologic phenomena in multiple personality and hypnosis. Am J Clin Hypn 26:124–137, 1983

Braun BG: Hypnosis creates multiple personality: myth or reality? Int J Clin Exp Hypn 32:191–197, 1984a

Braun BG: Uses of hypnosis with multiple personality. Psychiatric Annals 14:34–40, 1984b

Braun BG: Towards a theory of multiple personality and other dissociative phenomena. Psychiatr Clin North Am 7:171–193, 1984c

Braun BG: Issues in the psychotherapy of multiple personality, in Treatment of Multiple Personality Disorder. Edited by Braun BG, Washington, DC, American Psychiatric Press, 1986, pp 1–28

Braun BG, Sachs RG: The development of multiple personality disorder: predisposing, precipitating, and perpetuating factors, in Childhood Antecedents of Multiple Personality. Edited by Kluft RP. Washington, DC, American Psychiatric Press, 1985, pp 37–64

Carlson ET: The history of multiple personality in the United States (l): the beginnings. Am J Psychiatry 138:666–668, 1981

Caul D: Group and videotape techniques for multiple personality disorder. Psychiatric Annals 14:43–50, 1984

Caul D, Sachs RG, Braun BG: Group therapy in treatment of multiple personality disorder, in Treatment of Multiple Personality Disorder. Edited by Braun BG. Washington, DC, American Psychiatric Press, 1986, pp 143–156

Coons PM: The differential diagnosis of multiple personality. Psychiatr Clin North Am 12:51–67, 1984

Coons PM: Treatment progress in 20 patients with multiple personality disorder. J Nerv Ment Dis 174:715–721, 1986

Coons PM: Psychophysiologic aspects of multiple personality disorder: a review. Dissociation 1:47–53, 1988

Coons PM, Bradley K: Group psychotherapy with multiple personality patients. J Nerv Ment Dis 173:515–521, 1985

Coons PM, Milstein V: Psychosexual disturbances in multiple personality. J Nerv Ment Dis 47:106–110, 1986

Coons PM, Bowman ES, Milstein V: Multiple personality disorder: a clinical investigation of 50 cases. J Nerv Ment Dis 176:519–527, 1988

Ellenburger HF: The Discovery of the Unconscious. New York, Basic Books, 1970

Fagan J, McMahon PP: Incipient multiple personality in children. J Nerv Ment Dis 172:26–36, 1984

Fine CG: Thought on the congnitive perceptual substrates of multiple personality disorder. Dissociation 1(4):5–10, 1988a

Fine CG: The work of Antoine Despine: the first scientific report on the diagnosis of a child with multiple personality disorder. Am J Clin Hypn 31:33–39, 1988b

Franklin J: Diagnosis of covert and subtle signs of multiple personality disorder through dissociative signs. Dissociation 1(2):27–33, 1988

Frischholz EJ: The relationship among dissociation, hypnosis, and child abuse in the development of multiple personality disorder, in Childhood Antecedents of Multiple Personality. Edited by Kluft RP. Washington, DC, American Psychiatric Press, 1985, pp 99–126

Gmelin ET: Materiater Für die Anthropologie, Vol 1. Tübingen, Cotta, 1791, pp 3–89

Gruenewald D: On the nature of multiple personality: comparisons with hypnosis. Int Clin Hypn 32:170–190, 1984

Herman JL, Schatzow E: Recovery and verification of memories of childhood sexual trauma. Psychoanalytic Psychology 4:1–14, 1987

Hilgard ER: Divided Consciousness: Multiple Controls in Human Thought and Action, Expanded Edition. New York, John Wiley, 1986

Horevitz RP, Braun BG: Are multiple personalities borderline? Psychiatr Clin North Am 7:69–87, 1984

Kluft E, Poteat J, Kluft RP: Movement observations in multiple personality disorder: a preliminary report. American Journal of Dance Therapy 9:313–46, 1986

Kluft RP: Varieties of hypnotic intervention in the treatment of multiple personality. Am J Clin Hypn 24:230–240, 1982

Kluft RP: Aspects of the treatment of multiple personality disorder. Psychiatric Annals 14:51–55, 1984a

Kluft RP: An introduction to multiple personality disorder. Psychiatric Annals 14:19–24, 1984b

Kluft RP: Multiple personality in childhood. Psychiatr Clin North Am 7:121–134, 1984c

Kluft RP: Treatment of multiple personality disorder: a study of 33 cases. Psychiatr Clin North Am 7:9–29, 1984d

Kluft RP: The natural history of multiple personality disorder, in Childhood Antecedents of Multiple Personality. Edited by Kluft RP. Washington, DC, American Psychiatric Press, 1985, pp 197–238

Kluft RP: Personality unification in multiple personality disorder: a follow-up study, in Treatment of Multiple Personality Disorder. Edited by Braun BG. Washington, DC, American Psychiatric Press, 1986b, pp 29–60

Kluft RP: Treating children who have multiple personality disorder, in Treatment of Multiple Personality Disorder. Edited by Braun BG. Washington, DC, American Psychiatric Press, 1986b, pp 79–105

Kluft RP: First rank symptoms as diagnostic indicators of multiple personality disorder. Am J Psychiatry 144:293–298, 1987a

Kluft RP: Making the diagnosis of multiple personality, in Diagnostics and Psychopathology. Edited by Flach FF. New York, WW Norton, 1987b, pp 207–225

Kluft RP: The parental fitness of mothers with multiple personality disorder: a preliminary study. Child Abuse Negl 11:272–280, 1987c

Kluft RP: The simulation and dissimulation of multiple personality disorder. Am J Clin Hypn 30:104–118, 1987d

Kluft RP: An update on multiple personality disorder. Hosp Community Psychiatry 38:363–373, 1987e

Kluft RP: The dissociative disorders, in The American Psychiatric Press Textbook of Psychiatry. Edited by Talbott JA, Hales RE, Yudofsky SC. Washington, DC, American Psychiatric Press, 1988a, pp 557–585

Kluft RP: The phenomenology and treatment of extremely complex multiple personality disorder. Dissociation 1:47–58, 1988b

Kluft RP: The postunification treatment of multiple personality disorder: first findings. Am J Psychother 42:212–228, 1988c

Kluft RP: The phenomenology and treatment of extremely complex multiple personality disorder. Dissociation 1(4):47–58, 1988d

Kluft RP (ed): Dissociation: the David Caul Memorial Symposium symposium papers: iatrogenesis and MPD. Dissociation 2:66–104, 1989

Kluft RP, Braun BG, Sachs RG: Multiple personality, intrafamilial abuse, and family psychiatry. International Journal of Family Psychiatry 5:283–301, 1984

Kluft RP, Steinberg M, Spitzer RL: DSM-III-R revisions in the dissociative disorders: an exploration of their derivation and rationale. Dissociation 1:39–46, 1988

Loewenstein RJ, Hornstein N, Farber B: Open trial of clonazepam in the treatment of posttraumatic stress symptoms in multiple personality disorder. Dissociation 1:3–12, 1988

Miller SD: Optical differences in cases of multiple personality disorder. J Nerv Ment Dis 177:480–486, 1989

Nemiah JC: Dissociative disorders, in Comprehensive Textbook of Psychiatry, 3rd Edition. Edited by Kaplan H, Freedman A, Sadock B. Baltimore, MD, Williams & Wilkins, 1980, pp 1544–1561

Petetain JHD: Mémoire sur la découverte des phenomènes que presentent la catalepsie et le somnambulisme. Paris, Baillière, 1787

Putnam FW: The psychophysiologic investigation of multiple personality disorder. Psychiatr Clin North Am 7:31–40, 1984

Putnam FW: The Diagnosis and Treatment of Multiple Personality Disorder. New York, Guilford, 1989

Putnam FW, Loewenstein RJ, Silberman EK, et al: Multiple personality disorder in a hospital setting. J Clin Psychiatry 45:172–175, 1984

Putnam FW, Guroff JJ, Silberman EK, et al: The clinical phenomenology of multiple personality disorder: review of 100 recent cases. J Clin Psychiatry 47:285–293, 1986

Putnam FW, Zahn TP, Post RM: Differential autonomic nervous system activity in multiple personality disorder. Psychiatry Res (in press)

Riley RL, Mead J: The development of symptoms of multiple personality disorder in a child of three. Dissociation 1(3):41–46, 1988

Rosenbaum M: The role of the term schizophrenia in the decline of diagnoses of multiple personality disorder. Arch Gen Psychiatry 37:1383–1385, 1980

Ross CA: Multiple Personality Disorder: Diagnosis, Clinical Features, and Treatment. New York, John Wiley, 1989

Ross CA, Norton GR: Multiple personality disorder patients with a prior diagnosis of schizophrenia. Dissociation 1:39–42, 1988

Ross CA, Norton GR: Effects of hypnosis on the features of multiple personality disorder. Am J Clin Hypn 32:99–106, 1989

Ross CA, Heber S, Norton GR, et al: Differences between multiple personality disorder and other diagnostic groups on structured interview. J Nerv Men Dis 177:487–491, 1989a

Ross CA, Norton GR, Fraser GA: Evidence against the iatrogenesis of multiple personality disorder. Dissociation 2:61–65, 1989b

Ross CA, Norton GR, Wozney K: Multiple personality disorder: an analyis of 236 cases. Can J Psychiatry 34:413–418, 1989c

Sachs RG: The adjunctive role of social support systems in the treatment of multiple personality disorder, in Treatment of Multiple Personality Disorder. Edited by Braun BG. Washington, DC, American Psychiatric Press, 1986, pp 157–174

Sachs RG, Frischholz EJ, Wood JI: Marital and family therapy in the treatment of multiple personality disorder. Journal of Marital and Family Therapy 4:249–259, 1988

Schreiber FR: Sybil. Chicago, IL, Henry Regnery, 1973

Schultz R, Braun BG, Kluft RP: Multiple personality disorder; phenomenology of selected variables in comparison to major depression. Dissociation 2:45–51, 1989

Solomon RS, Solomon V: Differential diagnosis of multiple personality. Psychol Rep 51:1187–1194, 1982

Spiegel D: Multiple personality as a post-traumatic stress disorder. Psychiatr Clin North Am 7:101–110, 1984

Spiegel D, Hunt T, Dondershine HE: Dissociation and hypnotizability in posttraumatic stress disorder. Am J Psychiatry 145:301–305, 1988

Spiegel D, Bierre P, Rootenberg J: Hypnotic alteration of somatosensory perception. Am J Psychiatry 146:749–754, 1989

Spiegel H, Spiegel D: Trance and Treatment: Clinical Uses of Hypnosis (1978). Washington, DC, American Psychiatric Press, 1987

Steinberg M, Rounsaville B, Cicchetti DV: The structured clinical interview for DSM-III-R dissociative disorders: preliminary report on a new diagnostic instrument. Am J Psychiatry 147:76–82, 1990

Stern CR: The etiology of multiple personalities. Psychiatr Clin North Am 7:149–159, 1984

Stutman R, Bliss EL: The post-traumatic stress disorder (the Vietnam syndrome), hypnotizability, and imagery. Am J Psychiatry 142:741–743, 1985

Talbott JA, Hales RE, Yudofsky SC (eds): The American Psychiatric Press Textbook of Psychiatry. Washington, DC, American Psychiatric Press, 1988

Watkins JG, Watkins HH: Ego states and hidden observers. Journal of Altered States of Consciousness 5:3–18, 1979–1980

# Chapter 3

# Psychogenic Amnesia and Psychogenic Fugue: A Comprehensive Review

## by Richard J. Loewenstein, M.D.

This chapter discusses psychogenic amnesia and psychogenic fugue. Over the last century there have been a number of clinical reports and studies of these disorders in different populations ranging from soldiers in combat to civilians who present themselves to emergency services with complaints of loss of memory for personal identity. Unfortunately, contributions to this literature are shaped by differing theoretical biases, use a variety of methodologies and diagnostic criteria, and describe different clinical populations. Thus major questions remain about the etiology, phenomenology, psychodynamics, and course of psychogenic amnesia and psychogenic fugue. In this chapter, I will review conceptual and clinical issues in the study of amnesia and fugue with a particular focus on the relationship of these conditions to severe psychic trauma. The latter factor has only recently been systematically recognized as a significant determinant in the development of dissociative disorders (Putnam 1985; van der Kolk 1986).

## Amnesia and Fugue as Symptoms

Amnesia and fugue are unusual among the DSM-III and DSM-III-R (American Psychiatric Association 1980, 1987) disorders in that both are specific disorders, as well as symptoms of other disorders. For example, both are commonly described in multiple personality disorder (MPD) (Putnam 1989). In fact, amnesia will be one of the diagnostic criteria for this disorder in DSM-IV (Work Group on DSM-IV Dissociative Disorders, unpublished). Amnesia is even part of the diagnostic criteria for psychogenic fugue in DSM-III-R. Amnesia is not only a dissociative disorder and a dissociative symptom. It is also among the DSM-III-R diagnostic criteria for somatization disorder and posttraumatic stress disorder (PTSD). In part, this reflects the conceptual legacy of "classic hysteria" under which somatoform, posttraumatic, and dissociative disorders were subsumed in late 19th century and much of 20th century psychiatric nosology predating DSM-III.

In addition, amnesia can be understood as a concomitant of cognitive or intrapsychic defensive processes (Schacter and Kihlstrom 1989). Thus it can be viewed not only from a descriptive and psychopathologic perspective, but from an adaptational, process-oriented, psychodynamic one as well. Discussions of amnesia and fugue in the literature often blur the distinction between these ways of understanding dissociative phenomena leading to imprecision in conceptualization.

## Definitions of Terms

The discussion of the literature is much clearer if the reader is familiar with the current DSM-III-R diagnostic criteria for psychogenic amnesia and psychogenic fugue (Table 3-1). The DSM-III-R definitions for these disorders are different from those used in most pre-DSM-III studies. In addition, these early studies generally

Table 3-1.  DSM-III-R criteria for diagnostic criteria for psychogenic amnesia, psychogenic fugue, and dissociative disorder not otherwise specified

---

*Psychogenic Amnesia*
A.  The predominant disturbance is an episode of sudden inability to recall important personal information that is too extensive to be explained by ordinary forgetfulness.
B.  The disturbance is not due to multiple personality disorder or to an organic mental disorder (e.g., blackouts during alcohol intoxication).

*Psychogenic Fugue*
A.  The predominant disturbance is sudden, unexpected travel away from home or one's customary place of work, with inability to recall one's past.
B.  Assumption of a new identity (partial or complete).
C.  The disturbance is not due to multiple personality disorder or to an organic mental disorder (e.g., partial complex seizures in temporal lobe epilepsy).

*Dissociative Disorder Not Otherwise Specified (DDNOS)*
Disorders in which the predominant feature is a dissociative symptom (i.e., a disturbance or alteration in the normally integrative functions of identity, memory, or consciousness) that does not meet the criteria for a specific dissociative disorder.

*Examples:*
1)  Ganser's syndrome: the giving of "approximate answers" to questions, commonly associated with other symptoms such as amnesia, disorientation, perceptual disturbances, fugue, and conversion symptoms.
2)  Cases in which there is more than one personality state capable of assuming executive control of the individual, but not more than one personality state is sufficiently distinct to meet the full criteria for multiple personality disorder, or cases in which a second personality never assumes complete executive control.
3)  Trance states, i.e., altered states of consciousness with markedly diminished or selectively focused responsiveness to environmental stimuli. In children this may occur following physical abuse or trauma.
4)  Derealization unaccompanied by depersonalization.
5)  Dissociated states that may occur in people who have been subjected to periods of prolonged and intense coercive persuasion (e.g., brainwashing, thought reform, or indoctrination while the captive of terrorists or cultists).
6)  Cases in which sudden, unexpected travel and organized, purposeful behavior with inability to recall one's past are not accompanied by the assumption of a new identity, partial or complete.

---

*Note.*  Reprinted from DSM-III-R with permission from American Psychiatric Association (1987).

do not clearly differentiate amnesia from fugue or from more pleomorphic dissociative disorders such as MPD.

The current diagnostic criteria for amnesia and fugue are quite restrictive. For example, those for amnesia specify that the episode of amnesia must be "sudden" in onset. The criteria for fugue specify that a "new identity" must be assumed as part of the fugue. As will be discussed below, a frequent type of psychogenic amnesia is a retrospectively reported memory gap or series of gaps for part of the life history. Also, dissociating patients may engage in travel, wandering, or flight while in altered states of consciousness but never assume a new identity. Thus such cases are now subsumed under the dissociative disorder not otherwise specified (DDNOS) classification in DSM-III-R, rather than being placed in the conceptually more logical categories of amnesia or fugue. Fortunately, proposed revisions in the diagnostic criteria for psychogenic amnesia and fugue in DSM-IV will attempt to rectify these difficulties (Table 3-2).

In this chapter, the term *fugue-like* will be used to describe episodes that satisfy only the first criterion for psychogenic fugue in DSM-III-R. The term *psychogenic amnesia* will be used to describe episodes of sudden onset, as well as those reported retrospectively by history.

## What Is Psychogenic Amnesia?

Psychogenic amnesia is usually regarded as a more fundamental disturbance than fugue, since amnesia is a core part of fugue states and is generally considered to be the more common disorder (Putnam 1985). Psychogenic amnesia can be more broadly defined as a reversible memory impairment in which groups of memories for personal experience that would ordinarily be available for recall to the conscious mind cannot be retrieved or retained in a verbal form (or, if temporarily retrieved, cannot be wholly retained in consciousness). In addition, this disturbance is not primarily due to destruction or dysfunction of neurobiologic systems and structures that subserve memory or language but rather to a potentially reversible form of psychological inhibition.

The diagnosis of psychogenic amnesia generally connotes four factors. First, relatively large groups of memories and associated affects have become unavailable, not just single memories, feelings, or thoughts (Rapaport 1942). Second, the unavailable memories usually relate to day-to-day information that would ordinarily be a more-or-less routine part of conscious awareness: who I am, what I did, where I went, to whom I spoke, what was said, what I thought and felt at the time, and so on (Hilgard 1977). Three, the ability to remember new factual information, general cognitive functioning, and language capacity are usually intact (Lishman 1987). Finally, the dissociated memories frequently indirectly reveal their presence in more-or-less disguised form, such as intrusive visual images, somatoform symptoms, nightmares, conversion symptoms, and behavioral reenactments.

## Types of Psychogenic Amnesia

Following Janet (1901), the discussion of amnesia in DSM-III-R describes several types of disturbance in the process of recall in this disorder (Table 3-3). In addition, there are a variety of disturbances in the content of memory that characterize psychogenic amnesia. Most of these are forms of localized, selective, and systematized amnesias. These are listed with suggested pertinent mental status questions in Table 3-4. These amnesia symptoms are commonly found in patients with

Table 3-2.   Suggested DSM-IV diagnostic criteria for psychogenic amnesia, psychogenic fugue, and dissociative disorder not otherwise specified

*Psychogenic Amnesia*
A. The predominant disturbance is one or more episodes of inability to recall important personal information, usually of a traumatic or stressful nature, that is too extensive to be explained by ordinary forgetfulness.
B. The disturbance is not due to multiple personality disorder or to an organic mental disorder (e.g., blackouts during alcohol intoxication).

*Psychogenic Fugue*
A. The predominant disturbance is sudden, unexpected travel away from home or one's customary place of work, with inability to recall one's past and/or an assumption of new identity.
B. The disturbance is not due to multiple personality disorder or to an organic mental disorder (e.g., partial complex seizures in temporal lobe epilepsy).

*Dissociative Disorder Not Otherwise Specified (DDNOS)*
Disorders in which the predominant feature is a dissociative symptom (i.e., a disturbance or alteration in the normally integrative functions of identity, memory, or consciousness) that does not meet the criteria for a specific dissociative disorder.

*Examples:*
1) Cases similar to multiple personality disorder but failing to meet full criteria for this disorder. Examples include cases in which (a) not more than one personality state is sufficiently distinct; (b) a second personality never assumes complete executive control; (c) amnesia for important personal information does not occur.
2) Trance states, i.e., altered states of consciousness with markedly diminished or selectively focused responsiveness to environmental stimuli, leading to distress or dysfunction. This may include recurrent auto-hypnotic phenomena such as spontaneous trance, age regression, and positive and negative hallucinations.
3) Derealization unaccompanied by depersonalization.
4) Dissociated states that may occur in people who have been subjected to periods of prolonged and intense coercive persuasion (e.g., brainwashing, thought reform, or indoctrination while the captive of terrorists or cultists).
5) Ganser's syndrome: the giving of "approximate answers" to questions, associated with other symptoms such as amnesia, disorientation, perceptual disturbances, fugue, and conversion symptoms.
6) Dissociative and trance phenomena in which the specific characteristics of the disorders are indigenous to particular locations and cultures, and their predominant features involve a disturbance of the normally integrative functions of memory, identity, or consciousness (e.g., amok, bebainan, benzi mazurazura, guria, kupenga, kwechitsiko). Entry into altered states of consciousness, disremembered behavior, and the assumption of another identity or the sense of being possessed by some entity are common features of some of these indigenous conditions.

*Source.*   From Work Group on DSM-IV Dissociative Disorders (unpublished).

MPD but may also occur in other patients with recurrent dissociative symptoms short of full MPD who meet criteria for DDNOS. The importance of amnesia in MPD is emphasized in the proposed DSM-IV diagnostic criteria for MPD, which specify that amnesia must be present to make this diagnosis. Many patients meeting diagnostic criteria for psychogenic amnesia or fugue will actually have a far more extensive history of amnesia, fugue-like states, and dissociation if closely questioned in the clinical interview or followed up longitudinally (Kluft 1985).

The concepts of anterograde amnesia and retrograde amnesia can be confusing to apply to psychogenic amnesia. In neuropsychiatry, anterograde amnesia defines a neurobiologically based inability to acquire and retain new memories after a traumatic event or disease onset (Levin et al. 1982). Retrograde amnesia implies an organically based impairment in recall or previously retained information (Lishman 1987). In psychogenic amnesia, one can usually demonstrate intact anterograde and retrograde memory function once the amnesia is cleared (Schacter et al. 1982). To the extent that there is a traumatic event that precipitates the psychogenic amnesia, there usually is an anterograde psychogenic amnesia for the trauma and at least some subsequent events (Kluft 1988). There may also be an additional psychogenic retrograde amnesia for occurrences before the traumatic event (Janet 1901). In most cases, when the amnesic patient comes to clinical attention, the presentation is one of an amnesia retrograde to the time of clinical contact. This usually leads to characterization of the amnesia as a retrograde amnesia. In the rare cases of continuous psychogenic amnesia, there is a continuous psychogenic anterograde amnesia that mimics the organic amnestic syndromes (Kluft 1988). Ultimately, it may be more useful to devise a separate terminology to describe the temporal progression of the psychogenic amnesias so that the unique characteristics of these conditions may be more clearly delineated.

## Psychogenic Amnesia and Ordinary Forgetfulness

The DSM-III-R diagnostic criteria for psychogenic amnesia specify that the amnesic disturbance must be "too extensive to be explained by ordinary forgetfulness" (p. 275). This definition raises the question of what is meant by "ordinary forgetfulness"

Table 3-3. Types of psychogenic amnesia

---

Localized amnesia
  Inability to recall events related to a circumscribed period of time
Selective amnesia
  Ability to remember some, but not all, of the events during a circumscribed
    period of time
Generalized amnesia
  Failure to recall the whole life of the patient
Continuous amnesia
  Failure to recall successive events as they occur
Systematized amnesia
  Amnesia for certain categories of memory such as all memories relating to
    one's family or a particular person

---

*Source.* From American Psychiatric Association (1987), Janet (1901), Kluft (1988), and Nemiah (1985).

**Table 3-4.** The subjective experience of psychogenic amnesia

If the answers to the mental status questions (below) are positive, the patient should be asked to describe in detail his/her experience of the symptom including its relation to use of psychoactive substances.

*BLACKOUTS OR "TIME LOSS"
Mental Status Questions: "Do you 'lose time'?" "Do you have Blackouts?"

*REPORTS BY OTHERS OF DISREMEMBERED BEHAVIOR
Mental Status Questions: "Are you told of things you say and do for which you have no memory? Out of character behavior? Child-like behavior?"

*APPEARANCE OF UNEXPLAINED POSSESSIONS
Mental Status Questions: "Do you find things in your possession that you cannot explain? For example, clothes, tools, weapons, artwork, writings, items in your shopping basket, receipts, etc?"

*PERPLEXING CHANGES IN RELATIONSHIPS
Mental Status Questions: "Do you find that your relationships with people seem influenced by factors that you cannot recall? For example, do you find that people are angry with you or act closer to you apparently based on events for which you have no memory?"

*FUGUE-LIKE EPISODES
Mental Status Questions: "Do you find yourself in places with no idea how you got there? Do you set out to go somewhere but find yourself somewhere else without knowing how you got there? What is the longest period of time you have lost during such an experience?"

*EVIDENCE OF UNUSUAL FLUCTUATIONS IN ABILITIES, HABITS, TASTES, KNOWLEDGE
Mental Status Questions: "Does your ability to do things, such as athletics, artistic endeavors, mechanical tasks, work tasks, intellectual tasks, etc., fluctuate markedly in ways you cannot explain? Are you told that you do things you didn't know you could do?"

*FRAGMENTARY RECALL OF THE LIFE HISTORY
Mental Status Questions: "Are you aware of gaps in your memory for your life? Are you missing memories for important events in your life, like a wedding or a graduation? For your childhood? For events in wartime? For other important aspects of your adult life?"

*CHRONIC MISTAKEN IDENTITY EXPERIENCES
Mental Status Questions: "Do you find that you are approached by people whom you don't know, who insist they know you? Who say they have met you before? Who say they have done things with you? Who even call you by another name?"

*BRIEF ("MICRO") AMNESIAS DURING PERSONAL INTERACTIONS
Mental Status Questions: "Do you find that you do not remember all or part of your interactions/conversations with people? Like this interview? Do you/will you remember all or part of our conversation today?"

*Source.* From Bernstein and Putnam (1986), Kluft (unpublished), and Putnam (1989).

and how psychogenic amnesia differs from it. In addition, nonpathologic forms of amnesia have been described such as infantile and childhood amnesia, amnesia for sleep and dreaming, and hypnotic amnesia (Schacter and Kihlstrom 1989). A full discussion of these issues is impossible here. It is important for the reader to be aware, however, that little systematic research has been performed differentiating and characterizing different forms of psychogenic amnesia.

One major difficulty is that there is insufficient terminological clarity in this field of study. In extreme clinical or nonpathologic cases, one can fairly easily characterize a phenomenon as psychogenic amnesia. In borderline cases it becomes much murkier what should be termed amnesia, dissociation, repression, normal forgetting, and so on. Also, terminology (e.g., implicit memory, explicit memory) is not used uniformly in different studies of memory and amnesia. As noted above, it may be best to devise separate, or at least more clearly defined, terminologies to characterize organic and psychogenic amnesias, respectively. Use of the same terms to describe both types of conditions may actually limit exploration of unique aspects of the psychogenic amnesia process.

In the work of cognitive psychologists, memory has been conceptualized as having various subtypes (for a fuller discussion, see Squire 1987). For the purpose of this brief discussion, however, we will be concerned with the differentiation between intentional recall of previous experience such as autobiographical memory, in contrast to memory for skills, information, facts, concepts, and vocabulary that can be demonstrated without requiring recall of the temporal context in which the knowledge was acquired (Schacter and Kihlstrom 1989; Squire 1987). The former is termed explicit/episodic memory, whereas the latter is called implicit/semantic memory. Implicit/semantic memory may be preserved in cases of severe organic anterograde amnesia even when the explicit/episodic memory is markedly deficient (Schacter and Kihlstrom 1989; Squire 1987).

Basically, most forms of psychogenic amnesia are thought primarily to involve difficulties with the functioning of explicit/episodic memory not implicit/semantic memory (Schacter and Kihlstrom 1989). However, several studies have confirmed the clinical observation that subjects with pathologic psychogenic amnesia for their life history can demonstrate implicit, autobiographical memory while amnesic (Schacter and Kihlstrom 1989). For example, when asked to free associate, to imagine or to make up a story, or when exposed to projective tests, patients with psychogenic amnesia or MPD will include in their productions elements that contain autobiographical information without their necessarily being consciously aware of this. Thus psychogenic amnesia may appear to vary over time in the same patient.

Amnesic patients may also have intense reactions to stimuli that are emotionally significant without knowing consciously the reason for the reaction or the significance of the stimuli (Kaczniak et al. 1988; Schacter and Kihlstrom 1989). Clinically, this is most vividly demonstrated when a patient with PTSD has a behavioral reexperiencing episode triggered by an apparently benign everyday stimulus. Similar phenomena may also be observed in individuals who are generally not classified as having psychogenic amnesia, however, such as a person with an intense anniversary reaction who is not conscious of the anniversary.

In early studies of autobiographical memory, evidence has been acquired in several populations to support the notion that infantile and childhood amnesia can be experimentally documented (Rubin et al. 1986; Schacter and Kihlstrom 1989).

Later autobiographical memory is said to show a retention gradient for memory of the most recent 20 to 30 years of the subject's life, and a "reminiscence component for the subject's youth" in subjects over 35 (Rubin et al. 1986, p. 220).

Clinically, patients with psychogenic amnesia may describe exaggerated or extended forms of childhood amnesia. This finding has been documented in an experimental study of a cognitively normal MPD patient who, unlike normal controls, showed a virtual absence of memories for the first 10 years of her life (Schacter et al. 1989). In another study, a patient with a global psychogenic amnesia was evaluated with cognitive testing while amnesic and after memory recovery. As compared with an organically impaired control, the psychogenic amnesia patient was able to recall memories from various parts of the life history without the temporal gradient that characterized the retrograde amnesia of the organic patient (Schacter et al. 1982). Recall of autobiographical information while amnesic seemed related to life events with positive affects that were unconnected with the traumatic events precipitating the amnesia. Implicit autobiographical memory phenomena were documented as well in this patient.

Similar phenomena have been described in posthypnotic amnesia with implicit demonstration that the memories for which amnesia has been suggested have been encoded and stored, but without their being accessible directly for retrieval (Schacter and Kihlstrom 1989).

Theories of posthypnotic amnesia and pathologic forms of psychogenic amnesia overlap. Several theories have been posited, none of which may be mutually exclusive. They may simply describe aspects of the phenomena from different conceptual and theoretical vantage points. Psychoanalytically based theories focus on the issue of motivated psychological sequestration of unpleasant or conflictual memories and emotions to reduce psychic pain. Social-psychological theories suggest that amnesia is a product of "self-distraction and strategic self-presentation" (Schacter and Kihlstrom 1989, p. 222; see also Kirshner 1973). Schacter and Kihlstrom themselves developed a theory of amnesia that focuses on information processing. They described the dissociation of mental events in terms of a relative decrease in executive control or synthesis among groups of psychic or memory elements and the inhibition of "control elements" that can give access to information that is stored (see also Hilgard 1977; Janet 1901). Theories in the literature on trauma posit "state-dependent" effects such that psychogenic amnesia results when traumatic events are encoded during an altered state resulting in limited conscious access to these memories during the baseline state (Putnam 1989; Spiegel 1988b; van der Kolk 1986).

## HISTORICAL REVIEW

### Early History

In classic European accounts of demonic possession and exorcism, the possessed person is frequently described as showing amnesia for the period of possession and the exorcism (Ellenberger 1970; Laurence and Perry 1988). In addition, some of the culture-bound dissociative and psychotic disorders such as *piblokto* are described as demonstrating amnesia as part of the symptom picture (Lehmann 1985) (Table 3-2).

In Europe in the late 18th and early 19th centuries, amnesia was recognized as a concomitant of "artificial somnambulism," considered to be the prototype of modern hypnosis, developed by devotees of Mesmer's animal magnetism theories (Ellenberger 1970; Laurence and Perry 1988). In various countries during the 19th century, there were periods of great interest in artificial somnambulism and in "magnetic diseases" (i.e., spontaneously occurring disorders with symptoms similar to those that appeared in artificial somnambulism). These included nocturnal somnambulism and its waking counterpart, the ambulatory automatism or fugue. In these conditions, the person performed activities that were complex and coordinated, but apparently "cut off from the continuity of consciousness" (Ellenberger 1970, p. 124) with resultant amnesia.

## Later Developments: Hysteria, Amnesia, and Fugue

By the late 19th century, there was an interweaving of the notions of the somnambulistic magnetic disorders with the concept of hysteria. Since that time, the linkage of hysteria with dissociative conditions such as amnesia and fugue has been a cornerstone of psychiatric nosology and psychodynamic theory until the advent of DSM-III and its revision with its re-differentiation of the somatoform and the dissociative disorders.

In their classic descriptions of hysteria, both Briquet (1859) and Charcot (quoted in Janet 1901) underscored the frequent occurrence of amnesia, memory problems, and fugue in hysterical patients. Charcot put considerable effort in differentiating organic disorders of the nervous system from similar disorders caused by hysterical and posttraumatic factors (Ellenberger 1970). Outside of Europe during this time, there was interest in similar phenomena as well. For example, in the United States, William James described one of the paradigmatic cases of fugue with change of personal identity, that of Ansel Bourne (see Hilgard 1977).

## Janet

Janet was influenced by the work of the early "magnetizers" as well as by Charcot (van der Hart and Friedman 1989). His discussion of the phenomenology of amnesia, fugue, and other dissociative conditions remains one of the most comprehensive in the literature and is quite similar to more modern conceptualizations (American Psychiatric Association 1987; Fisher 1945; Fisher and Joseph 1949; Gill and Brenman 1959; Rapaport 1942). Janet regarded amnesia as a core aspect of hysterical and somnambulistic states (Janet 1901, 1907; van der Hart and Friedman 1989). He viewed amnesia as a basic part of the dissociative process in which complex subsystems of memories, feelings, thoughts, and ideas became autonomous through disconnection from the overall executive control of the total personality with failure to recognize these as part of the patient's own consciousness. Janet (1907) hypothesized that fugue was based on dissociation of more complex groups of mental functions than occurred in amnesia and was usually organized around a powerful emotion or feeling state that linked many trains of associations accompanied by a wish to run away.

## Freud

The description of complex psychogenic amnesia symptoms also can be found in the original case descriptions of hysterical patients by Breuer and Freud (1893–1895). For example, patients such as Anna O and Emmy von N were described as having blackouts; episodes of disremembered behavior; extensive amnesic gaps for the life history; fluctuations in handwriting, handedness, and language; and spontaneous age regression with amnesia.

The famous formulation "hysterics suffer mainly from reminiscences" (Breuer and Freud 1893–1895, p. 7) implies that hysterical patients suffer from considerable amnesia, since dissociated memories related to traumatic experiences were posited as the cause of the hysterical process. Breuer viewed hysterical symptoms as arising from spontaneous auto-hypnotic ("hypnoid") states caused by traumatic events. He discussed at length the separation and independent activity of the "psychical product of these states" (p. 216) and the resultant gross amnesia that occurs once the hysterical process has been established in the patient.

Freud (Breuer and Freud 1893–1895), on the other hand, proposed that the divisions in memory and awareness in hysteria occurred through an active process of "defence" in which incompatible or unacceptable ideas, feelings, and memories were separated from consciousness. Freud minimized the importance of hypnoid states, although he noted that the hypnoid state could operate as a form of defence: "I am unable to suppress a suspicion that somewhere or other the roots of hypnoid and defence hysteria come together and that there the primary factor is defence" (p. 286).

## Later Studies

Since the beginning of the 20th century, there have been a number of systematic studies and case reports about patients with amnesia and fugue. These studies have a multitude of methodological weaknesses. For example, some patients diagnosed with psychogenic amnesia in these studies actually had clear-cut fugue-like episodes and vice versa (Akhtar and Brenner 1979; Fisher 1945; Fisher and Joseph 1949; Geleerd et al. 1945; Jones 1909; Luparello 1970). Also, some of these cases more closely approximate modern diagnostic criteria for MPD or DDNOS rather than amnesia or fugue (Akhtar and Brenner 1979; Fisher 1945; Geleerd et al. 1945; Kirshner 1973; McKinney and Lange 1983; Menninger 1919). Other cases seem to have had other disorders such as epilepsy, a primary mood disorder, or a psychotic disorder that could account for the memory disturbances or pathologic wandering (Stengel 1939, 1941, 1943).

Systematic studies in the literature on amnesia and fugue are of two kinds. The first consists of studies of the differential diagnosis of patients presenting with fugue or amnesia for personal identity and/or personal circumstances (Akhtar and Brenner 1979; Croft et al. 1973; Kennedy and Neville 1957; Kiersch 1962; Leavitt 1935; Wilon et al. 1950). The second consists of attempts to study more homogeneous groups of patients with psychogenic amnesia or fugue who are without gross evidence of an organic mental disorder (Abeles and Schilder 1935; Berrington et al. 1956; Coons and Millstein 1989; Fisher 1945; Fisher and Joseph 1949; Geleerd et al. 1945; Kanzer 1937; Kirshner 1973; Parfitt and Carlyle-Gall 1944; Stengel 1939, 1941, 1943).

The variability among studies of the first type is shown by the different prevalences of a psychogenic etiology for amnesia and fugue: from less than 10% of a sample of 39 consecutive patients referred for neurologic consultation (Croft et al. 1973) to more than 50% of 74 consecutive amnesic patients self-referred either to a hospital emergency service or to police agencies (Kennedy and Neville 1957). Also, some authors were far more likely than others to diagnose malingering in amnesia and fugue patients. Most other patients in these studies had severe organic mental disorders accounting for their memory problems.

Abeles and Schilder (1935) and Kanzer (1939) studied 63 and 71 patients, respectively, who presented to Bellevue Hospital in New York with amnesia for personal identity. Patients with organic etiologies for the amnesia were said to have been excluded. Based on the clinical descriptions, some of these cases would meet the first DSM-III-R criteria for fugue, but not the second (i.e., they were DDNOS by current criteria).

The incidence of amnesia for personal identity was 0.26% in the Abeles and Schilder (1935) study. Severe life stresses engendering profound conflict, shame, guilt, disappointment, despair, and suicidal preoccupations were thought to be the major precipitants of the amnesic episodes. Abeles and Schilder viewed the amnesia as a form of "self-punishment arising from a feeling of guilt; it is a partial suicide" (p. 602) in which amnesia represents an alternative method of escape from intolerable situations and feelings.

Stengel (1939, 1941, 1943) described a total of 36 cases of fugue defined either as "a pathological compulsion to wander . . . to leave home . . . either [with] a complete loss of memory . . . or the memory is vague and dreamlike" (1941, p. 250) or "states of altered or narrowed consciousness with the impulse to wander" with variable post-fugue amnesia (p. 225). Stengel's patient group included seven patients with symptomatic epilepsy as well as a number of patients with alcoholism, organic brain disease, severe affective disorders suggestive of unipolar or bipolar disorders, or symptoms of paranoia and psychosis. One patient may have had MPD. Most of Stengel's patients described traumatic childhoods with parental conflict, neglect, abuse, desertion, or death. Stengel (1941, 1943) described many of his patients as "manic-depressive" with the fugue arising out of a psychotic manic or depressive states. These patients may actually have demonstrated wandering and memory problems related to state changes between mania, depression, and euthymia, not to a dissociative process.

Berrington et al. (1956) studied 37 cases of fugue based on retrospective chart review or their own "personal" experience and compared them to a "matched" control group. They found a similar percentage of "unhappy" childhoods in controls and fugue patients. Almost half of their fugue sample had a prior history of head injury with loss of consciousness and posttraumatic amnesia. Almost all patients described intense emotional conflicts related to specific precipitating events from which the patient felt unable to escape or fight.

Kirshner (1973) retrospectively studied the records of 30 patients seen between 1968 and 1970 at the Wright-Patterson Air Force Medical Center with "ego-alien behavior accompanied by varying degrees of amnesia" (p. 701). Twenty-three were active duty male servicemen and seven were female dependents. These 30 amnesia patients represented an incidence of 1.7% of the 1,795 psychiatric admissions during the study period. Seven patients were described as having fugue episodes. Kirshner described five cases in detail. There was a childhood history of physical abuse, emotional abuse, and/or possible sexual abuse in four of these cases. Frequent dissociative and trance-like episodes, depersonalization, and recurrent child-like behavior were described in the female patients, suggesting a more chronic dissociative condition such as MPD.

Despite the heterogeneity of these studies, most support the view of Abeles and Schilder (1935) that the psychosocial environment out of which psychogenic amnesia and fugue develop are massively stressful, with the patient experiencing intolerable emotions of shame, guilt, despair, rage, desperation, frustration, and conflict experienced as unresolvable without suicide or flight. The patients are frequently described as depressed or despairing, although virtually none of these studies provides sufficient data to ascertain whether modern criteria for a mood disorder could be met.

## Later Psychoanalytic Studies

Gill and Rapaport (1942), Rapaport (1942), Geleerd et al. (1945), Fisher (1945), Fisher and Joseph (1949), and Gill and Brenman (1959) described a number of cases of patients with amnesia, fugue, fugue-like episodes, and DDNOS by modern criteria. Bornstein (1946) reported a case of recurrent amnesia and fugue-like symptoms in an 8-year-old girl.

Fisher (1945) described three types of fugue: 1) fugue with awareness of loss of personal identity, 2) fugue with change of personal identity, and 3) fugue with retrograde amnesia. Similar typologies of the stages of episodes of amnesia and fugue were offered by Fisher as well as by Gill and Brenman (1959).

In stage 1 of amnesia-fugue, there is thought to be generation of an altered state of consciousness during which very complex activities may be engaged in, sometimes over long periods of time. A single idea that symbolizes or condenses a number of important ideas and emotions frequently dominates the patient's thinking in this stage. In stage 2, the patient becomes aware of the amnesia or loss of personal identity, at which point he or she frequently is brought for treatment. In this stage, amnesia is usually present for the first stage. In stage 3, the patient returns to his or her baseline state, usually with amnesia for the first stage and sometimes for the second as well.

Gill and Brenman (1959) described stage 2 either as a return to the baseline state with amnesia for stage 1, or a state in which there is awareness of loss of personal identity, change in personal identity, or return to a chronologically earlier period of life similar to a spontaneous hypnotic age regression. Gill and Brenman (1959) also hypothesized that traumatic war neuroses develop with a homologous set of phases, resulting in amnesia for the traumatic events.

Fisher (1945), Fisher and Joseph (1949), and Geleerd et al. (1945) suggested that the fugue can be understood as a kind of dream-like episode ("waking somnambulism") in which forbidden wishes can be expressed in a disguised, symbolic form with a "manifest and latent content" (Fisher and Joseph 1949, p. 489).

Traumatic circumstances surrounded the amnesia-fugue episodes in many of these patients. For example, among the cases of Fisher (1945) and Fisher and Joseph (1949), one patient began a series of fugues while in the midst of intense combat, although his terror of battle was a profound violation of his ideals about himself. Another patient with amnesia had a history of brutal treatment in childhood by his father and had also suffered severe war-related trauma for which he was amnesic in which he felt he had killed a severely wounded buddy who represented a substitute father. Another amnesia patient had been threatened with molestation and violence by her alcoholic brother-in-law. Among the patients of Geleerd et al. (1945) was an adolescent girl with episodes of running away with subsequent amnesia who had been sexually involved with a brother. The patient of Bornstein (1946) had contracted gonorrhea at the age of 4 after sexual abuse by an uncle. She also had been subject to violent insertion of vaginal douches by both parents for two years as "treatment" for the gonorrhea.

In addition to external dangers or traumas, the patients were often struggling with extreme emotions or impulses, such as overwhelming fear or intense incestuous, sexual, suicidal, or violent urges. Thus the patients were also described as suffering from massive psychological conflict from which fight or flight was impossible or psychologically unacceptable without dissociation.

In terms of severity of illness, patients with amnesia or fugue were thought to be intermediate between neurotic and psychotic patients (Fisher 1945; Geleerd et al. 1945). However, Fisher stated that: "It does not seem . . . that fugues are explicable in terms of the usual concepts of ego and superego; that ultimately other operational principles will have to be utilized when we know more about fugues" (p. 466).

A few other psychoanalytic case reports have stressed that amnesia, altered states of consciousness, "hypnoid states," and other forms of dissociation can be conceptualized as defensive reactions to childhood trauma, including childhood sexual abuse, physical abuse, and witness to violence (Bychowski 1962; Dickes 1965; Fliess 1953; Paley 1988; Shengold 1989; Silber 1979).

For the most part, however, contemporary psychoanalytic views of dissociation tend to accept, either implicitly or explicitly, Fairbairn's (1952) notions that "schizoid" processes underlie amnesia and fugue. In Fairbairn's view, "splitting of the ego" underlies amnesia and fugue as well as schizophrenia, thus linking these disorders together in terms of their hypothesized core characteristics. Because of the influence of this and related views in current psychoanalytic theorizing, the defenses of dissociation and "splitting" are commonly equated (Kernberg 1975). In addition, most psychoanalytic writing has minimized the importance of childhood abuse and severe adult psychic trauma in the genesis of psychopathologic states (Kluft 1988; Loewenstein 1990; Putnam 1985, 1989; Spiegel 1988b; van der Kolk 1986). Thus most psychoanalytic attempts to explain dissociation have been based solely on an object relations or splitting model, with many psychoanalytic authors automatically placing patients with posttraumatic or dissociative symptoms such as amnesia and fugue in the borderline or schizophrenic spectrum (Fairbairn 1952; Glover 1943; Goldberg 1987; Kernberg 1975).

## AMNESIA, FUGUE, AND TRAUMA

Greenberg and van der Kolk (1986) stated that: "Pathologies of memory are characteristic features of posttraumatic stress disorder" (p. 191). Although infrequently studied systematically, amnesia and fugue have been reported in a variety of traumatized populations, including soldiers exposed to combat (reviewed in detail below), concentration camp survivors (Jaffe 1968; Niederland 1968), victims of torture (Goldfeld et al. 1988), victims of rape (Coons et al. 1989; Kaszniak et al. 1988), sexually and physically abused children and adolescents (Goodwin 1982; Terr 1988), and adult survivors of sexual abuse (Briere and Conte 1989; Coons et al. 1989; Gelinas 1983). Virtually all patients with MPD, a group generally reporting the most extreme levels of childhood sexual, physical, and emotional abuse, report amnesia, and many also described fugues (Kluft 1988; Putnam 1989; Ross 1989).

### Combat-Related and Other Wartime Trauma

Acute forms of amnesia and fugue are frequent concomitants of wartime experiences. Amnesia was frequently described in association with "shell shock" and traumatic war neuroses in case reports about psychiatric problems among soldiers in World War I and World War II, respectively (Grinker and Spiegel 1945a, 1945b; Henderson and Moore 1944; Kardiner 1941; Kardiner and Spiegel 1947; Kubie 1943; Sargent and Slater 1941; Southard 1919; Thom and Fenton 1920; Tureen and Stein 1949). Similar reports have emerged about combatants in the Korean War, the Vietnam War, and the Arab-Israeli conflicts (Archibald and Tuddenham 1965; Cavenar and Nash 1976; El-Rayes 1982; Hendin et al. 1984; Kalman 1977; Kolb 1985; Sonnenberg et al. 1985; Spiegel 1988b). Grinker and Spiegel (1945b) reported that the extent of amnesia experienced by psychiatric battlefield casualties in World War II ranged from relatively brief localized or selective amnesias to complete generalized amnesia.

Sargent and Slater (1941) reported a 14.4% prevalence of amnesia as a "prominent symptom" in a consecutive series of 1,000 combat soldiers admitted to the neurologic unit of Sutton Emergency Hospital during World War II. Of the 87 soldiers subjected to the most severe combat stress, 35% had amnesia for war experiences, compared with 13% with "moderate" stress, and 6% with "trifling" stress. About 25% of all cases had a "trivial concussion or dazing" (p. 763) that seemed related to the onset of the amnesia or fugue. About 10% of the patients had a severe head injury that was related to development of symptoms.

In the American literature, Henderson and Moore (1944) noted a 5% prevalence of amnesia in 200 consecutive combat cases from the South Pacific theater in World War II. Torrie (1944) described an 8.6% prevalence of amnesia and fugue in 1,000 soldiers in the African campaigns. Parfitt and Carlyle-Gall (1944) described frequent amnesia and fugue in Royal Air Force personnel based in Britain during World War II. However, they tended to ascribe many of these episodes to malingering or a wish to escape danger or responsibility.

In the Sargent and Slater (1941) study, the intensity of combat exposure appeared to be the critical factor in the development of the amnesic syndrome. However, there appeared to be a group of patients with a prior personal or family history of dissociative disorders who had a lower threshold for overt amnesic disturbances in relation to combat. Soldiers with a prior history or family history of fugue or conversion symptoms were overrepresented in the group with dissociative symptoms with lesser combat exposure.

In the modern literature on chronic or delayed-onset PTSD in Vietnam veterans, Foy et al. (1987) described combat exposure as the major determinant of development of PTSD, although a similar threshold effect was seen. These findings indicate that some individuals with a preexisting childhood-related dissociative disorder or diathesis due to childhood trauma may have a lower threshold for development of overt dissociative and PTSD symptoms when retraumatized in combat or civilian life.

## Amnesia in Chronic and Delayed Posttraumatic Stress Disorder

Archibald and Tuddenham (1965) described a group of 77 World War II and Korean War veterans with a chronic "combat-fatigue syndrome," characterized by such symptoms as irritability, headaches, sleep disturbance, blackouts, overactive startle, and mistrust of others. They were compared with 60 patients without a combat history from the same clinic and with 20 nonpatient controls with a combat history but without known psychiatric disorder. Of the combat-stress group, 60% reported blackouts, a finding that was significantly more frequent than in both control groups. Of the combat-stress patients, 65% reported "memory difficulties," a finding significantly more frequent than in the combat controls.

Hendin et al. (1984) found that 20% of a sample of 100 Vietnam veterans with PTSD had chronic reexperiencing episodes, although the authors did not quantify how many of these also had amnesia. Their three clinical case examples all had amnesia for dissociative reexperiencing episodes. Laufer et al. (1984) suggested that Vietnam combat veterans with PTSD are more likely to show symptoms of "memory impairment" and "confusion in thinking" if they had witnessed "abusive violence" to noncombatants, whereas intrusive imagery and hyperarousal without such problems were more associated with combat exposure alone.

## Systematic Studies of Amnesia and Fugue in Other Traumatized Populations

Terr (1988) described 20 children who had experienced documented trauma before the age of 5, including physical trauma, sexual abuse, ritualistic abuse, kidnapping, and child pornography. Children's reports of trauma were compared with the documentary evidence. Single brief traumas were better remembered verbally, although little verbal memory was available for traumas that occurred before 28 months of age. Virtually all children, especially those traumatized repetitively, "remembered," often uncannily accurately, in behavioral reenactments of the trauma. Terr suggested that the data support the hypothesis that trauma may be preferentially encoded visually. This leads to a greater likelihood of remembering in imagery, dreams, and behavioral reenactments, not in verbal recall. These data support similar hypotheses advanced by Greenberg and van der Kolk (1986) and by Spiegel (1988a) about posttraumatic amnesia in both children and adults.

Coons and Milstein (1989) studied a consecutive series of 25 patients referred to a dissociative disorders clinic who met DSM-III criteria for psychogenic amnesia. Seventeen were inpatients; only two were men. Most patients had one to two episodes of amnesia. Patients also had symptoms of depression, somatization, depersonalization, and sexual dysfunction. Of the 25 patients, 72% had a history of child abuse, 52% had a history of sexual abuse, and 40% had a history of physical abuse. The child abuse was thought to be the precipitant of the amnesia in almost 40% of the cases.

Coons et al. (1989) studied the prevalence of adult and childhood trauma in various clinical populations diagnosed by DSM-III criteria. Eleven patients met criteria for psychogenic amnesia and six for atypical dissociative disorder (DDNOS). All DDNOS patients and 82% of psychogenic amnesia patients had suffered sexual abuse, physical abuse, verbal abuse, and/or neglect in childhood. About half of each group had also endured adult trauma (e.g., a rape). No patient in these groups had a history of combat. Patients in this study also completed the Dissociative Experiences Scale (DES) (Bernstein and Putnam 1986) and measures of PTSD and dissociative symptoms. Patients with a diagnosis of psychogenic amnesia had an average DES score of 26.2, essentially the same as the average DES score of the combat veterans with PTSD in this study. (In the original validation study of the DES, median scores were 4.38, 31.25, and 57.06 for normal controls, PTSD patients, and MPD patients, respectively.)

In a sample of 468 male and female clinical subjects with a reported history of childhood sexual abuse, Briere and Conte (1989) reported that 59.6% described an inability to remember the abuse at some time during their lives. Subjects with amnesia were more likely to have had more severe, early-onset, repetitive, physically injurious abuse with multiple perpetrators and direct threats of harm for disclosure. Subjects with a history of amnesia were more globally symptomatic as well.

## EPIDEMIOLOGY OF TRAUMA IN VARIOUS CLINICAL POPULATIONS

Modern data need to be acquired about the actual prevalence of amnesic syndromes in patients with trauma histories. Nonetheless, the epidemiologic data suggest that a large population is at risk for development of amnesic syndromes due to trauma.

Helzer et al. (1987) found PTSD diagnosed by DSM-III criteria in 1% of a general population sample of 2,493 adults. The prevalence was 3.5% in civilians exposed to physical attack and 20% in Vietnam veterans wounded in combat. A history of child abuse and/or childhood trauma was not explored in these subjects, although a diagnosis of PTSD in nonveterans was correlated with behavioral problems that began before the age of 15. Davidson et al. (1990) found a lifetime prevalence of PTSD of 1.3% in a community survey in North Carolina, "placing it above panic disorder, bipolar disorder, and schizophrenia with respect to lifetime frequency in the population sampled" (p. 259).

Russel (1983) studied 930 women in a random community sample using a structured interview. An episode of extrafamilial sexual abuse before the age of 18 was reported by 16% and an episode of extrafamilial sexual abuse before this age was reported by 31%. Father-daughter or stepfather-daughter incest was reported in 4.5% of cases. In addition, about 25% of the episodes of intrafamilial abuse were classified as "very serious" (meaning acts such as forced penetration, cunnilingus, fellatio). Amnesia and dissociation have been linked with more serious episodes of incestuous abuse (Briere and Conte 1989; Herman and Schatzow 1987).

The prevalence of a history of childhood sexual abuse among males is less well documented, but studies suggest that 2.5% to 16% may have been victimized sexually in some way in childhood, although girls are thought to be several times more likely than boys to be victimized (Finkelhor 1984, 1987). Physical abuse may also be linked to amnesia in some cases (Leventhal and Midelfort 1986). This form of abuse is reported to be about equally prevalent in females and males. On the other hand, males may be physically abused more frequently in earliest childhood, when a posttraumatic dissociative response is more likely (Loewenstein and Putnam 1986).

In studies of clinical populations, Herman (1986) found a history of physical or sexual victimization in 22% of 190 consecutive patients presenting to an outpatient clinic. Briere and Runtz (1987) found a history of childhood sexual abuse in almost 50% in a sample of women presenting to an outpatient crisis clinic. Briere and Zaidi (1989) found a 70% prevalence of childhood sexual abuse in a sample of 50 consecutive female patients in an urban emergency room setting where interviewers were trained to ask questions about abuse. Bryer et al. (1987) found a prevalence of 59% for physical and/or sexual abuse before the age of 16 in 66 female psychiatric inpatients identified in a prospective study; 72% of the sample reported abuse at some time in their lives. There are many other clinical studies that show high prevalences of childhood trauma and abuse in various inpatient and outpatient populations (Goodwin et al. 1990).

## TWO PRESENTATIONS OF PSYCHOGENIC AMNESIA AND FUGUE

The foregoing discussion can be summarized as follows. There are two major modes of presentation of the clinical syndromes of psychogenic amnesia and/or fugue. Although there may be overlap in some cases, it is helpful heuristically to make a clear distinction between them.

### *The "Classic" Presentation*

These patients are the textbook cases that form the image of dissociative disorders for most mental health professionals. The classic disorder is an overt, florid, dramatic dissociative disturbance that frequently results in the patient being brought quickly to medical attention specifically for symptoms related to the dissociative disorder. The paradigmatic case is that of the individual who is found without memory for identity or life history, often leading to media reporting of the case. This is a relatively rare disorder, although cases continue to be described primarily among patients in general hospital emergency services.

This presentation of amnesia or fugue is thought to develop in the context of profound conflict or emotional stress. An overwhelming or traumatic reality may engender affects or impulses in conflict with the patient's conscience or self-ideals. Depression and suicidal ideas are reported in many, but not all, cases. Despite this, there are no good data on the prevalence in these patients of intercurrent affective disorders, adjustment disorders, and other DSM-III or DSM-III-R Axis I or Axis II disorders. No single personality profile or antecedent history is consistently reported in these patients, although most studies suggest significant pathology in the patient's personal and family history. There may be a prior personal or family history of somatoform or dissociative symptoms.

In general, amnesia is more common in these patients than fugue or fugue-like states. The full DSM-III-R syndrome of fugue is probably very rare. It has been suggested, however, that fugue-like states may be much more common during wartime and times of natural disaster and dislocation (Putnam 1985). No data exist on this point, however.

Factors relating to avoidance of responsibility may be quite prominent in many of these cases, with sexual indiscretions, legal difficulties, financial problems, or fear of anticipated combat being part of the clinical matrix that surrounds the amnesia or fugue. There is a possible association in some cases with an antecedent history of head trauma with or without loss of consciousness, although this finding has never been studied rigorously using adequate controls.

Case reports suggest that many of these patients have histories of childhood or adult abuse or trauma. This has not been systematically studied, however. If carefully questioned, some of these patients will give a history of recurrent episodes of amnesia or fugue. Thus some will actually meet criteria for MPD or DDNOS. There are no data on the prevalence of PTSD symptoms in these patients.

## The "Nonclassic" Presentation

The nonclassic group of patients can be said to have a "covert" dissociative disorder since their primary complaints rarely relate directly to amnesia. Chronic, recurrent, or persistent psychogenic amnesia is the most common symptom in these cases, although some may describe a history of fugue-like states. For example, since a history of childhood sexual abuse is very common among adolescent runaways (McCormack et al. 1986), some of these episodes of running away may actually represent fugue-like periods (Goodwin et al. 1990).

Commonly, patients with the nonclassic presentation of amnesia will not reveal the presence of dissociative symptoms unless directly asked about them. These patients are often very uncomfortable when amnesia is inquired about and may minimize the presence or rationalize the importance of the symptom.

In these patients, the amnesia will often manifest itself as a circumscribed memory gap or series of memory gaps for the life history, primarily for times when traumatic events occurred (e.g., in childhood or during wartime). In the combat veteran with delayed-onset PTSD, amnesia may be discovered for behavioral disturbances re-lated to the reexperiencing of combat-related trauma (flashbacks), although exten-sive, circumscribed memory gaps for wartime events may also be described (Blank 1985).

These patients frequently come to treatment for a variety of symptoms, such as depression or mood swings, substance abuse, sleep disturbances, somatoform symptoms, anxiety and panic, suicidal or self-mutilatory impulses and acts, violent outbursts, eating problems, or interpersonal problems. Self-mutilation and violent behavior in these patients may also be accompanied by amnesia (Coons and Milstein 1989; Hendin et al. 1984).

There is frequently a history of childhood emotional, sexual, and/or physical abuse among many of these patients. Thus many will also meet criteria for chronic PTSD or, at least, will suffer from some posttraumatic stress symptoms. If carefully questioned or evaluated longitudinally, some of these patients will turn out to have a much more severe and chronic history of amnesia and dissociative and posttraumatic stress symptoms, leading to a diagnosis of MPD or DDNOS (Kluft 1985). Since the dissociative and PTSD symptoms are often unrecognized or misunderstood, these patients are frequently given only somatoform, affective, and/or personality disorder diagnoses.

The prevalence of this form of psychogenic amnesia is unknown. However, the high prevalence of childhood and adult trauma in both nonclinical and clinical populations suggests that this type of amnesic disorder may be quite common.

Etiologically, the amnesia can be understood as part of the dissociative response to trauma. This includes entering into a dissociative state while being traumatized and encoding of traumatic memories in iconic, sensorimotor, or other nonverbal forms (Greenberg and van der Kolk 1986; Spiegel 1988a, 1988b; Terr 1988). Thus full retrieval of the dissociated experiences in verbal form often does not occur without specific therapeutic interventions.

## DIFFERENTIAL DIAGNOSIS

There is no single test or examination that can establish absolutely whether a memory disorder is psychogenic, organic, malingered, or of mixed etiology. The clinician evaluating the amnesic patient must have a reasonable index of suspicion about any of these. In ambiguous cases, there should be careful reassessment of the clinical situation on an ongoing basis.

In actual clinical practice, however, most cases of psychogenic amnesia and fugue present very differently from other disorders with memory impairment or pathologic wandering (Blumer 1975; Lishman 1987). In the differential diagnosis of psychogenic amnesia and fugue, the clinician must strive primarily to rule out organic mental disorders, substance abuse disorders, seizure disorders, other dissociative disorders, somatoform disorders, and malingering (Kluft 1988). Rarely, the diagnosis of amnesia or fugue will be raised in the context of an anxiety disorder, psychotic disorder, or a recurrent affective disorder (Table 3-5).

## Baseline Evaluation

In the patient presenting with amnesia or fugue, it is important to perform a comprehensive clinical assessment. This includes a complete history, to the extent the patient can give it, including a developmental history and questioning about psychological trauma, including physical, sexual, and/or emotional abuse in childhood and adulthood. If possible, it may be crucial to obtain ancillary history from significant others and previous records.

The clinician should perform a complete physical and neurologic examination, a full mental status examination with cognitive testing, a baseline laboratory examination including an electrocardiogram, and toxicologic screening with a determination of blood alcohol level. Sequential observation in the hospital may also be helpful in clarifying the differential diagnosis. More specialized tests—including a full dementia workup, electroencephalogram, computed tomography scan, and/or magnetic resonance imaging scan—and neuropsychological testing may also be indicated. Rarely, intensive electroencephalogram monitoring in a specialized telemetry unit may be necessary to rule out an occult seizure disorder. It is unusual that a comprehensive baseline evaluation, ancillary history, and sequential observation fail to discriminate patients with psychogenic amnesia from those with organic disorders. The most problematic cases are those in which there is superimposition of psychogenic and organic deficits.

## Dementia, Delirium, and Organic Amnestic Disorders

In patients with dementia, organic amnestic disorders, and delirium, the memory loss for personal information is embedded in a far more extensive set of cognitive,

Table 3-5.  Differential diagnosis of psychogenic amnesia and fugue

---

Dementia, delirium, and amnestic syndromes
Discrete memory loss in organic disorders
  Posttraumatic amnesia
  Seizure disorders
  Psychoactive-substance-induced amnesia
  Transient global amnesia
Other dissociative disorders
Posttraumatic stress disorder and somatoform disorders
Malingering and amnesia for criminal behavior

---

language, attentional, behavioral, and memory problems. Loss of memory for personal identity is usually not found without evidence of a marked disturbance in many domains of cognitive function (Lishman 1987). Confabulation may be present to various degrees and is usually implausible or bizarre. Causes of organic amnestic disorders include Korsakoff's psychosis, amnestic stroke, postoperative amnesia, postinfectious amnesia, anoxic amnesia, and transient global amnesia (Benson 1978). Electroconvulsive therapy (ECT) may also cause a marked temporary amnesia as well as persistent memory problems in some cases (Benson 1978; Squire 1987).

## Discrete Memory Loss in Organic Disorders

Organic disorders with more clearly defined amnestic episodes include posttraumatic amnesia, transient global amnesia, amnesia related to seizure disorders, and blackouts related to alcohol, drugs, and other toxic factors. In general, the clinical picture and history will be sufficient to discriminate these disorders from psychogenic ones.

## Posttraumatic Amnesia

In posttraumatic amnesia due to brain injury, there is usually a history of a clear-cut physical trauma, a period of unconsciousness and/or amnesia, and objective clinical evidence of brain injury. In general, the length of the posttraumatic amnesia is a reasonable predictor of cognitive outcome. In general, the retrograde amnesia found in head injury cases is quite brief. An extensive retrograde amnesia out of proportion to the extent of the head injury suggests that a careful investigation for psychogenic factors should be undertaken (Lishman 1987). On the other hand, some studies have noted head injury of various degrees of severity as an antecedent to amnesia or fugue-like episodes in some cases (Berrington et al. 1956; Kopelman 1987a; Sargent and Slater 1941; Thom and Fenton 1920). No systematic modern data exist about this observation, however, and its importance remains to be clarified.

## Seizure Disorders

Seizure patients, especially those with complex-partial seizures, have been described as exhibiting complex behavior during seizures or in postictal states for which there is subsequent amnesia (Blumer 1975; Lishman 1987; Mayeux et al. 1979). Stressful life events may be associated with increased seizure frequency in some susceptible patients. Thus this factor alone is not sufficient to differentiate between psychogenic and epileptic amnesia-fugue states. In the vast majority of cases, however, ictal or postictal behaviors are brief, stereotyped, and only superficially purposeful (Blumer 1975; Lishman 1987). Patients have been reported to wander considerable distances during epileptic attacks and engage in semi-purposeful behavior. Unlike psychogenic fugue patients, however, epileptic patients in fugue episodes are usually recognized as showing abnormal behavior (Lishman 1987).

There has also been a hypothesis that temporal lobe pathology could predispose to the development of dissociative states and MPD (Mesulam 1981; Schenk and Bear 1981). Kiersch (1962) reported no higher than normal frequency of electroencephalogram abnormalities in 20 psychogenic amnesia-fugue patients as compared with data from the general population. Also, there are now three rigorous studies using structured interviews and/or standardized rating scales of dissociative symptoms comparing patients with MPD to those with well-documented complex partial seizure disorder (Devinsky et al. 1989; Loewenstein and Putnam 1988; Ross et al. 1989). In these studies, little phenomenological or psychometric similarity was found between the dissociative disorder patients and a total of about 100 seizure patients. These studies suggest that, in most patients, there is little relationship between the development of dissociative disorders and a seizure history.

## Psychoactive Substance-Induced Amnesia

A variety of substances and intoxicants have been implicated in the production of amnesia and fugue (for a review, see Good 1989). Offending agents include alcohol, sedative-hypnotics, anticholinergic agents, steroids, lithium carbonate, beta-blockers, pentazocine, phencyclidine, hypoglycemic agents, marijuana, psychedelics, methyldopa, and many others (Good 1989).

In most cases, a careful history both from the patient and ancillary sources, sequential clinical observation, and objective testing will clarify the etiology of the amnesia. In some instances of "pathologic intoxication" in which a small amount of alcohol or similar substance produces a major behavioral disinhibition, the alcohol may be producing its effect by facilitating the onset of a dissociative episode in a susceptible individual. This may be analogous to the disinhibition that occurs in a clinical amytal interview where attempts are made to uncover dissociated memories (Good 1989).

The most difficult differential diagnostic problem usually involves patients with a history of both substance-induced and psychogenic memory problems. In my experience, in the nonforensic context, patients with dissociative disorders such as MPD and the nonclassic forms of psychogenic amnesia often minimize the dissociative amnesia and emphasize the substance-induced problems as a rationalization for amnesia that could not have been related to substance abuse (e.g., extensive childhood amnesia that predated the onset of substance abuse in a patient without organic memory impairment). Clinically, the minimization of the dissociative amnesia in these cases usually seems related to avoidance of the painful memories and affects that are dissociated. However, the relative contribution of the substance abuse and the dissociation may only be fully clarified by sequential clinical observation once the patient has achieved sobriety.

## Transient Global Amnesia

Transient global amnesia may be mistaken for a psychogenic amnesia especially since stressful life events may precede either disorder. However, the clinical presentation and course of illness are quite different. In transient global amnesia, there is the sudden onset of anterograde amnesia, pronounced retrograde amnesia, preservation of memory for personal identity, anxious awareness of memory loss with repeated, often perseverative, questioning, overall normal behavior, lack of gross neurologic abnormalities in most cases, and rapid return of baseline cognitive function with a persistent short retrograde amnesia. The patient usually shows risk factors for cerebrovascular disease (Rollinson 1978).

## Dissociative Disorders

It is vital that clinicians have an index of suspicion that there have been recurrent amnesia or fugue episodes in patients who present with these symptoms. Systematic assessment of recurrent amnesia experiences should include inquiry about symptoms such as those described in Tables 3-3 and 3-4. In addition, dissociating patients should be evaluated for the presence of passive-influence experiences, auditory and visual hallucinations, and autohypnotic symptoms such as spontaneous trances, negative hallucinations, voluntary anesthesia, and out-of-body experiences (Kluft 1985; Loewenstein et al. 1988). The presence of recurrent amnesia and fugue with or without these other symptoms suggests a diagnosis of MPD or DDNOS.

## PTSD and Somatoform Disorders

Since many patients with amnesia and fugue have histories of trauma, the clinician should attempt to establish whether full or partial criteria for PTSD are met. I tend to make a comorbid dissociative disorder diagnosis in PTSD patients when the amnesia seems more extensive than can be accounted for by a particular traumatic event (e.g., for a whole year in combat as opposed to amnesia for a particular battle; for the first 10 years of childhood as opposed to specific events with an abusive babysitter).

In addition, since amnesia is a criterion for somatization disorder, a history of conversion symptoms or multiple physical complaints should be obtained in patients with amnesia or fugue. Many studies describe histories of sexual and/or physical abuse in childhood as well as complex psychogenic amnesia and frank MPD in patients with somatoform disorders such as Briquet's syndrome, somatoform pain disorder, and somatization disorder (Goodwin et al. 1990; Loewenstein 1990). These findings imply that some patients with somatoform disorders may be more parsimoniously understood as having dissociative disorders and PTSD related to childhood abuse, with the somatoform symptoms representing a nonverbal means of reexperiencing the trauma (Goodwin et al. 1990; Loewenstein 1990, Spiegel 1988a, 1988b; Terr 1988; van der Kolk 1986).

## Malingering and Amnesia for Criminal Behavior

There is no absolute way to differentiate true psychogenic amnesia from malingering. Malingerers have been noted to continue their deception even during hypnotically or barbiturate-facilitated interviews (Kluft 1988). Malingered amnesia is more common in patients presenting with classic forms of psychogenic amnesia than in those with the nonclassic type. As noted above, many of the classic cases were described as occurring in a clinical context of financial, sexual, and legal problems or in soldiers who wished to escape from combat.

On the other hand, in the clinical case reports, many malingerers quickly confessed their deceptions either spontaneously or when confronted by the examiner. In these nonforensic reports, the malingered amnesic patients were frequently pathetic individuals whose deception was transparent. It was often unclear where the conscious deception began and the unconscious defenses ended (Kopelman 1987b; Lishman 1987).

There have been several reviews of the problem of amnesia for criminal behavior (Kopelman 1987b; Rubinsky and Brandt 1986; Schacter 1986). From a legal standpoint, amnesia alone is not considered a sufficient factor to generate a finding of incompetence to stand trial or a verdict of not guilty by reason of insanity (Rubinsky and Brandt 1986). Psychogenic amnesia has been claimed by perpetrators in 30% to 40% of homicide cases and in a lesser percentage of other violent crimes (Kopelman 1987a, 1987b). Although malingering is often suspected in such cases, many of these individuals did little to avoid being charged with a crime and some even called the authorities themselves. In general, the murder cases with apparent true psychogenic amnesia were characterized by an unpremeditated assault in a state of high emotional arousal on a victim closely related to the perpetrator (Kopelman 1987b).

A variety of procedures have been suggested to differentiate objectively between forms of actual and malingered amnesia. At this point, none has achieved a definitive status in differentiating among these conditions (Kopelman 1987b). In general, clinicians have gotten into the most difficulty when they have confused the role of forensic examiner with that of treating therapist in assessment of accused criminals who claim amnesia or dissociation for criminal acts (Orne et al. 1984).

In terms of civil litigation, amnesia due to childhood abuse has recently been recognized as a legitimate factor in plaintiffs' failure to bring a timely tort action against their abusers within the usual statute of limitations. In several recent state and federal cases, courts have ruled that the statute of limitations for bringing suit against an abuser begins when the amnesic adult plaintiff becomes aware of the childhood abuse, not when the abuse first occurred (The Psychiatric Times 1990; The United States Law Week 1989). Cases of this type are likely to increase in frequency in the future.

## TREATMENT OF AMNESIA AND FUGUE

### Overview

The treatment of psychogenic amnesia and fugue is best understood if the clinician shifts from a psychopathologic frame of reference to one emphasizing psychological adaptation. In this section then, the terms *amnesia* and *fugue* will primarily refer not to disorders but to symptoms resulting from intrapsychic defensive and adaptational processes, usually to extreme, overwhelming, and/or traumatic circumstances.

Spiegel (1988b) stated that "dissociation has recently been understood as a defense not simply against memories or warded-off unconscious wishes but rather as a defense against the traumatic experience itself" (p. 22). With respect to psychogenic amnesia, this process can be understood as having several possible outcomes. First, after the acute traumatic events have passed, there may be a spontaneous recovery of memory, usually after the person is removed from the situation that generated the amnesia (Abeles and Schilder 1935; Grinker and Spiegel 1945b; Kennedy and Neville 1957; Sargent and Slater 1941). However, in many cases, the amnesia will persist, requiring specific treatment interventions for its resolution.

Once the dissociative process has become autonomous outside of the immediate traumatic circumstances, the interplay between amnesic symptoms and intrusive reexperiencing symptoms can be conceptualized using more standard views of intrapsychic defense (Horowitz 1986). Nonetheless, the key to therapeutic progress in many of these cases depends on the clinician's understanding that the patient's symptoms or apparent character pathology represent a posttraumatic adaptation rather than a developmental fixation or arrest (Arnold 1985; Briere 1989; Smith 1985; Spiegel 1988b; Terr 1988). It is also essential that the clinician bear in mind that critical historical data and core psychodynamic issues are generally concealed by the patient's amnesia (Smith 1985; Terr 1988). This is particularly true in the nonclassic presentations of persistent psychogenic amnesia secondary to childhood abuse, adult rape, or victimization and to wartime trauma.

In virtually all dynamic conceptualizations of psychogenic amnesia, the amnesia can be thought of as a kind of "safety valve" or "circuit breaker" that reflects the patient's ability to tolerate full conscious awareness of the dissociated material. Thus it is helpful for the therapist of the amnesic patient to discuss the adaptive nature of the amnesia early on treatment. It is not only the content of the dissociated memories that is experienced as painfully intolerable, however. For the most part, it is the overwhelming affects and the personal meaning of the traumatic events that reinforce the persistence of the amnesia (Spiegel 1988b; Terr 1988). Powerful and conflictual emotions of despair, grief, guilt, shame, rage, self-hatred, helplessness, and terror are commonly embedded in memories for which the person is amnesic. In addition, the traumatic events may cause profound shifts in the person's view of him or herself, significant others, and the nature of the world and all human relations (Briere 1989; Spiegel 1988b).

## Treatment of Acute Amnesic Symptoms in War

In the literature from World War II, a variety of interventions were reported for treatment of combat-related amnesia. Initially, the soldier was removed from combat and provided with food and sleep (Kardiner 1941; Kardiner and Spiegel 1947; Kubie 1943). If this was insufficient to resolve symptoms, more definitive treatment was undertaken, usually after removing the soldier from the frontlines.

Most authors emphasize establishment of a safe and supportive relationship between the treatment team and the amnesic patient as basic for successful treatment (Grinker and Spiegel 1945b; Kubie 1943). Some amnesias were said to lift in the course of taking the psychiatric history or merely with suggestion and reassurance (Tureen and Stein 1949). In more refractory amnesias, the patient was treated with psychotherapy to attempt derepression and integration of the dissociated experiences. Psychotherapy was often facilitated by hypnotherapy and/or narcosynthesis, usually with sodium amytal or pentothal, to attempt resolution of the amnesia itself (Grinker and Spiegel 1945a, 1945b; Henderson and Moore 1944; Kardiner 1941; Kardiner and Spiegel 1947; Kubie 1943; Perry and Jacobs 1982; Sargent and Slater 1941; Tureen and Stein 1949).

Kardiner (1941) stated that in 63% of patients with amnesia and/or fugue "rest, sedatives, and hypnosis were effective" in ameliorating symptoms (p. 218). Lambert and Rees (1944, cited in Perry and Jacobs 1982) reported that 82% of soldiers with amnesia who were treated with drug-facilitated interviews had complete resolution of the symptom.

In addition to individual psychotherapy, Kardiner (1941) described the use of group psychotherapy and hypnotherapy to promote recovery. Highly supportive, structured, reassuring, and "reeducative" approaches were often used by the therapist to attempt to accomplish return of the patient to a functional status and to prevent chronic disability (Grinker and Spiegel 1945b; Kardiner 1941; Kardiner and Spiegel 1947).

Some modern authors have questioned the necessity for somatic treatments such as narcosynthesis in many of these cases. They have voiced concern that such techniques actually reinforce the soldier's perception of having a severe illness rather than an understandable reaction to overwhelming events (Jones and Hales 1987). On the other hand, others have questioned whether the failure to use such techniques during the Vietnam War is among the factors that have led to the large number of Vietnam veterans with chronic and/or delayed-onset PTSD (Cavenar and Nash 1976).

## Acute Amnesia in Civilians: The Classic Presentations

The literature on treatment of acute generalized and localized psychogenic amnesia in civilians emphasizes similar issues. In the series of Abeles and Schilder (1935), about 75% of their 63 cases were said to have had rapid spontaneous remission of amnesia for personal identity. However, residual amnesia occurred in some of these cases (Abeles and Schilder 1935; Fisher 1945; Gill and Brenman 1959).

In cases with persistent generalized or severe localized amnesia, the initial therapeutic goal is to restore knowledge of personal identity and to gain at least an outline of the patient's history (Fisher and Joseph 1949). After this, more extensive work can be done to lift residual amnesia gradually and to clarify the events leading to the acute dissociative episode. Fisher and Joseph underscored the necessity of establishing a good therapeutic relationship with the patient. They emphasized respecting the protective function of the amnesia and pacing the therapeutic work; extremely intense emotions and powerful suicidal impulses may emerge as acute amnesias are relieved (see also Kaszniak et al. 1988).

Hypnotherapy and amytal narcosynthesis are the most common adjunctive methods used to facilitate recovery of dissociated memories in these cases (Abeles and Schilder 1935; Fisher 1945; Fisher and Joseph 1949; Garver et al. 1981; Herman 1938; Kennedy and Neville 1957; Kluft 1988; Mac Hovec 1981; Perry and Jacobs 1982; Ruedrich et al. 1985; van der Hart 1985). However, a variety of other methods also have been used to diminish amnesia, including suggestion, intensive history taking, automatic writing, and word association (Abeles and Schilder 1935; Jones 1909; Kennedy and Neville 1957; Ruedrich et al. 1985).

It is difficult to find acceptable data in the literature on acute combat-related or civilian amnesia to clarify variables that predict response to psychotherapy alone, psychotherapy plus hypnotherapy, psychotherapy plus narcosynthesis, and so on. Patients in these reports vary with respect to many factors, including intensity of combat exposure or traumatic experiences, prior history of child abuse or a dissociative disorder, length of time from being traumatized until definitive treatment, and so on. Therapist variables also were important; some authors are clearly more skilled than others at psychotherapeutic and/or hypnotherapeutic approaches to these patients.

With few exceptions, the reports on patients with acute amnesia are without follow-up or long-term treatment data.

## Treatment of Patients With Nonclassic Presentations of Psychogenic Amnesia

Dissociative symptoms in patients with the nonclassic, covert amnesia presentations generally should be treated in the framework of a longer-term psychotherapy directed at resolution of the complex psychological sequellae of the events producing the amnesia, usually severe traumatization due to childhood abuse, combat, or other forms of adult victimization (Briere 1989; Courtois 1988; Kluft 1988; Smith 1985; Spiegel 1988b; van der Kolk 1986).

The first tasks of treatment with these patients include restoration of the patient's physical well-being and safety and attempts at establishment of a therapeutic working alliance. The clinician must be prepared to intervene actively if the patient is acutely dangerous to self or others or if the patient is abusing substances in an uncontrollable way. Hospitalization may be necessary to stabilize such situations.

In my experience, these patients may de-escalate if they sense that the clinician is sensitive to and knowledgeable about issues relating to trauma. The clinician can often convey this by including tactful, sensitive history taking about relevant areas such as combat experiences and/or a history of childhood abuse (see Blank 1985; Briere 1989; Courtois 1988). This history taking may be sufficient to begin to alleviate the amnesia or at least to focus the patient's awareness that amnesia is present for crucial aspects of the life history.

It is best for the therapist not to rush prematurely to undo amnesias in such patients unless there is an emergency, such as imminent danger to self or others, that can be resolved only by overcoming the amnesia. Most of these patients have profound issues concerning trust, boundaries, control, and affect tolerance that are basic to their difficulties (Briere 1989; Smith 1985). The first task of the therapy is to establish a working alliance with a patient who is often profoundly mistrustful, ashamed, embittered, and demoralized (Briere 1989; Smith 1985).

In this regard, it is usually helpful for the clinician to reframe positively for the patient that his or her amnesia and posttraumatic symptoms are part of an internal survival and helping system, not something bad or crazy. It is useful for the therapist to be active, informative, and educative about the nature and dynamics of posttraumatic, amnesic, and dissociative symptoms. In addition, the therapist may need to help actively to structure and pace the therapy so that the patient is not overwhelmed by premature derepression of too much material (Briere 1989; Kluft 1988; Smith 1985).

In work with these patients, the clinician should never underestimate the effect of the traumatic experiences on the patient's overall adaptation. Further, since much of the critical data for understanding these patients are hidden by amnesia, the patient's difficulties may be ascribed solely to other Axis I or Axis II disorders or to more nonspecific development or characterological factors. This is especially true if the patient is demanding, angry, provocative, self-destructive, impulsive, treatment-refractory, or noncompliant (Briere 1989; Smith 1985; Spiegel 1988b).

Many of these patients may be able to overcome their amnesia completely without adjunctive methods, simply in the course of a well-constructed long-term therapy for their posttraumatic and dissociative disorders (Blank 1985; Briere 1989; Futterman and Pumpian-Mindlin 1951; Hendin et al. 1984; Kardiner and Spiegel 1947). On the other hand, hypnotherapy has been widely used adjunctively to help alleviate amnesia and to aid in symptom control in combat veterans with PTSD as well as in adult survivors of childhood sexual abuse (Brende and Benedict 1980; Courtois 1988; Kluft 1988; Putnam 1989; Spiegel 1988a, 1988b, 1989). Kolb (1985) described indications and contraindications for amytal narcosynthesis as an adjunctive method to overcome severe, refractory amnesia symptoms in combat veterans with delayed-onset and/or chronic PTSD (see also Cavenar and Nash 1976).

Group therapy may be a helpful treatment for many combat veterans with PTSD as well as for some survivors of childhood abuse (Briere 1989; Courtois 1988; Goodwin and Talwar 1989; Smith 1985). During group sessions, patients may recover memories for which they have had amnesia. Supportive interventions by the group members and/or group therapist may powerfully facilitate integration and mastery of the dissociated material (Goodwin and Talwar 1989).

Many clinical reports suggest a good outcome for those who can undertake and continue with a treatment focused on trauma-related issues (Briere 1989; Courtois 1988; Kluft 1988; Putnam 1989; Smith 1985; Spiegel 1988b). Nonetheless, little systematic outcome data have been collected on treatment for these patients.

## Somatic Therapies

There is no known pharmacotherapy for psychogenic amnesia and fugue other than drug-facilitated interviews (Loewenstein et al. 1988; Perry and Jacobs 1982; Ruedrich et al. 1985). A variety of agents have been used for this purpose, including sodium amytal, pentothal, oral benzodiazepines, and amphetamines (Ruedrich et al. 1985). At the present time, there have been no adequately controlled studies to assess the efficacy of any of these agents in comparison with one another, with other treatment methods, or with placebo (Ruedrich et al. 1985). Taking the literature as a whole, however, the current state of the evidence supports the use of intravenous sodium amytal as the safest and most effective agent as an adjunctive pharmacologic treatment for psychogenic amnesia (Perry and Jacobs 1982; Ruedrich et al. 1985). Appendix 1 outlines the procedure for drug-facilitated interviewing with sodium amytal.

A number of pharmacologic agents have been suggested for the adjunctive treatment of PTSD symptoms primarily in combat veterans (Davidson et al. 1990; Friedman 1987; Loewenstein et al. 1988; van der Kolk 1986). Although none of these agents are likely to target amnesia symptoms per se, amelioration of affective, anxiety, or posttraumatic symptoms may be useful in the overall stabilization of the patient with amnesia, permitting more effective work in psychotherapy.

A recent case report describes amelioration of some symptoms of apparent psychogenic amnesia with successful ECT treatment in a patient with a severe, refractory major depression (Daniel and Crovitz 1986). Convulsive treatments with ECT, insulin, and pentylenetetrazole were occassionally prescribed for refractory combat-related disorders during World War II (Kubie 1943), although modern military psychiatrists see no indication for such procedures (Jones and Hales 1987). At the present time, there appears to be no indication for treatment of psychogenic amnesia or acute or chronic posttraumatic disorders with ECT.

# CONCLUSIONS

Despite more than a century of clinical case reports and studies, the modern systematic understanding of patients with psychogenic amnesia and fugue has just begun. There are limited rigorous clinical, experimental, or epidemiologic data available about these conditions, although a few recent studies begin to provide a data base for further investigations. Many of the classic early studies of amnesia and fugue are clinically rich but methodologically problematic and require contemporary replication.

In particular, studies are needed to define the prevalence, clinical characteristics, and treatment outcome of patients presenting with various forms of amnesia and fugue. Also, there needs to be much more careful experimental characterization of psychogenic amnesia and its relationship to nonpathologic forms of amnesia, organic brain impairments, repression, and normal memory processes and forgetting.

The heuristic classification arrived at in this review implies that there may be at least two subgroups of these disorders: 1) a common one, with amnesia primarily related to traumatization, and 2) a rarer form, where amnesia develops in the context of overwhelming psychological conflict in an individual predisposed to dissociate. On the other hand, the predisposition to dissociate itself may be related to prior traumatization in these cases. Thus this may be the determining factor, even in most of the cases where intrapsychic conflict appears to be the immediate precipitant of the dissociation.

It is hoped that with the development of more clinically realistic diagnostic criteria to distinguish among these clinical entities in DSM-IV and beyond, definitive research studies will be undertaken to clarify these issues and to establish a more rigorous knowledge base about psychogenic amnesia and fugue.

## REFERENCES

Abeles M, Schilder P: Psychogenic loss of personal identity. Archives of Neurology and Psychiatry 34:587–604, 1935

Akhtar S, Brenner I: Differential diagnosis of fugue-like states. J Clin Psychiatry 40:381–385, 1979

American Psychiatric Association: Diagnostic and Statistical Manual of Mental Disorders, 3rd Edition. Washington, DC, American Psychiatric Association, 1980

American Psychiatric Association: Diagnostic and Statistical Manual of Mental Disorders, 3rd Edition, Revised. Washington, DC, American Psychiatric Association, 1987

Archibald HC, Tuddenham RD: Persistent stress reaction after combat. Arch Gen Psychiatry 12:475–481, 1965

Arnold AL: Diagnosis of post-traumatic stress disorder in Viet Nam veterans, in The Trauma of War: Stress and Recovery in Viet Nam Veterans. Edited by Sonnenberg SM, Blank AS Jr, Talbott JA. Washington, DC, American Psychiatric Press, 1985, pp 99–123

Benson DF: Amnesia. South Med J 71:1221–1227, 1978

Bernstein EM, Putnam FW: Development, reliability, and validity of a dissociation scale. J Nerv Ment Dis 174:727–735, 1986

Berrington WP, Liddell DW, Foulds GA: A re-evaluation of the fugue. Journal of Mental Science 102:280–286, 1956

Blank AS: The unconscious flashback to the war in Viet Nam veterans: clinical mystery, legal defense, and community problem, in The Trauma of War: Stress and Recovery in Viet Nam Veterans. Edited by Sonnenberg SM, Blank AS Jr, Talbott JA. Washington, DC, American Psychiatric Press, 1985, pp 293–308

Blumer D: Temporal lobe epilepsy and its psychiatric significance, in Psychiatric Aspects of Neurological Disease. Edited by Benson DF, Blumer D. New York, Grune & Stratton, 1975, pp 171–198

Bornstein B: Hysterical twilight states in an eight-year old child. Psychoanal Study Child 2:229–241, 1946

Brende JO, Benedict BD: The Vietnam combat delayed stress syndrome: hypnotherapy of "dissociative symptoms." Am J Clin Hypn 23:34–40, 1980

Breuer J, Freud S: Studies in hysteria (1893–1895), in The Standard Edition of the Complete Psychological Works of Sigmund Freud, Vol 2. Translated and edited by Strachey J. London, Hogarth Press, 1955, pp 1–309

Briere J: Therapy for Adults Molested as Children: Beyond Survival. New York, Springer, 1989

Briere J, Conte J: Amnesia in adults molested as children: testing theories of repression. Paper presented at the annual meeting of the American Psychological Association, New Orleans, LA, August 1989

Briere J, Runtz M: Post sexual abuse trauma: data and implications for clinical practice. Journal of Interpersonal Violence 2:367–369, 1987

Briere J, Zaidi LY: Sexual abuse histories and sequelae in female psychiatric emergency room patients. Am J Psychiatry 146:1602–1607, 1989

Briquet P: Traite Clinique et Therapeutique a l'Hysterie. Paris, J-B Balliere & Fils, 1859

Bryer JB, Nelson BA, Miller JB, et al: Childhood sexual and physical abuse as factors in adult psychiatric illness. Am J Psychiatry 144:1426–1430, 1987

Bychowski G: Escapades: a form of dissociation. Psychoanal Q 131:155–173, 1962

Cavenar JO, Nash JL: The effects of combat on the normal personality: war neurosis in Vietnam returnees. Compr Psychiatry 17:647–653, 1976

Coons PM, Milstein V: Psychogenic amnesia: a clinical investigation of 25 consecutive cases, in Proceedings of the Sixth Annual International Conference on Multiple Personality and Dissociation. Edited by Braun BG. Chicago, Dissociative Disorders Program, Department of Psychiatry, Rush University, 1989, p 36

Coons PM, Bowman ES, Pellow TA, et al: Post-traumatic aspects of the treatment of victims of sexual abuse and incest. Psychiatr Clin North Am 12:325–337, 1989

Courtois CA: Healing the Incest Wound: Adult Survivors in Therapy. New York, WW Norton, 1988

Croft B, Healthfield KWG, Swash M: Differential diagnosis of transient amnesia. Br Med J 4:593–596, 1973

Daniel WF, Crovitz HF: ECT-induced alteration of psychogenic amnesia. Acta Psychiatr Scand 74:302–303, 1986

Davidson J, Kudler H, Smith R, et al: Treatment of posttraumatic stress disorder with amitriptyline and placebo. Arch Gen Psychiatry 47:259–266, 1990

Devinsky O, Putnam F, Grafman J, et al: Dissociative states and epilepsy. Neurology 39:835–840, 1989

Dickes R: The defensive function of an altered state of consciousness: a hypnoid state. J Am Psychoanal Assoc 13:356–403, 1965

Ellenberger HF: The Discovery of the Unconscious. New York, Basic Books, 1970

El-Rayes MES: Traumatic war neurosis: Egyptian experience. Journal of the Royal Army Medical Corps 128:67–71, 1982

Fairbairn WRD: Psychoanalytic Studies of Personality. London, Routledge & Kegan Paul, 1952

Finkelhor D: Child Sexual Abuse: New Research and Theory. New York, Free Press, 1984

Finkelhor D: The sexual abuse of children: current research reviewed. Psychiatric Annals 17:233–241, 1987

Fisher C: Amnesic states in war neurosis: the psychogenesis of fugue. Psychoanal Q 14:437–468, 1945

Fisher C, Joseph ED: Fugue with awareness of loss of personal identify. Psychoanal Q 18:480–493, 1949

Fleiss R: The hypnotic evasion. Psychoanal Q 22:497–511, 1953

Foy DW, Resnick HS, Sipprelle RC, et al: Premilitary, military, and postmilitary factors in the development of combat-related posttraumatic stress disorder. The Behavior Therapist 10:3–9, 1987

Friedman MJ: Toward rational pharmacotherapy for posttraumatic stress disorder. Am J Psychiatry 145:281–285, 1987

Futterman S, Pumpian-Mindlin E: Traumatic war neuroses five years later. Am J Psychiatry 108:401–408, 1951

Garver RB, Fuselier GD, Booth TB: The hypnotic treatment of amnesia in an Air Force basic trainee. Am J Clin Hypn 24:3–6, 1981

Geleerd ER, Hacker FJ, Rapaport D: Contribution to the study of amnesia and allied conditions. Psychoanal Q 14:199–220, 1945

Gelinas DJ: The persistent negative effects of incest. Psychiatry 46:312–332, 1983

Gill M, Brenman M: Hypnosis and Related States. New York, International Universities Press, 1959

Gill M, Rapaport D: A case of amnesia and its bearing on the theory of memory. Character and Personality 11:166–172, 1942

Glover E: The concept of dissociation. Int J Psychoanal 24:7–13, 1943

Goldberg P: The role of distractions in the maintenance of dissociative mental states. Int J Psychoanal 68:511–523, 1987

Goldfeld AE, Mollica RF, Pesavento BH, et al: The physical and psychological sequelae of torture: symptomatology and diagnosis. JAMA 259:2725–2729, 1988

Good MI: Substance-induced dissociative disorders and psychiatric nosology. J Clin Psychopharmacol 9:88–93, 1989

Goodwin J: Sexual Abuse: Incest Victims and Their Families. Littleton, MA, Wright/PSG, 1982

Goodwin J, Talwar N: Group psychotherapy for victims of incest. Psychiatr Clin North Am 12:279–295, 1989

Goodwin J, Cheeves K, Connell V: Borderline and other severe symptoms in adult survivors of incestuous abuse. Psychiatric Annals 20:22–32, 1990

Greenberg MS, van der Kolk BA: Retrieval and integration of traumatic memories with the "painting cure," in Psychological Trauma. Edited by van der Kolk B. Washington, DC, American Psychiatric Press, 1986, pp 191–215

Grinker RR, Spiegel JP: Men Under Stress. Philadelphia, PA, Blakiston, 1945a

Grinker RR, Spiegel JP: War Neuroses. Philadelphia, PA, Blakiston, 1945b

Helzer JE, Robins LN, McEvoy L: Post-traumatic stress disorder in the general population. N Engl J Med 317:1630–1634, 1987

Henderson JL, Moore, M: The psychoneuroses of war. N Engl J Med 230:273–279, 1944

Hendin H, Haas AP, Singer P, et al: The reliving experience in Vietnam veterans with posttraumatic stress disorder. Compr Psychiatry 25:165–173, 1984

Herman JL: Histories of violence in an outpatient population: an exploratory study. Am J Orthopsychiatry 56:137–141, 1986

Herman JL, Schatzow E: Recovery and verification of memories of childhood sexual trauma. Psychoanalytic Psychology 4:1–14, 1987

Herman M: The use of intravenous sodium amytal in psychogenic amnesic states. Psychiatr Q 12:738–742, 1938

Hilgard ER: Divided Consciousness. New York, John Wiley, 1977

Horowitz MJ: Stress Response Syndromes, 2nd Edition. Northvale, NJ, Jason Aronson, 1986

Jaffe R: Dissociative phenomena in former concentration camp inmates. Int J Psychoanal 49:310–312, 1968

Janet P: The Mental State of Hystericals. New York, Putnam, 1901 (Reprinted Washington, DC, University Publications of America, 1977)

Janet P: The Major Symptoms of Hysteria. New York, Macmillan, 1907

Jones E: Remarks on a case of complete autopsychic amnesia. J Abnorm Psychol 4:218–235, 1909

Jones FD, Hales RE: Military combat psychiatry: a historical review. Psychiatric Annals 17:525–527, 1987

Kalman G: On combat neurosis: psychiatric experience during the recent Middle East war. Int J Soc Psychiatry 23:195–203, 1977

Kanzer M: Amnesia: a statistical study. Am J Psychiatry 96:711–716, 1939

Kardiner A: The Traumatic Neuroses of War. New York, Paul B. Hoeber, 1941

Kardiner A, Spiegel H: War Stress and Neurotic Illness. New York, Hoeber, 1947

Kaszniak AW, Nussbaum PD, Berren MR, et al: Amnesia as a consequence of male rape: a case report. J Abnorm Psychol 97:100–104, 1988

Kennedy A, Neville J: Sudden loss of memory. Br Med J 2:428–433, 1957

Kernberg O: Borderline Conditions and Pathological Narcissism. Northvale, NJ, Jason Aronson, 1975

Kiersch TA: Amnesia: a clinical study of ninety-eight cases. Am J Psychiatry 119:57–60, 1962

Kirshner LA: Dissociative reactions: an historical review and clinical study. Acta Psychiatr Scand 49:698–711, 1973

Kluft RP: The natural history of multiple personality disorder, in Childhood Antecedents of

Multiple Personality. Edited by Kluft RP. Washington, DC, American Psychiatric Press, 1985, pp 197–238

Kluft RP: The dissociative disorders, in The American Psychiatric Press Textbook of Psychiatry. Edited by Talbott JA, Hales RE, Yudofsky SC. Washington, DC, American Psychiatric Press, 1988, pp 557–585

Kolb LC: The place of narcosynthesis in the treatment of chronic and delayed stress reactions of war, in The Trauma of War: Stress and Recovery in Viet Nam Veterans. Edited by Sonnenberg SM, Blank AS Jr, Talbott JA. Washington, DC, American Psychiatric Press, 1985, pp 211–226

Kopelman MD: Amnesia: organic and psychogenic. Br J Psychiatry 150:428–442, 1987a

Kopelman MD: Crime and amnesia: a review. Behavioral Sciences and the Law 5:323–342, 1987b

Kubie LS: Manual of emergency treatment for acute war neuroses. War Medicine 4:582–598, 1943

Laufer RS, Brett E, Gallops MS: Post-traumatic stress disorder reconsidered: PTSD among Vietnam veterans, in Post-Traumatic Stress Disorder: Psychological and Biological Sequelae. Edited by van der Kolk BA. Washington, DC, American Psychiatric Press, 1984

Laurence JR, Perry C: Hypnosis, Will, and Memory. New York, Guilford, 1988

Leavitt FH: The etiology of temporary amnesia. Am J Psychiatry 91:1079–1088, 1935

Lehmann HE: Unusual psychiatric disorders, atypical psychoses, and brief reactive psychoses, in Comprehensive Textbook of Psychiatry, 4th Edition. Edited by Kaplan HI, Sadock BJ. Baltimore, MD, Williams & Wilkins, 1985, pp 1224–1238

Leventhal BL, Midelfort HB: The physical abuse of children: a hurt greater than pain. Adv Psychosom Med 16:48–83, 1986

Levin HS, Benton AL, Grossman RG: Neurobehavioral Consequences of Closed Head Injury. New York, Oxford University Press, 1982

Lishman WA: Organic Psychiatry, 2nd Edition. Cambridge, MA, Blackwell Scientific, 1987

Loewenstein RJ: Somatoform disorders in victims of incest and child abuse, in Incest-Related Disorders of Adult Psychopathology. Edited by Kluft RP. Washington, DC, American Psychiatric Press, 1990, pp 75–111

Loewenstein RJ, Putnam FW: A comparison study of dissociative symptoms in patients with complex partial seizures, MPD, and posttraumatic stress disorder. Dissociation 1:17–23, 1988

Loewenstein RJ, Hornstein N, Farber B: Open trial or clonazepam in the treatment of posttraumatic stress symptoms in MPD. Dissociation 1:3–12, 1988

Luparello TJ: Features of fugue: a unified hypothesis of regression. J Am Psychoanal Assoc 18:379–398, 1970

Mac Hovec FJ: Hypnosis to facilitate recall in psychogenic amnesia and fugue states: treatment variables. Am J Clin Hypn 24:7–13, 1981

Mayeux R, Alexander MP, Benson DF, et al: Poriomania. Neurology 29:1616–1619, 1979

McCormack A, Janus M, Burgess AW: Runaway youths and sexual victimization: gender differences in an adolescent runaway population. Child Abuse Negl 10:387–395, 1986

McKinney KA, Lange MM: Familial fugue: a case report. Can J Psychiatry 28:654–656, 1983

Menninger KA; Cyclothymic fugues: fugues associated with manic-depressive psychosis: a case report. J Abnorm Psychol 14:54–63, 1919

Mesulam MM: Dissociative states with abnormal temporal lobe EEG: multiple personalities and the illusion of possession. Arch Neurol 38:176–181, 1981

Nemiah J: Dissociative amnesia: a clinical and theoretical reconsideration, in Functional Disorders of Memory. Edited by Kihlstrom JF, Evans FJ. Hillsdale, NJ, Lawrence Erlbaum, 1979, pp 303–323

Nemiah J: Dissociative disorders, in Comprehensive Textbook of Psychiatry, 4th Edition. Edited by Kaplan HI, Sadock BJ. Baltimore, MD, Williams & Wilkins, 1985, pp 942–957

Niederland WG: Clinical observations on the "survivor syndrome." Int J Psychoanal 49:313–315, 1968

Orne MT, Dinges DF, Orne EC: On the differential diagnosis of multiple personality in the forensic context. Int J Clin Exp Hypn 32:118–169, 1984

Paley AN: Growing up in chaos: the dissociative response. Am J Psychoanal 48:72–83, 1988

Parfitt DN, Caryle-Gall CM: Psychogenic amnesia: the refusal to remember. Journal of Mental Science 379:519–531, 1944

Perry JC, Jacobs D: Overview: clinical applications of the amytal interview in psychiatric emergency settings. Am J Psychiatry 139:552–559, 1982

The Psychiatric Times: Adults molested as children are given additional time limit to bring suit. March 1990, p 30

Putnam FW Jr: Dissociation as a response to extreme trauma, in Childhood Antecedents of Multiple Personality. Edited by Kluft RP. Washington, DC, American Psychiatric Press, 1985, pp 65–97

Putnam FW: Diagnosis and Treatment of Multiple Personality Disorder. New York, Guilford, 1989

Rapaport D: Emotions and Memory. Baltimore, MD, Williams & Wilkins, 1942

Rollinson RD: Transient global amnesia: a review of 213 cases from the literature. Aust N Z J Med 8:547–549, 1978

Ross CA: Multiple Personality Disorder: Diagnosis, Clinical Features, and Treatment. New York, John Wiley, 1989

Ross CA, Heber S, Anderson G, et al: Differentiating multiple personality disorder and complex partial seizures. Gen Hosp Psychiatry 11:54–58, 1989

Rubin DC, Wetzler SE, Nebes RD: Autobiographical memory across the lifespan, in Autobiographical Memory. Edited by Rubin DC. Cambridge, Cambridge University Press, 1986, pp 202–225

Rubinsky EW, Brandt J: Amnesia and criminal law: a clinical overview. Behavioral Sciences and the Law 4:27–46, 1986

Ruedrich SL, Chu C-C, Wadle CV: The amytal interview in the treatment of psychogenic amnesia. Hosp Community Psychiatry 36:1045–1046, 1985

Russel DEH: The incidence and prevalence of intrafamilial and extrafamilial sexual abuse of female children. Child Abuse Negl 7:133–146, 1983

Sargent W, Slater E: Amnesic syndromes in war. Proceedings of the Royal Society of Medicine 34:757–764, 1941

Schacter DL: Amnesia and crime: how much do we really know? Am Psychol 41:286–295, 1986

Schacter DL, Kihlstrom JF: Functional amnesia, in Handbook of Neuropsychology, Vol 3. Edited by Boller F, Grafman J. Amsterdam, Elsevier Science, 1989, pp 209–231

Schacter DL, Wang PL, Tulving E, et al: Functional retrograde amnesia: a quantitative study. Neuropsychologia 20:523–532, 1982

Schacter DL, Kihlstrom JF, Kihlstrom LC, et al: Autobiographical memory in a case of multiple personality. J Abnorm Psychol 98:508–514, 1989

Shengold L: Soul Murder: The Effects of Childhood Abuse and Deprivation. New Haven, CT, Yale University Press, 1989

Schenk L, Bear D: Multiple personality and related dissociative phenomena in patients with temporal lobe epilepsy. Am J Psychiatry 138:1311–1316, 1981

Silber A: Childhood seduction, parental pathology, and hysterical symptomatology: the genesis of an altered state of consciousness. Int J Psychoanal 60:109–116, 1979

Smith JR: Individual psychotherapy with Viet Nam veterans, in The Trauma of War: Stress and Recovery in Viet Nam Veterans. Edited by Sonnenberg SM, Blank AS Jr, Talbott JA. Washington, DC, American Psychiatric Press, 1985, pp 125–163

Sonnenberg SM, Blank AS Jr, Talbott JA: The Trauma of War: Stress and Recovery in Viet Nam Veterans. Washington, DC, American Psychiatric Press, 1985

Southard EE: Shell-Shock and Other Neuropsychiatric Problems. Boston, MA, WM Leonard, 1919

Spiegel D: Dissociating damage. Am J Clin Hypn 29:123–131, 1988a

Spiegel D: Dissociation and hypnosis in posttraumatic stress disorders. Journal of Traumatic Stress 1:17–33, 1988b

Spiegel D: Hypnosis in the treatment of victims of sexual abuse. Psychiatr Clin North Am 12:295–307, 1989

Squire L: Memory and Brain. New York, Oxford University Press, 1987

Stengel E: Studies on the psychopathology of compulsive wandering. Br J Med Psychol 18:250–254, 1939

Stengel E: On the aetiology of the fugue states. Journal of Mental Science 87:572–599, 1941

Stengel E: Further studies on pathological wandering (fugues with the impulse to wander). Journal of Mental Science 89:224–241, 1943

Terr L: What happens to early memories of trauma? A study of twenty children under the age five at the time of documented traumatic events. J Am Acad Child Adolesc Psychiatry 27:96–104, 1988

Thom DA, Fenton N: Amnesias in war cases. American Journal of Insanity 76:437–448, 1920

Torrie A: Psychosomatic casualties in the Middle East. Lancet 1:139–143, 1944

Tureen LL, Stein M: The base section psychiatric hospital. Bulletin of the US Army Medical Department 9 (suppl): 105–137, 1949

The United States Law Week: *Doe v Doe*, Calif Ct App 6th Dist, No H003404, 11/30/89, 58 LW 2356, 12/19/89

van der Hart O: Metaphoric and symbolic imagery in the hypnotic treatment of an urge to wander: a case report. Australian Journal of Clinical Experimental Hypnosis 13:83–95, 1985

van der Hart O, Friedman B: A reader's guide to Pierre Janet on dissociation: a neglected intellectual heritage. Dissociation 2:3–16, 1989

van der Kolk B: Psychological Trauma. Washington, DC, American Psychiatric Press, 1986

Wilson G, Rupp C, Wilson WW: Amnesia. Am J Psychiatry 106:481–485, 1950

**Appendix 1.** Procedure for sodium amytal interviewing for psychogenic amnesia and fugue

---

The reader should review the articles cited below for a full discussion of indications, contraindications, and risks of this procedure.

1. Obtain informed consent (including potential risks such as respiratory depression and intense, upsetting emotional reactions) for the procedure and for audiotaping and/or videotaping if this is to be done as part of the interview.

2. Have the patient recline in comfortable surroundings.

3. Insert an intravenous line.

4. Instill a 5% solution of sodium amytal (500 mg amytal dissolved in 10 cc of sterile water) at a rate no faster than 1 cc (50 mg) per minute to prevent sleep or respiratory depression.

5. Infusion of amytal continues until slurring of speech, lateral nystagmus, and/or drowsiness occurs. The usual dose is 150 to 350 mg for this to occur. Patients with histories of alcohol and/or hypnotic-sedative abuse may require higher doses of amytal. Infusion of 25 to 50 mg of amytal may be continued every 5 minutes or so to maintain narcosis.

6. It is generally recommended to begin the interview by discussing neutral topics and to move relatively slowly into the areas for which the patient is amnestic. Hypnotic-like suggestions, for example to move back in time or to visualize upsetting memories as if on a screen, may be helpful in some cases to obtain the history and/or to modulate affective discharge.

7. Affect-laden or traumatic material may be worked over repeatedly as clinically indicated.

8. After termination of the interview, have the patient monitored until he or she is able to walk without supervision.

9. You may wish to review the audiotape or videotape of the interview with the patient as clinically warranted.

---

*Source.* From Kluft (1988), Kolb (1985), Perry and Jacobs (1982), and Ruedrich et al. (1985).

# Chapter 4

# The Spectrum of Depersonalization: Assessment and Treatment

*by Marlene Steinberg, M.D.*

## OVERVIEW

### Symptom of Depersonalization

First described in 1872 by Krishaber, the symptom of depersonalization was not named until 1898, when Dugas contrasted "the feeling of loss of the ego" with a "real loss" (Dugas 1898; Krishaber 1872; Saperstein 1949). Ackner (1954) noted that depersonalization lacked clear-cut boundaries and, to correct this lack, described four salient features of depersonalization: 1) the feeling of unreality or strangeness regarding the self; 2) the retention of insight and lack of delusional elaboration; 3) the affective disturbance resulting in a loss of all affective response ("numbness") except discomfort in regard to the depersonalization; and 4) the unpleasant quality that may vary in intensity inversely with the patient's familiarity with the symptom. These four features continue to be generally accepted. Episodes of depersonalization may precipitate a panic attack and/or agoraphobia (Ambrosino 1973), or may also be associated with dysphoria (Roth 1959, 1960); chronic depersonalization often results in the patient's resignation to or acceptance of the symptom. Depersonalization is reported to be a normal sequela of life-threatening events (Noyes et al. 1977) and is also frequent among victims of sexual abuse, political imprisonment, torture, and cult indoctrination (Jacobson 1959; Spiegel 1984). Depersonalization is encountered in association with hypnosis (Wineburg and Straker 1973), hypnogogic and hypnopompic states, sleep deprivation (Bliss et al. 1959), sensory deprivation (Reed and Sedman 1964), hyperventilation (Cohen 1988), and drug or alcohol use (Good 1989).

Patients describe depersonalization as a feeling of being unreal, of being dead, of parts of the body being disconnected, of observing or watching a movie of the self, or of being an automaton; frequently, they complain of a lack of all feelings (Ackner 1954; Fewtrell 1986; Jacobson 1959; Mayer-Gross 1935; Saperstein 1949) and many attribute this numbness to depression (Roth 1960). The sense of depersonalization is evident in the following excerpts from a study by Steinberg et al. (1990) using the Structured Clinical Interview for DSM-III-R Dissociative Disorders (SCID-D) (Steinberg 1986):

> It's really weird. Its sort of like I'm here, but I'm really not here and that I kind of stepped out of myself, like a ghost. . . . I feel really light, you know. I feel kind of empty and light, like I'm going to float away. . . . Sometimes I really look at myself that way. . . . It's kind of a cold, eerie feeling. I'm just totally numbed by it. (SCID-D interview, unpublished transcript)

I felt like I do not belong in this body. I, I'm in the wrong body. I don't know how to explain that. . . . I feel that I was not supposed to have been born into this body. Which body it is, I don't know. It was not this body. . . . I always felt I had the wrong face. (SCID-D interview, unpublished transcript)

Depersonalization is typified by the "as if" quality of the experience, and, although patients may report feeling "as if" the self were dead, unreal, or automated, reality testing remains intact (Ackner 1954; Fewtrell 1986; Saperstein 1949). A patient suffering from depersonalization often expresses general puzzlement, since "these changes always remain incredible to the patient" (Galdston 1947). Depersonalization has been noted to be quite elusive and is frequently not a presenting complaint (Ackner 1954; Mayer-Gross 1935; Shimizu and Sakamoto 1986).

> Depersonalization is an elusive phenomenon in the sense that it involves a strange absence of feeling and an apparent reduction of vividness and reality. It is therefore difficult for many people to articulate. Whereas most subjects can readily describe an anxiety bout or feelings of morbid depression, a curious state of non-being is much more difficult to put into words. (Fewtrell 1986, p. 264)

Many people do not report these feelings spontaneously, although they may suffer from chronic depersonalization. Patients may fear that the clinician will think they are crazy and may be reluctant to report their experiences (Ackner 1954; Edwards and Angus 1972; Shorvon et al. 1946). The feelings of detachment that underlie the depersonalized state may be described by people in many different ways (Ackner 1954; Fewtrell 1986). Some patients complain mainly of feelings they are unreal; others may state that they feel as if they are an automaton. Some people adapt to their chronic depersonalization and may actually find it comforting. Patients who exhibit persistent or recurrent depersonalization may or may not experience distress in association with the depersonalization episode.

Depersonalization has been reported to be the third most common complaint among psychiatric patients, following depression and anxiety (Cattell and Cattell 1974). "It is difficult to determine the incidence of depersonalization experiences because of the relative strangeness of the symptoms and the attendant problems of patients communicating them to the psychiatrist" (Cattell and Cattell 1974, p. 767). Detection is also complicated by the fact that, "in contrast to many other disturbances, it is not marked by altered external or social behavior, but by an altered state of consciousness or perception" (Levy and Wachtel 1978, p. 292). Although this symptom is common among psychiatric patients and although there is a large body of literature that describes the symptom and theorizes about etiology, there exist few systematic investigations of the incidence of the symptom and of the disorders in which it exists. Brauer et al. (1970) utilized a self-administered questionnaire containing 49 items relating to depersonalization and derealization to study the frequency of depersonalization in 84 psychiatric inpatients: 26 with personality disorder, 25 schizophrenia, 13 neurotic depression, 11 psychotic depression, 3 manic-depressive illness, and 6 other psychiatric diagnoses. Of these inpatients, 80% experienced depersonalization and 12% reported "severe and lasting experiences" (p. 511) of depersonalization. A history of depersonalization was "only elicited from detailed examination of the patient" and had not been included in the initial psychiatric evaluation. In another study, outpatients in a hospital in Bombay were evaluated for depersonalization using Dixon's self-administered depersonalization questionnaire; 7.6% (32 of 288) of these patients were noted to experience depersonalization, with 22% of these patients (7 of 32) experiencing persistent depersonalization (Parikh et al. 1981).

## Depersonalization Disorder

Depersonalization neurosis was defined as a freestanding syndrome in DSM-II (American Psychiatric Association 1968) and described as "dominated by a feeling of unreality and of estrangement from the self, body, or surroundings." Depersonalization disorder was included in the new dissociative disorder section introduced in DSM-III (American Psychiatric Association 1980). The criteria in DSM-III required one or more episodes of depersonalization sufficient to produce impairment and not due to any other disorder. To clarify these basic features of depersonalization disorder, DSM-III-R (American Psychiatric Association 1987) criteria were expanded (Table 4-1).

Depersonalization disorder has a chronic, yet variable course. Level of functioning is thought to range from slight to severe impairment and may be related to the coexistence of other symptoms and syndromes. There are few reports of depersonalization in children (Elliott et al. 1984; Fast and Chethik 1976; Salfield 1958), but a growing number of case reports of depersonalization as a predominant symptom in adolescents and adults (Ackner 1954; Davidson 1964; McKellar 1978; Meares and Grose 1978; Shimizu and Sakamoto 1986; Shorvon et al. 1946), with some investigations reporting on samples of up to 120 cases (Shimizu and Sakamoto 1986). Depersonalization disorder is typically thought to begin in adolescence (Kluft 1988), although it may have undetected onset in childhood (Shimizu and Sakamoto 1986). Incidence and prevalence are unknown.

Since depersonalization occurs within a variety of psychiatric disorders, there has been some controversy as to whether depersonalization disorder exists as a distinct syndrome. Numerous case reports with depersonalization as the predominant

Table 4-1.  DSM-III-R diagnostic criteria for depersonalization disorder

---

A. Persistent or recurrent experiences of depersonalization as indicated by either (1) or (2):
   (1) an experience of feeling detached from, and as if one is an outside observer of, one's mental processes or body
   (2) an experience of feeling like an automaton or as if in a dream
B. During the depersonalization experience, reality testing remains intact.
C. The depersonalization is sufficiently severe and persistent to cause marked distress.
D. The depersonalization experience is the predominant disturbance and is not a symptom of another disorder, such as Schizophrenia, Panic Disorder, or Agoraphobia without History of Panic Disorder but with limited symptom attacks of depersonalization, or temporal lobe epilepsy.

---

*Source.* Reproduced, with permission, from the Diagnostic and Statistical Manual of Mental Disorders, 3rd Edition, Revised. Copyright 1987 American Psychiatric Association.

symptom, however, support the existence of depersonalization disorder as a primary disturbance (Ackner 1954; Davidson 1964; Shorvon et al. 1946; Shimizu and Sakamoto 1986). Difficulties in the detection of depersonalization disorder may be due to 1) prior lack of a reliable diagnostic tool for the assessment of depersonalization disorder; 2) the multifaceted presentation of the symptom, resulting in a variety of external complaints (Ackner 1954); 3) the need for interview strategies specifically designed to elicit histories of dissociative symptoms (Edwards and Angus 1972); 4) overlap of depersonalization symptoms with a wide variety of psychiatric and organic disorders (Ackner 1954; Cattell and Cattell 1975); and 5) the fact that depersonalization is rarely the presenting complaint (Cattell and Cattell 1975; Edwards and Angus 1972; Shorvon et al. 1946; Waltzer 1972). Difficulties in the detection of depersonalization disorder may have led to the misconception that the syndrome is rare, and misdiagnosis may be supported by the presence of a secondary, but highly visible, symptom that masks the depersonalization (Moran 1986). Variations in reported incidence and prevalence may also be a result of interview strategies; a British researcher reported "the less structured the interview, the more likely it is that there will be inconsistencies in the frequency with which depersonalization is recognized" (Edwards and Angus 1972, p. 243). During training, minimal emphasis is placed on taking a history of dissociative symptoms, and clinical exposure to the accurate detection of depersonalization disorder has been limited, resulting in a widely varying level of clinician knowledge of the diagnosis.

## Theories of Etiology

Various biological and psychodynamic theories have been advanced for the etiology of depersonalization (Sedman 1972). First, depersonalization may originate from physiologic or anatomical disturbance, as evidenced by feelings of depersonalization produced by temporal lobe dysfunction and various metabolic and toxic (i.e., drug) states (Ackner 1954; Sedman 1970). Second, depersonalization may result from a "preformed functional response of the brain," adaptive to overwhelming traumata, as evidenced by the occurrence of depersonalization in a variety of psychiatric disorders and in nonpsychiatric populations (Mayer-Gross 1935). Third, analytic theories assign depersonalization a role as a defense against painful and conflictual affects (Cattell and Cattell 1975; Frances et al. 1977; Shraberg 1977). These affects may include guilt, phobic anxiety, anger, rage, paranoia, conflictual ego identifications, primitive fusion fantasies, and exhibitionism (Stamm 1962). Oberndorf (1950) believed depersonalization masked anxiety resulting in loss of affect. He viewed anxiety accompanying depersonalization as secondary to the patient's fears of going crazy. Fourth, a split between observing and participating self has been hypothesized to account for the depersonalized state (Noyes and Kletti 1976). Such a split allows the patient to become a detached observer of the self. "Thus in the face of mortal danger we find individuals becoming observers of that which is taking place, effectively removing themselves from danger" (Noyes and Kletti 1976, p. 108). Finally, Mann and Havens (1987) hypothesized that depersonalization is likely to occur when a child is raised in an environment that "systematically fails to know some part of [the child who then] goes into the world with that part feeling tentative, not quite real. (p. 148)" Due to these distortions, the child then is unable to accurately assess themself.

To date, systematic research into theories of etiology is limited, and further research is necessary to clarify the etiology of depersonalization and to establish conclusive support for any of the current theories of etiology.

## Transient Depersonalization Syndromes

Depersonalization frequently appears as a response to life-threatening danger such as accidents, serious illnesses, cardiac arrests, anaphylactic reactions, and complications of surgery (Noyes and Kletti 1977; Noyes et al. 1977).

> The data presented suggest that depersonalization is, like fear, an almost universal response to life threatening danger. It develops instantly upon the recognition of danger and vanishes just as quickly when the threat to life is past. Its contrasting subjective effects appear to be manifestations, as Roth and Harper [1962] have suggested, of heightened arousal on the one hand and dissociation of consciousness from that arousal on the other. It is an adaptive mechanism that combines opposing reaction tendencies, . . . one serving to intensify alertness and the other to dampen potentially disorganizing emotion. (Noyes and Kletti 1977, p. 382)

Although patients with posttraumatic stress disorder (PTSD) may have survived life-threatening danger as described in the Noyes research, the systematic assessment of depersonalization in patients with PTSD awaits new research. Depersonalization appears to occur commonly in conjunction with PTSD flashbacks and is frequently reported by survivors of severe physical, emotional, or sexual abuse. Patients report that at the time of the sexual abuse they may feel as if they are outside of their body observing the abuse occurring in another individual. Adult patients with depersonalization are able to recall this occurring at the time of childhood abuse. (Spiegel 1988a)

Noyes et al. (1977) found that a transient depersonalization syndrome developed in "nearly one third of [normal] persons exposed to life threatening danger (accident victims) and close to 40% of a group of hospitalized psychiatric patients" (p. 401). Accident victims who had experienced loss of consciousness or amnesia for the accident were excluded. The psychiatric patients were interviewed within the first week of hospitalization or as soon thereafter as possible. "Accident victims were asked if they had experienced depersonalization between the time they became aware that an accident was about to take place and the moment it was complete (median 5 seconds) . . . [Psychiatric] patients were asked if such effect had occurred during the symptomatic period of their illness (median 6 months)" (p. 402). The authors found that the syndrome of depersonalization appeared very similar in normal persons exposed to danger and in psychiatric patients, "suggesting a degree of uniformity irrespective of the substrate from which it arises" (p. 407). Analysis of subject responses revealed three meaningful factors: 1) detachment related to the body or self, 2) alertness directed toward the threatening environment, and 3) mental clouding that contained panoramic memory. The authors noted an association between anxiety and depersonalization and suggested that anxiety that is severe and potentially disorganizing may play an etiologic role.

> The split between the observing and participating self that has been hypothesized to account for the depersonalized state received support from

participants in this study. As they became detached observers, they felt distant from their bodies and seemed to lose contact with their emotions and bodily sensations. Thus, distancing or dampening effects appeared to accompany the experience of the observing self. It was this self that the depersonalized individual identified as himself and the one he maintained subjective awareness of throughout.

The most common feature (72% of subjects) of depersonalization was a feeling of strangeness or unreality. Three features of depersonalization appear to be more common in experiences associated with life-threatening danger: 1) panoramic memory commonly occurring with the depersonalization experience; 2) isolated episode immediately following trauma; and 3) the pleasurable nature of the episode along with reported enhancement of the survivor's appreciation of life.

## The Spectrum of Depersonalization: Normal Versus Abnormal

Depersonalization is a nonspecific symptom and not pathognomonic of any clinical disorder (Brauer et al. 1970; Fleiss et al. 1975). Studies of young normal adults indicate that depersonalization may occur among normal individuals under a variety of circumstances (Dixon 1963; Myers and Grant 1972; Roberts 1960; Trueman 1984b). These findings, in combination with descriptions of depersonalization in normal adults following life-threatening traumas (Noyes and Kletti 1977), increase the need for clarification of the spectrum of depersonalization from general, normal experiences to disabling, pathognomonic episodes. In college students, brief episodes of depersonalization were noted to occur in 8.5% (Myers and Grant 1972) to 34% (Trueman 1984a) to 46% (Dixon 1963). Variation in range of depersonalization may be a function of the different samples, different questionnaires, different rates of response, or different methods of verifying episodes. Depersonalization in college students was associated with the occurrence of anxiety, déjà vu, agoraphobia, and recent disturbances in emotional health (Dixon 1963; Myers and Grant 1972; Trueman 1984b) and with religious experience or meditation (Trueman 1984b). All of these studies were of a normal group of subjects and included no comparison group of subjects with psychiatric disorders.

In a study by Steinberg et al. (1990), normal controls were compared to psychiatric patients on the SCID-D. The normal controls experience absent to isolated, transient depersonalization episodes that follow stressful events; psychiatric patients with nondissociative disorders experience mainly isolated and occasional depersonalization episodes that vary in duration and stressor; and patients with dissociative disorders experience recurrent to persistent depersonalization. Although some aspects of depersonalization in normal college students and psychiatric patients are shared (i.e., feelings of unreality, detachment, strangeness, and self-observation), the SCID-D research indicates that the quality of the depersonalization experience in patients with a dissociative disorder has key distinguishing features. The SCID-D study found that such abnormal depersonalization is often associated with ongoing and recurrent interactive dialogues between the observing and participating self.

I start to argue with somebody that's in that chair, but I see that person in that chair and I see it's me. I see that person and he's looking at me and he's laughing at me, and he's calling me on to fight him, and fight him, and fight him, and I don't want to fight him. . . . I see me outside myself, in other words, and he's laughing at me, calling out saying, "come on punk, fight me, come on punk, fight me."

Well, like I'll be talking about watching a baseball game, and I'll say "now this guy is going to hit a home run," and then I'll hear, "this guy is not going to hit a home run. This guy is going to strike out" and I'll turn around and look in the chair and say, "I'm telling you watch it. I'll bet you ten dollars he's going to hit a home run" and the person sitting there, which is me, will turn around and say, "he's going to strike out and the ten dollars is up." "Well, put the money up" I tell him. Those kinds of conversations. (SCID-D interview, unpublished transcript)

These dialogues appear to be unrelated to stressful events. Normal depersonalization, however, appears to be transient with no ongoing dialogues. When dialogues do occur in normal depersonalization, they typically retain features of memory, either the memory of an actual prior conversation or an imagined dialogue with a real person known to the subject. The SCID-D research indicates that it is both the persistence and the nature of depersonalization that differ from normal to abnormal subjects (Table 4-2).

## DIFFERENTIAL DIAGNOSIS

The differential diagnosis of patients who experience recurrent or persistent depersonalization should include the dissociative disorders, a variety of other psychiatric disorders, and possible organic etiology. Since depersonalization is rarely the chief or presenting complaint, depersonalization disorder may go undetected (Edwards and Angus 1972). The difficulty in assessing depersonalization may also lead to misdiagnosis supported by a secondary, but highly visible symptom. Common initial diagnoses include depression due to characteristic lack of affect (Ackner 1954; Lower 1972; Roth 1960) and panic and anxiety disorders due to frequent coexistence of panic and anxiety (Ambrosino 1973; Cassano et al. 1989; Roth 1959). Accurate differential diagnosis and appropriate treatment depends on systematic assessment to determine the primary symptom.

### Dissociative Disorders

Depersonalization disorder, multiple personality disorder, and dissociative disorder not otherwise specified should be included in the differential diagnosis of a patient suffering from the symptom of depersonalization. A complete assessment of coexisting dissociative symptoms (amnesia, derealization, and identity confusion and identity fragmentation, including the presence of alternate personalities) is essential in ruling out the dissociative disorders (Steinberg et al. 1990). Patients with depersonalization disorder will experience recurrent to persistent depersonalization, variable derealization, and absent to mild amnesia and identity fragmentation. Identity confusion, if present, occurs mainly in association with the depersonalization. These patients do not suffer from alternate personalities. In contrast, patients with multiple personality disorder suffer from frequent to persistent amnesia, depersonalization, derealization, persistent identity confusion, and severe fragmentation with the existence of several personalities, at least two of which take control of the individual's behavior. Patients with dissociative disorder not otherwise specified suffer from depersonalization in conjunction with a variety of combinations of the other dissociative symptoms.

## Anxiety Disorders

Symptoms of depersonalization frequently coexist with symptoms of anxiety, panic, and/or agoraphobia (Ambrosino 1973; Roth 1959, 1960). Roth and Harper (1962) noted a correlation between severe acute anxiety states and depersonalization-derealization in a sample of phobic anxious patients with panic attacks. Deper-

Table 4-2.    Distinguishing between normal and abnormal depersonalization

| Common mild depersonalization | Transient depersonalization | Abnormal depersonalization |
|---|---|---|
| **I. Context** Occurs as an isolated symptom | Occurs as an isolated symptom | Occurs within a constellation of other dissociative or non-dissociative symptoms |
| **II. Frequency** One or few episodes | One episode that is transient | Persistent or recurrent depersonalization |
| **III. Duration** Depersonalization episode is brief. Lasts seconds — minutes | Of limited duration (minutes — weeks) | Chronic and habitual depersonalization lasting up to many years |
| **IV. Precipitating Factors** —Extreme fatigue —Sensory deprivation —Hypnogogic and hypnopompic states —Drug or alcohol intoxication —Sleep deprivation —Medical illness/ toxic states —Severe psychosocial stress | Life-threatening danger. This is a syndrome noted to occur in 33% of individuals immediately following exposure to life-threatening danger, such as near-death experiences, auto accidents (Noyes J, et al. 1977). Single, severe psychological trauma | Not associated with precipitating factors in column 1. May be precipitated by a traumatic memory. May be precipitated by a stressful event, but occurs even when there is no identifiable stress. Occurs in the absence of a single immediate severe psychosocial trauma. |

*Source.*    Reprinted with permission from Steinberg et al. (1987).

sonalization-derealization was found in 34% of 150 patients with panic disor-
der/agoraphobia during the panic attacks (Cassano et al. 1989). Patients with
depersonalization-derealization were noted to have an earlier age of onset of panic
disorder/agoraphobia, and to exhibit more frequent and more severe forms of
avoidance behavior (Cassano et al. 1989). "The experience of depersonalization is
often accompanied by considerable secondary anxiety, and frequently, patients fear
that their symptoms are a sign that they are going insane" (Nemiah 1989, p. 1042).
On the other hand, primary anxiety may result in depersonalization and derealization and is an indication that extremely high levels of anxiety have been attained
(Cassano et al. 1989). "This cycle of anxiety followed by depersonalization or
derealization may become semi-autonomous; thoughts of impending episodes
arouse anxiety and consequent dissociative experiences" (Trueman 1984b, p. 91).

A review of patients with depersonalization found that phobic anxiety symptoms
were the symptoms most commonly associated with depersonalization (Roth 1960).
The frequent coexistence of phobic anxiety, panic attacks, and depersonalization
has led some authors to describe a phobic anxiety-depersonalization syndrome
(Ambrosino 1973; Roth 1959) that is thought to be relatively common. These patients
suffer from panic attacks, phobic anxiety, anticipatory anxiety, depersonalization,
derealization, somatic preoccupation, and reactive depression (Ambrosino 1973).
Phobic symptoms develop because crowded places or open country may tend to
intensify feelings of unreality and depersonalization (Roth and Argyle 1988). "It is
in the early and acute phases that depersonalization and related features are most
often prominent. They tend to fade, appear intermittently or not at all as the disorder
enters a chronic phase" (Roth and Argyle 1988, p. 39). This syndrome has been noted
to be more common in women, with the typical age of onset in the late 20s. Typical
precipitants to this syndrome included severe emotional trauma, such as bereave-
ment or serious illness of a close relative, with 12% of women having onset during
pregnancy or following childbirth (Roth 1959). One author noted that 10% of his
patients during a 10-year period could be described as having this syndrome
(Ambrosino 1973). Although the syndrome has been well described, the sequence
of these symptoms is not as clear (Linton and Estock 1977). These studies warrant
further investigation into the clinical features and historical development of panic
disorder/agoraphobia with and without depersonalization to determine whether
separate consideration of these groups, with therapeutic and prognostic implications, is indicated. One study suggested that panic and depersonalization may
respond selectively to pharmacologic agents (Hollander et al. 1989). "Studies of
depersonalization may shed light on some of the basic psychological and
physiological mechanisms underlying this whole group of disorders" (Roth and
Argyle 1988, p. 40).

The overlap in symptoms of anxiety and depersonalization may contribute to the
patient's initial difficulty in distinguishing or reporting on which symptom came
first. In fact, although depersonalization may be the primary symptom, the patient
may present with the more common and easily described complaint of anxiety
and/or panic attacks (Moran 1986). Usually the sequence becomes more apparent
following the systematic assessment of the course, age of onset, context, and
associated features of depersonalization and anxiety. Repeated evaluations and
longitudinal follow-up may also provide historical information helpful in accurate
assessment. For accurate differential diagnosis and appropriate treatment, the

crucial issue is the identification of the primary symptom. Did the depersonalization result in subsequent anxiety, or did anxiety lead to subsequent depersonalization?

## Depression

Depression is noted to be the most common misdiagnosis of patients suffering from prominent depersonalization and phobic anxiety (Roth 1960). Patients with symptoms of depersonalization as well as depersonalization disorder may appear to be suffering from a major depression or may have a coexisting depression. Depersonalization may 1) mimic the symptoms of depression (Roth 1960), 2) coexist with depression, or 3) be a feature of depression of later life (Anderson 1936). Accurate differential diagnosis and appropriate treatment depend on systematic assessment to determine which symptom is primary. Specifically, systematic assessment of the onset, course, associated features, and other symptoms should prevent such confusion. "A careful analysis of the symptomatology should prevent [the clinician's] mistaken diagnosis, for retardation, self-deprecatory, nihilistic or hypochondriacal delusions and true diurnal variation with early morning awakening are all very rare [with depersonalization]" (Roth 1960, p. 297).

Aspects of the symptom of depersonalization may mimic the loss of feeling seen in patients with depression. Several investigators noted that all patients with depersonalization experienced emotional numbness resulting in varying degrees of affective loss (Ackner 1954; Jacobson 1959; Lower 1972; Mayer-Gross 1935; Saperstein 1949). "Indeed in many [cases of depersonalization] the sense of emotional numbness, of being dead or detached from life around them, was the primary complaint, and the disturbance in the sense of self [specifically feeling unreal, or as if an observer of oneself] was uncovered only on questioning" (Lower 1972, p. 569). The emotional detachment or numbness of a depersonalization episode is often experienced as an absence of feeling or pronounced loss of affect, expecting only the discomfort the patient may experience due to the depersonalization (Ackner 1954). Typical descriptions include: "I'm doing things, but it's as though I'm standing off from things, not involved—as though I'm not real." "It's like watching a not very interesting mildly amusing movie. It's not painful; it's just an absence of all feelings." "Feeling frozen and numb." The alteration of the sense of self (i.e., seeing self outside of self or feeling unreal), pathognomonic of depersonalization, can best be understood as the result of affective isolation (Lower 1972). There are important implications for patients who are perceived as having intractable depression; in the presence of predominant depersonalization and phobic anxiety, the "illness will not behave as a primary affective disorder and ECT [electroconvulsive therapy] may worsen the feelings of depersonalization (Roth 1960).

## Obsessions and Hypochondriacal Symptoms

Several investigators have noted the frequent occurrence of obsessional traits (Roth 1959; Shorvon et al. 1946; Torch 1978) as well as hypochondriacal features (Torch 1978) in patients with depersonalization. Torch suggested that continued preoccupation with the self may lead to feelings of unreality and that obsessional thinking may play a role in the etiology of depersonalization. The exact relationship between depersonalization and obsessional and hypochondriacal traits remains unknown, and further research is needed for clarification.

## Schizophrenia

Although research indicates that depersonalization is nonspecific (Brauer et al. 1970; Fleiss et al. 1975), this symptom was once thought to be a prodromal symptom of schizophrenia (Galdston 1947). This misconception may continue to contribute to misdiagnosis of some patients with dissociative disorders who experience depersonalization. Depersonalization is a common occurrence in patients with schizophrenia. While 42% of a group of schizophrenic patients reported out-of-body experiences, on follow-up 14% were noted to have had typical out-of-body experiences that matched those of the control group (Blackmore 1986). In another study, 11% of schizophrenic patients were noted to experience depersonalization (Sedman and Kenna 1963). Although a variety of body boundary disturbances are common in patients with schizophrenia (Blackmore 1986), the depersonalization seen in patients with schizophrenia can be distinguished from depersonalization in patients with depersonalization disorder since reality testing is lost in schizophrenia and the depersonalization is incorporated into the delusional system. In schizophrenia, the patient may believe that self and body have, in fact, been detached or separated.

## Borderline Personality Disorder

Depersonalization occurred in 11 of 13 patients with a borderline personality disorder who had experienced transient psychotic episodes (Chopra and Beatson 1986). Severe dissociative experiences, including depersonalization and derealization, have been thought to be particularly common and discriminating of borderline personality and are given added weight in the Diagnostic Interview for Borderline Patients (Gunderson et al. 1981). These studies of patients with borderline personality, however, do not include a group of patients with dissociative disorders in the patient sample and thus cannot evaluate whether or not the Diagnostic Interview for Borderline Patients discriminates a group of patients with borderline personality from another group with dissociative disorders. Pope et al. (1985) noted that "this raises the possibility that multiple personality and other dissociative disorders may have existed but went unrecognized in some members of our cohort" (p. 1289). Thus the coexistence of depersonalization disorder may have gone undetected in the existing studies of borderline personality disorder.

## Substance Abuse Disorders

Acute intoxication or withdrawal from a variety of drugs or alcohol can result in symptoms of depersonalization that are indistinguishable from those characteristic of depersonalization disorder (Good 1989). "The presentations of substance induced dissociative states may resemble those of functional dissociative disorders or organic and psychogenic factors may coexist and be intertwined or indistinguishable" (Good 1989, p. 88). Depersonalization has been most commonly reported in association with marijuana (Moran 1986; Szymanski 1981) and hallucinogens such as LSD (Ludwig 1966; Waltzer 1972), and mescaline (Guttman and Maclay 1936), and may also occur with alcohol, cocaine, phencyclidine, narcotics, sedatives, and stimulants (Good 1989). Acute intoxication with these drugs may also intensify preexisting feelings of depersonalization. In addition, prolonged depersonalization (occurring months after only a few occasions of marijuana use) have been reported to occur, especially when use occurred at times of stress, and such patients were diagnosed as meeting DSM-III criteria for a variety of psychiatric disorders, including depersonalization disorder (Keshaven and Lishman 1986; Szymanski 1981). Also, recurrent depersonalization that was initially experienced by marijuana use has been associated with the development of agoraphobia. "A fear of this 'uncontrolled' depersonalization resulted in considerable anticipatory anxiety and panic attacks. Patients ultimately presented for treatment of agoraphobia" (Moran 1986, p. 187). Ludwig (1966) hypothesized that a subset of patients with chronic depersonalization and alienation may self-medicate with LSD in an attempt to alleviate these feelings. In these patients, he found that LSD resulted in an improved sense of reality and ability to feel.

A history of drug and alcohol use and of the temporal history of depersonalization is essential for accurate diagnosis. The patient that experiences alcohol- or drug-induced depersonalization should be evaluated for the occurrence of these symptoms without drugs or alcohol. As coexisting psychiatric disorders are common in individuals with drug and alcohol abuse, the presence of an underlying psychiatric disorder in which depersonalization is a symptom should be ruled out. Szymanski (1981) reported that although depersonalization may initially be understood as a pharmacologic effect of marijuana, "after the patients had experienced depersonalization, external stressors and intrapsychic factors may have contributed to its continued use as a defense mechanism."

## Seizure Disorders

Depersonalization, along with a variety of other psychiatric symptoms, may be seen in patients with seizure disorders, particularly temporal lobe epilepsy (Bear and Fedio 1977; Flor-Henry 1976; Slater et al. 1963). A variety of dissociative phenomena, including fugue states, amnesia, depersonalization, and derealization, have been reported to occur in the seizure disorders (Bear and Fedio 1977; Flor-Henry 1976; Slater et al. 1963). These phenomena may be seen during pre-ictal, interictal, or postictal states and have been most commonly associated with temporal lobe epilepsy. An investigation utilizing the Dissociative Experiences Scale (DES) (Bernstein and Putnam 1986) noted that there was a 20% overlap in DES scores of seizure disorders and multiple personality disorder, indicating that one in five patients with epilepsy "have significant dissociative experiences" (Devinsky et al. 1989). Other investigations have noted the misdiagnosis of epilepsy in patients whose psychiatric disorders manifest dissociative symptoms (Roth and Harper 1962). In one study, depersonalization occurred in 11 of 30 patients with temporal lobe epilepsy and in 17 of 30 patients with the phobic anxiety depersonalization syndrome (Roth and Harper 1962). Derealization occurred only in the psychiatric group. Age of onset for epileptics was commonly under the age of 20, whereas age of onset of phobic anxiety depersonalization group was over the age of 20. The authors also noted that earlier age of onset, predominance in males, automatic stereotypic behavior, and loss of consciousness characterized patients with temporal lobe epilepsy and not patients who had phobic anxiety depersonalization syndrome (Harper and Roth 1962). The appearance of dissociative disorders in individuals with seizures was reported in two case studies (Mesulam 1981; Schenck and Bear 1981). At present, it is not known whether these associations are coincidental or causal.

Standard clinical practice currently relies on an index of suspicion based on history suggestive of a seizure disorder. An electroencephalogram (EEG) is then performed to rule out presence of a seizure disorder. Although depersonalization may occur in the seizure disorders, it may be differentiated from depersonalization as it occurs in the major psychiatric disorders and in normal controls. The depersonalization present in patients with psychiatric disorders may be quite complex and elaborate. For example, a patient may report watching himself from a distance and engaging in a dialogue with himself, and the episode may last for hours to days. Depersonalization in the seizure disorders, however, is usually brief (lasting from seconds to minutes), with stereotypic and repetitive content that is rarely elaborated. Although automatic behavior and speech may occur with depersonalization within the psychiatric disorders, it is typically complex and elaborate, purposeful, and well organized (Harper and Roth 1962). In the seizure disorders, there is also perceived automatic behavior and automatic speech, but it is typically purposeless and repetitive (e.g., lip smacking), or speech automatism in which the "patient utters a mixture of words and sentences which may be linguistically correct but bear no appropriate relation to the present situation" (Bingley 1958).

## *Organic Illnesses*

Life-threatening medical illnesses, trauma, and illness resulting in disturbances or fluctuations in consciousness may precipitate a depersonalization episode (Noyes and Kletti 1977). Depersonalization may be a relatively common symptom in postconcussional syndrome (Grigsby 1986). Depersonalization has been reported in cases of structural pathology (i.e., brain tumor) (Ghadirian et al. 1986), infectious causes (i.e., encephalitis), and metabolic abnormalities (i.e., hypoglycemia) (Cohen 1988). It is not uncommon for depersonalization to accompany migraine headaches and, in some cases, may be a migraine equivalent (Shraberg 1977). In one case report, depersonalization and anxiety attacks were related to the development of a right temporal lobe meningioma; this depersonalization disappeared following removal of the tumor (Ghadirian et al. 1986). Depersonalization has also been noted to accompany complaints of vertigo presumably as a function of vestibular dysfunction and has been reported in association with two cases of Ménière's disease, a disorder characterized by episodic vertigo, progressive hearing loss, and fullness in the ear usually associated with tinnitus (Grigsby and Johnston 1989). Depersonalization may also occur in cases of acute and chronic organic syndromes such as cerebral arteriopathy and Korsakoff's psychosis (Kenna and Sedman 1965).

## *Medication Side Effects*

Case reports have noted depersonalization as a side effect of a variety of medications, including the neuroleptic haloperidol (Lukianowicz 1967), the anti-inflammatory agent indomethacin (Schwartz and Moura 1983), alpha methyldopa (Lukianowicz 1967), and the amphetamine-like agent fenfluramine (Imlah 1970). Such drug-induced depersonalization is usually transient and commonly disappears on discontinuation of the medication. However, these case reports did not systematically evaluate the baseline level of depersonalization prior to the initiation of medication therapy. Therefore, it is unclear whether these medications resulted in the new depersonalization or exacerbated preexisting depersonalization, or whether the association is coincidental.

## SYSTEMATIC ASSESSMENT

The symptom of depersonalization poses special problems for the diagnostician. It may be difficult for a subject whose major defense is depersonalization to volunteer an accurate history because of the close intercorrelation of depersonalization with other dissociative symptoms, such as amnesia (Steinberg et al. 1990). In addition, patients may seek to minimize or hide episodes of depersonalization due to fears of being thought crazy (Ackner 1954; Fewtrell 1986). Also, patients may have difficulty describing this elusive symptom (Ackner 1954; Fewtrell 1986; Torch 1987). To overcome difficulties in systematic assessment, new instruments have been developed for the evaluation of depersonalization and the diagnosis of depersonalization disorder.

## Mental Status Examination and Psychiatric History

In addition to the routine psychiatric history and mental status examination, depersonalization requires additional specific strategies for detection and evaluation (Table 4-3).

## Biological Testing

The diagnostic workup of the patient with recurrent depersonalization should include a complete physical examination and laboratory testing including complete blood count, electrolytes, liver function tests, and thyroid function tests. Depersonalization may occur in hypoglycemia and has also been associated with hyperventilation (Cohen 1988). EEG and other brain-imaging techniques are indicated in those patients who exhibit recurrent or persistent depersonalization along with symptoms suggesting organic etiology. An EEG utilizing nasopharygeal electrodes is indicated if there is an index of suspicion for temporal lobe epilepsy. Computed tomography is indicated to rule out a variety of brain lesions. If there is an index of suspicion of substance abuse, drug toxicology screens may be helpful in ruling out substance-induced depersonalization. Drug screens will also confirm the presence

Table 4-3.  Specific strategies for the detection and evaluation of depersonalization

---

1. Use patient's own name for/description of depersonalization in asking questions about the symptom.
2. Take thorough history of symptom including age of onset, frequency, duration, course, and precipitating factors.
3. Rule out drugs, alcohol, medical illness, or head trauma.
4. Evaluate presence/absence of psychotic symptoms, affective symptoms, and of the other dissociative symptoms.
5. Take history of traumatic experiences.
6. Word initial questions in an open-ended manner, with more specific follow-up questions.
7. Ask questions in several different ways, in order to allow for differences in patient's descriptive styles. For example, patients may variously describe depersonalization as watching the self from outside of the body, being a stranger, or feeling like an automaton. The same patient may endorse one of these descriptions while denying the others.
8. Note nonverbal cues such as a trancelike or automatic appearance.

---

*Source.*  Reprinted with permission from Steinberg et al. (1987) (rev. 1990).

of a prescribed medication, such as a neuroleptic, which may produce a side effect of depersonalization.

## Screening Tools and Structured Interviews

Until recently there were no tools for the assessment of depersonalization or the diagnosis of depersonalization disorder. Recent advances in systematic detection of the dissociative disorders have included the development of several instruments, including screening tools and structured interviews for the diagnosis of the dissociative disorders. Screening instruments possess the advantage of ease and cost effectiveness. Self-report formats, however, may be limited by patients' reluctance to describe depersonalization. Screening instruments should be followed by thorough clinical evaluation via a more comprehensive instrument, such as a structured interview. Several investigations have utilized self-report questionnaires and interviews that focus on the symptom of depersonalization. These questionnaires have provided the base of descriptive papers on depersonalization in college students (Dixon 1963; Myers and Grant 1972; Roberts 1960); psychiatric patients (Brauer et al. 1970); and survivors of life-threatening trauma (Noyes and Kletti 1977; Noyes et al. 1977). Statistical analysis has not been used to evaluate the questionnaires as screening instruments. Nonetheless, these questionnaires have played an important role in describing the characteristic features of depersonalization and in understanding the phenomenology of this symptom.

Recent self-report screening instruments for dissociative symptoms include the symptom of depersonalization with a variety of dissociative experiences (Bernstein and Putnam 1986; Riley 1988). These instruments have been statistically evaluated and have reported good reliability and validity. These instruments include the DES, mentioned earlier in the section on seizure disorders, and the Questionnaire of Experiences of Dissociation (Riley 1988). The DES consists of 28 items in the format of a visual analogue scale. Subjects obtain a score ranging from 0 to 100, which rates reported dissociative experiences. The Questionnaire of Experiences of Dissociation includes 26 true-false items. The Perceptual Alteration Scale (Sanders 1986) is in the preliminary stages of development and includes items from the Minnesota Multiphasic Personality Inventory (MMPI) (Hathaway and McKinley 1970) relevant to dissociation. The Perceptual Alteration Scale was reported to discriminate between college students who had normal eating habits and those who were binge eaters.

The Structured Clinical Interview for DSM-III-R Dissociative Disorders (SCID-D) is a semi-structured interview that evaluates five dissociative symptoms (amnesia, depersonalization, derealization, identity confusion, and identity alteration) and diagnoses the dissociative disorders. Good to excellent reliability and discriminant validity have been reported for the SCID-D (Steinberg 1986b; Steinberg et al. 1990). Boon and Draijer have completed a cross-national replication and extension study of the SCID-D and also reported good-excellent reliability (Boon and Draijer, in press). Overall assessment using the SCID-D yields a total score ranging from 5 to 20, with a severity rating for each of five dissociative symptoms. The symptom of depersonalization is systematically rated for severity and possible clinical significance for dissociative disorder diagnosis. The SCID-D contains 40 items related to depersonalization, with follow-up items for endorsed symptoms. The SCID-D scoring and interpretation manual contains severity ratings for depersonalization in terms of a variety of factors, including the frequency and duration of episodes and the presence or absence of precipitating stressors. Diagnostic score sheets are also provided for the systematic assessment of the presence or absence of depersonalization disorder. Reported results of interexaminer reliability for the symptom of depersonalization note an observed agreement of 95% and a weighted kappa of .88. Depersonalization obtained the highest interexaminer reliability of the five symptoms assessed (Steinberg et al. 1990).

The Dissociative Disorders Interview Schedule (Ross et al. 1989) is a structured interview developed to assess dissociative disorders along with major depressive episode, borderline personality, and somatization disorder. Items on the interview closely parallel the DSM-III criteria for the disorders assessed. Poor interrater reliability ($r = .56$) was reported for depersonalization disorder using this interview schedule.

## THERAPY

### Overview

Therapy for depersonalization is indicated if the depersonalization is recurrent or results in impairment of function or in distress. If depersonalization is secondary to an underlying primary disorder, treatment of the depersonalization may occur by treating the underlying illness (Walsh 1975). In the case of primary depersonalization that is nonresponsive to the treatment of the presumed primary disorder, avoidance of precipitating factors may be helpful (Walsh 1975). Depersonalization is thought to be a state of low rather than high arousal (Lader and Wing 1966), and formal relaxation techniques are not recommended and may exacerbate the depersonalization (Fewtrell 1984). Treatment of depersonalization and depersonalization disorder is based on a steadily increasing number of clinical reports. Supportive psychodynamic therapy (Fewtrell 1984; Lehmann 1974; Torch 1987), pharmacologic treatment (Fewtrell 1984; Hollander et al. 1989; King and Little 1959; Noyes et al. 1987; Nuller 1982; Stein and Uhde 1989; Torch 1975), behavioral and directive techniques (Blue 1979; Dollinger 1983; Sookman and Solyom 1978), hypnosis (Spiegel 1988), and family interventions (Dollinger 1983) have been described, but their relative effectiveness has not yet been evaluated. In addition, there are no controlled studies of the pharmacotherapy of depersonalization or depersonalization disorder. Further research is required using newly available diagnostic instruments for systematic assessment of depersonalization.

### Psychodynamic Psychotherapy

Therapy in which the patient identifies the underlying dynamics to achieve control over his or her symptom is reported to be effective (Lehmann 1974; Torch 1987). Since depersonalization has been theorized to develop as a defense against overwhelming stressors, the principles of traditional psychotherapy are used to guide this treatment. Work is centered on the abreaction of the traumatic memories that resulted in the depersonalization (Torch 1987). The understanding of the origins of the depersonalization allows the patient an increased sense of control, which then decreases the need to continue to use the defense.

The psychotherapeutic approach to treatment has been extensively reviewed by Torch (1987). He cited Schilder's (1939) statement that analysts predict analysis for a patient with depersonalization disorder to be double the duration of that for obsessive-compulsive neurosis and noted the pessimistic tone of previous descriptions of therapy. Patients with depersonalization disorder were noted often to seek help via consultations with a variety of physicians or other therapists and to severely restrict activity so as to decrease the risk of loss of control (Torch 1987). The fear of being regarded as insane resulted in somatic symptoms such as headaches, fainting, and fatigue, any of which may be the presenting complaint (Shorvon et al. 1946). Self-destructive behaviors such as drug or alcohol abuse and wrist slashing have been reported as attempts to self-medicate or "feel alive" (Miller and Bashkin 1974; Torch 1987). Patients with chronic depersonalization often accommodate to the symptoms, and these patients may feel little need for treatment (Torch 1981). If the depersonalization worsens, however, patients are more likely to feel distress. Torch stated that it is important not only "to explore underlying dynamics (including feelings of worthlessness and helplessness), but to give unusually strong credence to the contents resulting from an obsession with the self." The most important focus should be on control issues, as in "an obsessional way the patient is actually caricaturing a compulsive ritual of which he is the focus" (Torch 1987). In psychodynamic psychotherapy, the patient explores the origins of his or her feelings of worthlessness and helplessness and ultimately acknowledges that these feelings relate to unrealistic parental expectations. With more realistic standards of acceptability, the patient's sense of self can be rendered more acceptable (Torch 1987).

> Dissociation, as a defense, ceases to be necessary as a protection from feelings of external rejection. (Torch 1987, p. 142).

Cattell and Cattell (1974) noted that traditional analysis is contraindicated in depersonalization since the patients' feeling of unreality about themselves may be aggravated by the lack of visual contact with the therapist.

Identifying the patient's depersonalization and then educating the patient about the symptom is often very helpful (Fewtrell 1986; Torch 1987).

> Many clients who have such experiences are being encouraged to articulate the subjective sensations for the very first time, resulting in great relief. (Fewtrell 1986, p. 266)

Fewtrell also recommended that patients be encouraged to accept "the experience for what it is" rather than attempt to change it directly.

> Often the patient, despite the treatment, has not ever been approached with the concept of depersonalization, and no more relief, at least in quantitative terms, will ever be noted in these individuals than that accorded by simply putting the intangible feeling into words for the first time. (Torch 1987, p. 136)

Levy and Wachtel (1978) noted the importance of learning to accept and tolerate the depersonalization:

> If the patient can tolerate the experience of unrealness for a time, he can make for himself a new reality which is more solidly grounded in his own needs and perceptions, and in a sense more "real" than his old compromises were, however comfortable and familiar they might have felt. (p. 298)

## Hypnosis

Hypnosis may be useful as an important adjunct to the psychotherapy of depersonalization. The experience of dissociation, which is a feature of the hypnotic trance, may be used to "demonstrate to such patients how to control dissociation and to begin a process of communication which, in the context of well structured psychotherapy, can eventually lead to a reduction in such spontaneous dissociative symptoms" (Spiegel 1988b, p. 911). In addition, hypnosis remains an effective tool for gaining access to traumatic memories in a controlled manner; the goal of treatment is the full integration of these dissociated memories (Spiegel 1988a; Spiegel 1988b).

## Behavioral Therapy

Dollinger (1983) presented a case report of depersonalization disorder in an adolescent who was treated with family therapy and behavior modification. The patient was asked to record her depersonalization experiences in conjunction with a reward contingency plan. (The patient was allowed to drive for 30 minutes with the reward of an additional 30 minutes conditional on a reduction in depersonalization episodes from the previous week.) Depersonalization experiences were decreased from 6 to 10 per day prior to this treatment to none over a period of 15 weeks of this treatment. On 3-year follow-up, the patient was still symptom free. The importance of individualizing treatment with relevant reward contingency plans is noted. Indirectly this method assisted the patient in achieving a sense of self-control over her recurrent depersonalization.

Blue (1979) reported on the use of a 7-week directive therapy in the successful treatment of depersonalization disorder. This patient was asked to engage in an unpleasant chore (i.e., housecleaning) whenever she had a depersonalization episode. The patient reported a marked decrease in her symptoms. On the fifth session the patient was given an assignment to create the feelings of depersonalization within herself. This suggestion of a relapse allowed her to learn that she could control her symptoms. The following week the patient reported only minimal feelings of strangeness. At 3-month follow-up she was free of these symptoms.

Behavior therapy was also reported by Sookman and Solyom (1978) in two cases of intractable depersonalization. Treatment by flooding using taped narrative of depersonalization episodes was effective in nearly eliminating depersonalization in one patient. In the second patient, exposure to situations that provoked his depersonalization was less effective in decreasing the depersonalization per se, but was effective in decreasing obsessive symptoms, which usually followed a depersonalization episode. Thus flooding in imagination was more effective than flooding in vivo in decreasing the severity of the depersonalization episode. The authors suggested that since depersonalization is itself an experience of the imagination, it may be more effectively treated in imagination.

Further studies are needed to identify the indication for and efficacy of behavior therapy in the treatment of depersonalization. "Behavioral techniques may prove to be especially helpful in cases in which anticipatory anxiety, phobic avoidance, and obsessive perseveration are exacerbating features" (Sookman and Solyom 1978, p. 1545).

## Pharmacologic Treatment

In addition to psychosocial and intrapsychic factors, biological factors also appear to play an important role in depersonalization. There may be a physiologic predisposition to the depersonalization in some patients (Stein and Uhde 1989). Systematic studies of the pathophysiology of depersonalization are sparse.

> The presence of depersonalization in toxic states, temporal lobe epilepsy, and tumors and other related disturbances of the parietal temporal areas has been adduced as evidence of the presence of an organic substrate for depersonalization. The neuroanatomical pathway has appeared to involve the limbic structures. . . . Both functional and organic depersonalization were found to be end products that result from transient release of higher cortical functions and an uninhibited or facilitated expression of lower limbic ones. . . . This Jacksonian framework has emphasized the adaptational phylogenetic significance of depersonalization. It has supported those who have considered depersonalization a preformed functional response of the brain which therefore has a useful biological function, particularly in stressful or calamitous situations. (Shraberg 1977, pp. 37–38)

Davison (1964) noted nonspecific EEG changes during attacks of depersonalization similar to those seen in migraine attacks. Further research is need to determine whether a subset of depersonalization episodes may be a migraine equivalent (Shraberg 1977).

Depersonalization frequently occurs in depressive illness (Noyes et al. 1987) and is also common in anxiety disorders (Noyes et al. 1987; Oberndorf 1950). This association suggest that antidepressants and antianxiety agents may prove effective in the treatment of depersonalization. Depression scores have been shown to fall as symptoms of depersonalization decrease (Sedman 1972). These results provide a conceptual basis for use of antidepressants. Noyes et al. (1987) reported the successful treatment of a patient with depersonalization disorder with the tricyclic antidepressant desipramine (raised to 200 mg/day). Although the depersonalization followed an episode of depression, the authors suggested that until the relationships between depersonalization and depression are clarified, comorbidity should be taken into account. Walsh (1975) and Hollander et al. (1989) noted that antidepressants may be effective in the treatment of depersonalization. Hollander et al. (1989) reported that imipramine and alprazolam resulted in resolution of panic attacks in one patient, but the depersonalization disorder remained unchanged. Fluoxetine was started and gradually increased to 60 mg/day over a 6-week period. By the 11th week after starting fluoxetine, the patient had a marked reduction in depersonalization symptoms. "This report suggests that panic and depersonalization may respond selectively to pharmacological agents, even when both kinds of symptoms are present in the same patient" (Hollander et al. 1989, p. 402). Panic symptoms responded to imipramine and alprazolam, while the depersonalization remained unchanged. The depersonalization responded to fluoxetine, a selective serotonin reuptake blocker, while the panic remained in remission. "This suggests difference and similarities in the pathophysiology of panic and depersonalization and calls into question the statement in DSM-III-R that the diagnosis of depersonalization disorder is not made when panic is present" (Hollander et al. 1989,

p. 402). In patients with endogenous depression, severe depersonalization appears to increase the resistance to antidepressive therapy and leads to lingering depressive phases. In other words, patients with endogenous depression and depersonalization may be less responsive to antidepressants and may require pharmacotherapy directed at the depersonalization (Nuller 1982).

Stein and Uhde (1989) reported a detailed psychobiological investigation of a single patient with depersonalization disorder. A single-blind therapeutic trial of carbamazepine and clonazepam found that the anticonvulsant carbamazepine was not effective and the benzodiazepine anticonvulsant clonazepam was effective in reducing the depersonalization. Anticonvulsants were chosen for these studies because of the clinical links between the experience of depersonalization-derealization and temporal lobe epilepsy (Gloor et al. 1982). The patient described feeling nearly free of her chronic depersonalization and derealization symptoms following 1 to 2 weeks of clonazepam (raised to 1 mg/day). The same investigators also performed a caffeine challenge to explore there hypothesis that depersonalization disorder might share a common pathophysiology with panic disorder, which is known to be exacerbated by caffeine administration. They found that oral caffeine (240 mg) resulted in an increase in self-rated derealization, which was significantly decreased by clonazepam treatment but not be carbamazepine treatment. This response to caffeine has not been well studied in other psychiatric disorders and may not be specific for panic or anxiety disorders. The finding that clonazepam was effective whereas carbamazepine was not is similar to treatment of panic disorder, where potent benzodiazepines are effective (Ballenger et al. 1988; Spier et al. 1986) but carbamazepine is less effective in most patients (Uhde et al. 1988). This "might suggest the preferential importance of central type benzodiazepine receptors (Weiss et al. 1985) over peripheral type benzodiazepine receptors in the pathogenesis and treatment of depersonalization disorder" (Stein and Uhde 1989, p. 318). The authors noted that the patient's first-degree family history of panic disorder (mother) and response to clonazepam may suggest a shared heritability for panic and depersonalization. Because they are based on a single case report, these speculations remain tentative. Nuller (1982) reported in a separate study that phenazepam, a benzodiazepine derivative, (3–6 mg/day; in some patients, 2–30 mg/day), was found to be effective in reducing depersonalization episodes in 34 of 43 patients with severe depersonalization.

Mixed results have been reported with the use of neuroleptics, although systematic trials have not yet been performed (Cattell and Cattell 1975). Ambrosino (1973) noted that neuroleptics are ineffective in the treatment of depersonalization. Nuller (1982) reported that clozapine, a neuroleptic known for its strong anxiolytic effect, was administered orally or intramuscularly (150–600 mg/day) to 15 patients with severe depersonalization as the predominant symptom. In 9 of 15 patients, the clozapine was moderately effective in reducing the depersonalization in 4 to 6 weeks after beginning of clozapine administration. Positive effects from the clozapine tended to occur at the beginning of the depersonalization syndrome, and cases of chronic depersonalization appeared to be less responsive to this medication.

A variety of medications no longer commonly used due to significant side effects were previously reported to be effective in studies on patients with severe depersonalization, including pentylenetetrazole (Metrazol) (Schilder 1939), intravenous methamphetamine (Methedrine) with ECT (Davison 1964), pentathol injections (King and Little 1959), D-amphetamine and amobarbitol (Cattell and Cattell 1975;

Harper and Roth 1962), and intramuscular thiopentone (King and Little 1959). In addition, ECT may worsen symptoms of depersonalization (Roth 1959). A study of 38 cases with predominant depersonalization noted improvement in 6 cases following ECT, no change in 22 cases, and 10 cases in which patients reported feeling worse (Shorvon et al. 1946). In a study of 15 patients with severe depression and depersonalization, depression improved following ECT but depersonalization was unaffected (Ambrosino 1973).

Preliminary data on pharmacologic treatments show much potential promise. Given the preliminary nature of the treatment research, current treatment of patients with recurrent depersonalization should include a flexible individualized approach incorporating the strategies reviewed and adapted to the diagnostic features, needs, and history of the patient. A variety of pharmacologic treatments may be effective in the treatment of recurrent depersonalization. As the clinical reports cited are primarily uncontrolled, controlled double-blind studies with larger samples are needed before definite conclusions are made regarding the specific pharmacotherapy of depersonalization. The possible mechanism of action of the medications and relative efficacy of differing treatments also require further investigation. These studies reflect preliminary efforts. Therapeutic trials of medication for depersonalization disorder and other psychiatric disorders with recurrent depersonalization should include assessments of 1) diagnosis utilizing reliable diagnostic tools such as the SCID-D; 2) systematic ratings of depersonalization, depression, phobias, anxiety, and panic recorded at baseline (prior to medication trials) and at several intervals throughout the clinical trial, and 3) systematic outcome measures, including the ratings of symptoms. "Controlled drug trials should be undertaken for the treatment of this chronic, often disabling, disorder" (Stein and Uhde 1989).

In summary, depersonalization is a common experience that is encountered within a spectrum of clinical severity ranging from normal transient depersonalizations following traumatic events to the severe, chronic depersonalization encountered in depersonalization disorder. Systematic study of both the symptom and the syndrome of depersonalization is in the early stages, due in part to changing definitions, diagnostic criteria, and to the lack, up to this time, of a standard measure. New instruments for the systematic assessment of depersonalization are now available; however, the majority of reports available remain anecdotal. Pharmacologic research, although able to indicate positive potential for some medications, awaits systematic clinical trials. At present, the psychotherapy of depersonalization is designed to help the patient integrate traumatic memories and to decrease the anxiety associated with the symptom. The relative efficacy of each of the available forms of treatments also awaits systematic clinical testing.

## REFERENCES

Ackner B: Depersonalization, I: aetiology and phenomenology. Journal of Mental Science 100:838–853, 1954

Ambrosino S: Phobic anxiety-depersonalization syndrome. NY State J Med 73:419–425, 1973

American Psychiatric Association: Diagnostic and Statistical Manual of Mental Disorders, 2nd Edition. Washington, DC, American Psychiatric Association, 1968

American Psychiatric Association: Diagnostic and Statistical Manual of Mental Disorders, 3rd Edition. Washington, DC, American Psychiatric Association, 1980

American Psychiatric Association: Diagnostic and Statistical Manual of Mental Disorders, 3rd Edition, Revised. Washington, DC, American Psychiatric Association, 1987

Anderson EW: Prognosis of the depression of later life. Journal of Mental Science 82:559, 1936

Ballenger J, Burrows G, Dupont R Jr, et al: Alprazolam in panic disorder and agoraphobia: results from a multicenter trial, I: efficacy in short term treatment. Arch Gen Psychiatry 45:413–422, 1988

Bear D, Fedio P: Quantitative analysis of interictal behavior in temporal lobe epilepsy. Arch Neurol 34:454–467, 1977

Bernstein E, Putnam F: Development, reliability, and validity of a dissociation scale. J Nerv Ment Dis 174:727–735, 1986

Bingley T: Mental symptoms in temporal lobe epilepsy and temporal lobe gliomas. Acta Psychiatrica Neurologica 33 (suppl 120):1–151, 1958

Blackmore S: Out of body experiences in schizophrenia: a questionnaire survey. J Nerv Ment Dis 174:615–619, 1986

Bliss E, Clark L, West C: Studies of sleep deprivation: relationship to schizophrenia. Archives of Neurologica Psychiatry 81:348–359, 1959

Blue F: Use of directive therapy in the treatment of depersonalization neurosis. Psychol Rep 45:904–906, 1979

Boon S, Draijer N: Diagnosing dissociative disorders in the Netherlands: a pilot study with the Structured Clinical Interview for DSM-III-R Dissociative Disorders. Am J Psychiatry (in press)

Brauer R, Harrow M, Tucker G: Depersonalization phenomena in psychiatric patients. Br J Psychiatry 117:509–515, 1970

Cassano G, Petracca A, Perugi G, et al: Derealization and panic attacks: a clinical evaluation on 150 patients with panic disorder/agoraphobia. Compr Psychiatry 30:5–12, 1989

Cattell JP, Cattell JS: Depersonalization: psychological and social perspectives, in American Handbook of Psychiatry. Edited by Arieti S. New York, Basic Books, 1974, pp 767–799

Chopra H, Beatson J: Psychotic symptoms in borderline personality disorder. Am J Psychiatry 143:1605–1607, 1986

Cohen S: The pathogensis of depersonalization: a hypothesis (letter). Br J Psychiatry 152:578, 1988

Davison K: Episodic depersonalization: observations on 7 patients. Br J Psychiatry 110:505–513, 1964

Devinsky O, Putnam F, Grafman J, et al: Dissociative states and epilepsy. Neurology 39:835–840, 1989

Dixon J: Depersonalization phenomena in a sample population of college students. Br J Psychiatry 109:371–375, 1963

Dollinger S: A case report of dissociative neurosis (depersonalization disorder) in an adolescent treated with family therapy and behavior modification. J Consult Clin Psychol 51:479–484, 1983

Dugas L: Un cas de depersonalization. Revue Philosophique 45:500–506, 1898

Edwards G, Angus J: Depersonalization. Br J Psychiatry 120:242–244, 1972

Elliott G, Rosenberg M, Wagner M: Transient depersonalization in youth. Social Psychology Quarterly 47:115–129, 1984

Fast I, Chetnik M: Aspects of depersonalization-derealization in the experience of children. Int Review of Psycho-analysis 3:483–490, 1976

Fewtrell W: Relaxation and depersonalization. Br J Psychiatry 145:217, 1984

Fewtrell W: Depersonalization: a description and suggested strategies. British Journal of Guidance and Counseling 14:263–269, 1986

Fleiss JL, Gurland BJ, Goldberg K: Independence of depersonalization-derealization. J Consult Clin Psychol 43:110–111, 1975

Flor-Henry P: Epilepsy and psychopathology, in Recent Advances in Clinical Psychiatry. Edited by Granville-Grossman K. Edinburgh, Churchill Livingstone, 1976, pp 262–295

Frances A, Sacks M, Aronoff M: Depersonalization: a self relations perspective. Int J Psychoanal 58:325–331, 1977

Galdston I: On the etiology of depersonalization. J Nerv Ment Dis 105:25–39, 1947

Ghadirian A, Gauthier S, Bertrand S: Anxiety attacks in a patient with a right temporal lobe meningioma. J Clin Psychiatry 47:270–271, 1986

Gloor P, Oliver A, Quesney L, et al: The role of the limbic system in experiential phenomena of temporal lobe epilepsy. Ann Neurol 12:129–144, 1982

Good M: Substance-induced dissociative disorders and psychiatric nosology. J Clin Psychopharmacol 9:88–93, 1989

Grigsby JP: Depersonalization following minor closed head injury. International Journal of Clinical Neuropsychology 8:65–68, 1986

Grigsby J, Johnston C: Depersonalization, vertigo and Meniere's disease. Psychol Rep 64:527–534, 1989

Gunderson J, Kolb J, Austin V: The diagnostic interview for borderline patients. Am J Psychiatry 138:896–903, 1981

Guttmann E, Maclay WS: Mescalin and depersonalization. Journal of Neurology and Psychopathology 16:193–212, 1936

Harper M, Roth M: Temporal lobe epilepsy and the phobic anxiety-depersonalization snydrome. Compr Psychiatry 3:129–151, 1962

Hathaway SR, McKinley JC: Minnesota Multiphasic Personality Inventory, Revised. Minneapolis, MN, University of Minnesota, 1970

Hollander E, Fairbanks J, Decaria C, et al: Pharmacological dissection of panic and depersonalization. Am J Psychiatry 146:402, 1989

Imlah N: Unusual effect of fenfluramine. Br Med J 2:178–179, 1970

Jacobson E: Depersonalization. J Am Psychoanal Assoc 7:581–610, 1959

Kenna J, Sedman G: Depersonalization in temporal lobe epilepsy and the organic psychoses. Br J Psychiatry 111:293–299, 1965

Keshaven M, Lishman W: Prolonged depersonalization following cannabis abuse. Br J Addict 81:140–142, 1986

King A, Little J: Thiopentone treatment of the phobic anxiety depersonalization syndrome. Proceedings of the Royal Society of Medicine 52:595–596, 1959

Kluft R: Dissociative Disorders, in The American Psychiatric Press Textbook of Psychiatry. Edited by Talbott JA, Hales RE, Yudofsky SC. Washington, DC, American Psychiatric Press, 1988, pp 557–585

Krishaber M: De la nevropathie cerebro-cardique. Gaz Sci Med Bordeaux 1872

Lader M, Wing L: Physiological Measures, Sedative Drugs and Morbid Anxiety. Maudsley Monograph No. 14. London, Ozodoes University Press, 1966

Lehmann L: Depersonalization. Am J Psychiatry 131:1221–1224, 1974

Levy J, Wachtel P: Depersonalization: an effort at clarification. Am J Psychoanal 38:291–300, 1978

Linton P, Estock R: The anxiety phobic depersonalization syndrome: role of the cognitive-perceptual style. Disease of the Nervous System 38:138–141, 1977

Lower R: Affect changes in depersonalization. Psychoanal Rev 59:565–577, 1972

Ludwig A: Altered states of consciousness. Arch Gen Psychiatry 15:225–233, 1966

Lukianowicz N: "Body image" disturbances in psychiatric disorders. Br J Psychiatry 113:31–47, 1967

Mann D, Havens L: Discussion of Dr. Torch's paper: depersonalization and the pathology of the self. Hillside J Clin Psychiatry 9:144–151, 1987

Mayer-Gross W: On depersonalization. Br J Med Psychol 15:103–126, 1935

McKellar A: Depersonalization in a 16-year-old boy. South Med J 71:1580–1581, 1978

Meares R, Grose D: On depersonalization in adolescence: a consideration from the viewpoints of habituation and identity. Br J Med Psychol 31:335–347, 1978

Mesulam M: Dissociative states with abnormal temporal lobe EEG. Arch Neurol 38:176–181, 1981

Miller F, Bashkin E: Depersonalization and self-mutilation. Psychoanal Q 43:638–649, 1974

Moran C: Depersonalization and agoraphobia associated with marijuana use. Br J Med Psychol 59:187–196, 1986

Myers D, Grant G: A study of depersonalization in students. Br J Psychiatry 121:59–65, 1972

Nemiah J: Dissociative disorders (hysterical neurosis, dissociative type), in Comprehensive Textbook of Psychiatry, Fifth edition. Edited by Kaplan HI, Sadock BJ. Baltimore, MD, Williams & Wilkins, 1989, pp 1028–1044

Noyes R Jr, Kletti R: Depersonalization in the face of life-threatening danger: an interpretation. Omega 7:103–114, 1976

Noyes R Jr, Kletti R: Depersonalization in response to life-threatening danger. Compr Psychiatry 18:375–384, 1977

Noyes R Jr, Hoenk P, Kuperman S, et al: Depersonalization in accident victims and psychiatric patients. J Nerv Ment Dis 164:401–407, 1977

Noyes R Jr, Kuperman S, Olson S: Desipramine: a possible treatment for depersonalization disorder. Can J Psychiatry 32:782–784, 1987

Nuller Y: Depersonalization: symptoms, meaning, therapy. Acta Psychiatr Scand 66:451–458, 1982

Oberndorf C: Role of anxiety in depersonalization. Int J Psychoanal 31:1–5, 1950

Parikh A, Sheth F, Apte J: Depersonalization (a phenomenological study in psychiatric patients). J Postgrad Med 27:226–230, 1981

Pope H, Jonas J, Hudson J, et al: An empirical study of psychosis in borderline personality disorder. Am J Psychiatry 142:1285–1290, 1985

Reed G, Sedman G: Personality and depersonalization under sensory deprivation conditions. Percept Mot Skills 18:659–660, 1964

Riley K: Measurement of Dissociation. J Nerv Ment Dis 176:449–450, 1988

Roberts W: Normal and abnormal depersonalization. Journal of Mental Science 106:478–493, 1960

Ross C, Heber S, Norton G, et al: The Dissociative Disorders Interview Schedule: a structured interview. Dissociation 2:169–189, 1989

Roth M: The phobic anxiety-depersonalization syndrome. Proceedings of the Royal Society of Medicine 52:587–595, 1959

Roth M: The phobic anxiety-depersonalization syndrome and some general aetiological problems in psychiatry. Journal of Neuropsychiatry 1:293–306, 1960

Roth M, Argyle N: Anxiety, panic, and phobic disorders: an overview. J Psychiatr Res 22:33–54, 1988

Roth M, Harper M: Temporal lobe epilepsy and the phobic anxiety-depersonalization syndrome, II: practical and theoretical considerations. Compr Psychiatry 3:215–226, 1962

Salfield D: Depersonalization and altered disturbances in childhood. Journal of Mental Science 104:472–476. 1958

Sanders S: The Perceptual Alteration Scale: a scale measuring dissociation. Am J Clin Hypn 29:95–102, 1986

Saperstein J: On the phenomenon of depersonalization. J Nerv Ment Dis 110:236–251, 1949

Schenck L, Bear D: Multiple personality and related dissociative phenomena in patients with temporal lobe epilepsy. Am J Psychiatry 138:1311–1326, 1981

Schilder P: The treatment of depersonalization. Bull NY Acad Med 15:258–272, 1939

Schwartz J, Moura R: Severe depersonalization and anxiety associated with indomethacin. South Med J 76:679–680, 1983

Sedman G: Theories of depersonalization: a reappraisal. Br J Psychiatry 117:1–14, 1970

Sedman G: An investigation of certain factors concerned in the etiology of depersonalization. Acta Psychiatr Scand 48:191–219, 1972

Sedman G, Kenna J: Depersonalization and mood changes in schizophrenia. Br J Psychiatry 109:669–673, 1963

Shimizu M, Sakamoto S: Depersonalization in early adolescence. Jpn J Psychiatry Neurol 40:603–608, 1986

Shorvon H, Hill J, Burkitt E, et al: The depersonalization syndrome. Proceedings of the Royal Society of Medicine 39:779–792, 1946

Shraberg D: The phobic anxiety-depersonalization syndrome. Psychiatric Opinion 14:35–40, 1977

Slater E, Beard A, Glitheroe E: The schizophrenia-like psychoses of epilepsy. Br J Psychiatry 109:95–150, 1963

Sookman D, Solyom L: Severe depersonalization treated by behavior therapy. Am J Psychiatry 135:1543–1545, 1978

Spiegel D: Multiple personality as a post-traumatic stress disorder. Psychiatr Clin North Am 7:101–110, 1984

Spiegel D: Dissociation and hypnosis in post-traumatic stress disorders. Journal of Traumatic Stress 1:17–33, 1988a

Spiegel D: Hypnosis, in The American Psychiatric Press Textbook of Psychiatry. Edited by Talbott JA, Hales RE, Yudofsky SC. Washington, DC, American Psychiatric Press, 1988b, pp 907–928

Spier S, Tesar G, Rosenbaum J, et al: Treatment of panic disorder and agoraphobia with clonazepam. J Clin Psychiatry 47:238–242, 1986

Stamm J: Altered ego states allied to depersonalization. J Am Psychoanal Assoc 10:762–783, 1962

Stein M, Uhde T: Depersonalization disorder: effects of caffeine and response to pharmacotherapy. Biol Psychiatry 26:315–320, 1989

Steinberg M: The Structured Clinical Interview for DSM-III R Dissociative Disorders. New Haven, CT, Department of Psychiatry, Yale University School of Medicine, 1986

Steinberg M, Howland F, Cicchetti D: The Structured Clinical Interview for DSM-III-R Dissociative Disorders: a preliminary report, in Dissociative Disorders: Proceedings of the Third International Conference on Multiple Personality/Dissociative States. Edited by Braun B. Chicago, IL, Rush University, 1986, p 125

Steinberg M, Rounsaville B, Cicchetti D: Scoring and Interpretation Manual: The Structured Clinical Interview for DSM-IIIR Dissociative Disorders. New Haven, CT, Department of Psychiatry, Yale University School of Medicine, 1987

Steinberg M, Rounsaville B, Cicchetti D: The Structured Clinical Interview for DSM-III-R Dissociative Disorders: preliminary report on a new diagnostic instrument. Am J Psychiatry 147:76–81, 1990

Szymanski H: Prolonged depersonalization after marijuana use. Am J Psychiatry 138:231–233, 1981

Torch E: Alternative treatments for depersonalization (letter). Am J Psychiatry 132:1334, 1975

Torch E: Review of the relationship between obsession and depersonalization. Acta Psychiatr Scand 58:191–198, 1978

Torch E: Depersonalization syndrome: an overview. Psychiatr Q 53:249–258, 1981

Torch E: The psychotherapeutic treatment of depersonalization disorder. Hillside J Clin Psychiatry 9:133–143, 1987

Trueman D: Anxiety and depersonalization and derealization experiences. Psychol Rep 54:91–96, 1984a

Trueman D: Depersonalization in a non-clinical population. J Psychol 116:107–112, 1984b

Uhde T, Stein M, Post R: Lack of efficacy of carbamazepine in the treatment of panic disorder. Am J Psychiatry 145:1104–1109, 1988

Walsh R: Depersonalization: definition and treatment. Am J Psychiatry 132:873–874, 1975

Waltzner H: Depersonalization and the use of LSD: a psychodynamic study. Am J Psychoanal 32:45–52, 1972

Weiss S, Post R, Patel J, et al: Differential mediation of the anticonvulsant effects of carbamazepine and diazepam. Life Sci 36:2413–2419, 1985

Wineburg E, Straker N: An episode of acute, self-limiting depersonalization following a first session of hypnosis. Am J Psychiatry 130:98–100, 1973

# Chapter 5

# Dissociation, Conversion, and Somatization

*by John C. Nemiah, M.D.*

The modern descriptive term *dissociative disorders* is derived from *dissociation,* a translation from the French of the word *désagrégation* introduced by Janet (1889) more than a hundred years ago to refer to a psychological process found in association with a variety of clinical symptoms. In this chapter I turn from the descriptive aspects of the individual dissociative disorders to the nature of dissociation itself.

Dissociation provides an unusually clear window on the psychological processes that underlie clinical symptoms. The study of patients with dissociative disorders opens to direct view the mechanisms of symptom formation and permits the empirical observation of psychodynamic phenomena that complement and amplify the findings of descriptive psychiatry. In what follows, we shall demonstrate those phenomena and indicate their implications for psychiatric diagnosis, treatment, and research.

## DISSOCIATION

The traditional marriage of conversion and dissociative hysteria was annulled in 1980 with the publication of DSM-III (American Psychiatric Association 1980), which elevated dissociative hysteria to a major category in its own right (dissociative disorders) and transported conversion hysteria, renamed conversion disorder, into the entirely separate and unrelated category of somatoform disorders. There was apparent justification for their divorce, given DSM-III's central emphasis on phenomenology as the basis for establishing psychiatric diagnoses. On the face of it, the two syndromes were clearly different; conversion disorder was characterized by a variety of *somatic* symptoms, whereas the symptomatic manifestations of dissociative disorders involved disturbances in major *mental* functions (e.g., memory, identity, and consciousness). This purely descriptive distinction, however, overlooks the fact that both conversion and dissociative symptoms may be found in close relation to one another in the same patient, as the following clinical experience bears out.

### A Patient With a Dissociative Disorder

As reported elsewhere (Frankel 1976; Nemiah 1979), Martha G was 35 years old when, during a minor car accident, she "hurt her back" and became totally unable to walk. After being confined to her bed and a wheelchair for some 6 months, she was admitted to the orthopedic service of a general hospital for evaluation. Her casual mention to the orthopedic resident that she occasionally heard a voice that told her to "say things and do things" led to an urgent call for psychiatric consultation.

Psychiatric examination disclosed interesting new findings. Despite her total incapacitation and demonstrated inability to walk, to work, or to engage in the activities of daily living and self-care, the patient was able to stand steadily on both feet without support. Examination of her lower extremities, moreover, revealed full and normal function of her musculature, a normal range of motion of her limbs when she was lying or sitting, the absence of any muscular wasting, and normal reflexes. She was, however, unable to experience sensation in her legs. As she said, "My legs, they're not there. There's no feeling in my legs. The only way I can tell that they're there is by looking at them." Furthermore, throughout her illness, the patient had maintained full and normal function of her bladder and bowels.

On the basis of these findings, it could be concluded that the patient's sensorimotor symptoms were not the result of underlying pathology in her nervous or muscular tissue. Her primary difficulty, the inability to walk, arose not from a lack of localized physiologic function in her legs but from a loss of the coordinated pattern of movements that comprises walking. Her disability, in other words, stemmed from a disturbance in higher-order central, conceptual psychological function, not from specific localized, peripheral anatomical lesions. From a clinical point of view, her dysfunction was a conversion symptom, and her disturbance in gait, although lacking the characteristic loss of balance and dramatic, staggering, ataxic locomotion of astasia-abasia, was a manifestation of that disorder, with an emphasis on the abasia.

The exploration of the patient's auditory hallucination revealed equally interesting findings. The presence of hallucinations, of course, alerts clinicians to the possibility that the patient is suffering from a major psychotic disorder. Apart, however, from this single symptom, Martha G gave no evidence from her clinical history or mental status examination of a psychotic disturbance. Although she reported that she had undergone a significant change in her inner life when, 3 years before her admission, she had joined a local evangelical church and "gave up smoking, drinking, and partying" (simple pleasures that she had complacently indulged in during her prior existence), she disclosed no personal or family history of psychotic illness. Nor were there any signs of it on examination. She related well and warmly to her psychiatrist and others, had a full range of affect without manifestations of depression or mania, gave no hint of disordered thinking, and maintained consistently good reality testing throughout her diagnostic interviews.

It was not entirely clear from Martha G's description whether the "voice" was perceived as being internal or was a vividly externalized auditory perception, but she left no doubt in the examiner's mind that it was entirely outside of the boundaries of her sense of self and came to her as an alien, unwanted intrusion into her consciousness. "It's a terrible voice," she complained. "It makes you say things and do things you don't want to . . . like say mean things to your husband or get mad at the doctors. That's not me, because I like to cooperate with my doctors. And if I don't do what it wants me to, sometimes the voice overcrowds me, overshadows me. It feels sometimes like it wants to take over me completely."

In response to the patient's last remark, the doctor made an intervention that produced a dramatic, unexpected, and instructive reaction. "Why don't you let it take over," he remarked quietly. Muttering a curt, "OK," the patient gripped the arms of her chair and threw back her head in a series of convulsive jerks, as if in a desperate internal struggle. For the next 30 seconds, she was out of contact with those around her and appeared to be in a state of mild trance. Suddenly she "came to" and looked boldly about her. Asked how she felt, she replied cheerfully, "I feel fine . . . and we've got rid of that other one that stays sick all the time."

It rapidly became apparent that another personality, who called herself "Harriet," had emerged on the scene. In contrast to the more passive and subdued Martha, Harriet was piquantly lively in spirit and speech and declared that she enjoyed smoking, social drinking, and "partying and night-clubbing." She was vocally scornful of Martha for having given up these pleasures and was annoyed at the restrictions that Martha's illness imposed on her own freedom of activity. Two observations were particularly striking. At one point Harriet remarked that she "felt like dancing." Asked if she could walk (let alone dance), she replied, "Sure!" and immediately stood up and walked briskly across the room and back to her chair. Furthermore, she commented that she frequently "talked to Martha. I tell her little jokes . . . tell her to say mean things to her husband, and do things like that. I make her *so* miserable!"

A short while thereafter, the examining psychiatrist suggested that Harriet allow Martha to "come back." With a mild demurrer, Harriet entered a brief lapse of consciousness characterized by the same convulsive jerking of her head and signs of internal struggle as before, and then suddenly opened her eyes as Martha. She now once again had all her symptoms back and exhibited, in addition, a total amnesia for the period of 10 minutes during which Harriet had been in the ascendancy.

This brief clinical account cannot do full justice to all the events that occurred during the hour-long examination of Martha G, but it is sufficient to underscore several important points. In the first place, it was now apparent that diagnostically the patient fell into the category of multiple personality disorder as evidenced by the alternating personalities of Martha and Harriet—a diagnosis that had not been suspected before the dramatic events of the clinical interview. At the same time, she manifested classic sensorimotor conversion symptoms in both the dysfunctioning of her legs and her hallucinated voice. Although the underlying source of her motor disturbance was not readily apparent, the voice that Martha heard was patently an ego-alien derivative of the underlying Harriet's telling her "to say mean things to her husband and do things like that." It was furthermore apparent that the patient's phenomenologically disparate symptoms of conversion disorder and multiple personality disorder were not only closely related as integral parts of her overall psychiatric illness, but that both aspects of her clinical syndrome resulted from the operation of the basic underlying psychological mechanism of dissociation. We must, therefore, turn our attention to a brief consideration of that mechanism.

## The Nature of Dissociation

Although the clinical phenomena related to the concept of dissociation had been recognized for nearly half a century before his clinical investigations, it was Pierre Janet who, more than a hundred years ago, first elaborated the concept itself in the concluding chapters of his volume, *L'automatisme psychologique* (Janet 1889). His formulation, which formed a basis for much of the subsequent evolution of psychodynamic psychiatry, is still a foundation stone of modern psychodynamic observation and theory. The term *dissociation* refers to the exclusion from consciousness and the inaccessibility of voluntary recall of mental events, singly or in clusters, of varying degrees of complexity, such as memories, sensations, feelings, fantasies, and attitudes. Although rendered unconscious (or "subconscious" as Janet termed it) by the dissociative process, these mental elements are not thereby removed from the sum total of mental contents. Far from being permanently erased from existence ("forgotten" in the common sense of the word), they are, on the contrary, preserved in their unconscious state, with the potential of being subsequently recalled to consciousness under special circumstances. Furthermore, they have the capacity in their unconscious state to intrude on and affect consciousness in a variety of disguises that may take the form of ego-alien symptoms. We shall return presently to the role of dissociation in the production of Martha G's disorder, but first let us turn our attention to a couple of simpler clarifying clinical examples in which unconscious mental elements are quite patently related to the production of clinical symptoms.

## CONVERSION

### A Patient With a Conversion Disorder

Janet's (1889) famous patient Marie suffered from a variety of somatic symptoms, among them a total blindness in her left eye and numbness of the left side of her face:

> I wished to explore the blindness in her left eye, but Marie objected to it when she was awake, stating that she had been that way since birth. It was easy to demonstrate by hypnotic somnambulism that she was mistaken. If one changed her into a small child of five by the usual procedures [i.e., hypnotic age regression], she recovered the sensation she had had at that age, and one could observe that she saw very well with both eyes. It was when she was six that the blindness had begun. What were the circumstances? Marie persisted in saying, when she was awake, that she had absolutely no idea. During hypnotic trance, however, . . . I determined that the blindness had begun at a specific moment in connection with a trifling incident. She had been forced, despite her screams of protest, to sleep with a child of her own age *the left side of whose face was covered with scabs* [italics in original]. Marie herself developed similar scabs some time afterwards, which appeared almost identical and had exactly *the same distribution* [italics in original]. These scabs reappeared for several years and then were completely cured, but it was noticed that from that point on *the left side of her face was anesthetic and she was blind in her left eye* [italics in original]. She has since always retained this anesthesia. . . . I made the same attempt as before [i.e., in treating other somatic symptoms that Marie manifested]. I brought her back [i.e., in hypnosis] to the period of contact with the child of whom she had had such horror. I caused her to believe that the child was very attractive and had no scabs, but she was only half convinced. After having her repeat the scene twice, I was successful, and she fearlessly caressed the imaginary child. The sensation in the left side of her face reappeared without difficulty, and when I woke her up, Marie saw clearly with her left eye. (pp. 439–440) [Author's translation]

This clinical episode is instructive in several ways. In the first place, we find the origins of a conversion symptom in a traumatic event—Marie's being forced to sleep with her disfigured playmate despite the disgust and horror this aroused in her. Second, the memory images of that event had been dissociated from consciousness. Third, although the memory of this event was beyond Marie's normal conscious, voluntary recall, it had not been entirely erased from her mind but could be raised into consciousness again in the hypnotic state. Fourth, once the memory was hypnotically restored to consciousness and thereby made available for observation, it could directly and immediately be seen how the content of the memory was reproduced in the derivative conversion symptom of anesthesia and blindness in the same anatomical location as that of the playmate's horrifying lesion. The content of the dissociated memory image, in other words, was the source and determining factor of the form of Marie's conversion symptom. Finally, it could be observed how Janet, guided by this knowledge of the symptom's pathogenesis, was able to remove it by altering the patient's imagery through suggestion—a psychotherapeutic technique curiously reminiscent of some aspects of modern cognitive therapy.

## The Origin of a Conversion Symptom: An Autobiographical Account

In the following clinical observations, we can see even more directly how unconscious thoughts and imagery produce and determine the form of conversion symptoms. Morton Prince, one of America's foremost investigators of dissociative phenomena in the early years of this century, has provided a detailed account of a woman patient ("B.C.A."), who suffered from multiple personality disorder ("B.C.A." 1908–1909). Summarizing several years of observation, Prince wrote:

> When first seen the case presented the ordinary picture of so-called neurasthenia, characterized by persistent fatigue and the usual somatic symptoms, and by moral doubts and scruples. This phase was termed ... complex A. Later, another state, spoken of as complex B, suddenly developed. Complex A had no memory for complex B, but the latter not only had full knowledge of A, but presented co-consciously when A was present. B was therefore both an alternating and a co-conscious state. Besides differences in memory, A and B manifested distinct and markedly different characteristics, which included moods, tastes, points of view, habits of thought and controlling ideas. In place, for instance, of the depression, fatigue, and moral doubts and scruples of A, B manifested rather a condition of exaltation, and complete freedom from neurasthenia and its accompanying ideas. (p. 240)

From this brief description it will be noted that the B personality had a complete memory not only of its own experiences but of those of personality A as well. This was in contrast to personality A, who had many amnesic gaps in her memory covering those periods when B was in the ascendancy. In addition, B experienced herself as a separate personality from A, not only with continuity of that identity but with a self-awareness of her own trains of thought during the period when A was in the ascendancy—a phenomenon to which Prince gave the term *co-consciousness* and that has been described in other patients and by other investigators

(Hilgard 1977; Prince 1906; Schreiber 1974). In an autobiographical account ("B" 1908-1909), personality B writes thus of that phenomenon:[1]

> When I am not here as an alternating personality, my thoughts still continue during the [life] of A . . . although [she is] not aware of them. . . . I still go on thinking my own thoughts and retain all my memories of my life as B, and of my previous co-conscious life. I think my own thoughts, which are different from [hers], and at the same time I know [her] thoughts and what [she does] (p. 322). . . . My train of thought may be, and usually is, quite different from [A's]. When [A] is ill, for instance, she is thinking about her headache, and how hard life seems and how glad she will be when it is over, and I am thinking how tiresome it is to lie in bed when I am just aching to go for a long tramp or do something gay. We rarely have the same opinion about any book we are reading, though we may both like it. [A], however, enjoys some writers whom I find very tiresome, Maeterlinck, for example. She considers him very inspiring and uplifting, and I think he writes a lot of nonsense and is extremely depressing. (p. 326)

Although, as B reported, "ordinarily the two streams of thought run on side by side without interfering with each other," there were occasions on which B could modify A's thoughts and behavior without A's being aware of it. B wrote:

> As an example of involuntary influence, I will take the following incident, as it is fresh in my memory. A few days ago Dr. Putnam[2] kindly allowed [A] to see a patient of his who is suffering from a form of hysteria. She could not put her feet down flat on the floor, but turned her toes up and tried to walk on her heels and the sides of her feet, and as she walked she trembled all over and breathed irregularly.[3] I was much interested in the matter, and after we got home kept wondering how the girl managed to walk that way—it seemed so difficult. There was in my mind a picture of the girl with her toes turned up, trembling and breathing hard; I was imagining how it would seem to walk that way and to tremble all over, etc. I was not paying any attention to [A's] train of thought, being absorbed in my own, and did not consider how my thoughts might affect her until I became aware that she was trembling from head to foot, that her toes were all curled up, and that she could hardly keep her feet flat on the floor. . . . She was so much disturbed that she telephoned Dr. Prince, asking him to help her steady herself. I did not intend to produce such an effect. It would seem plain that my train of thought influenced her. (pp. 331–332)

---

[1]Throughout this account, the author refers to three personalities, A, B, and C. As Prince ("B" 1908–1909) commented in a footnote, personality C was the result of a partial integration, but was "not absolutely normal or a complete integration" (p. 313). Both A and C had the same amnesic gaps for B's existence and experiences and may therefore be considered closely associated in their relation to B. To avoid confusion, and to conform to Prince's designations in the passage quoted immediately above, A alone is used in the following quotations to designate the author's references to A or C, singly or in combination. Such changes in the original text are indicated by brackets.
[2]James Jackson Putnam, the famous neurologist, and a contemporary of Morton Prince.
[3]A case of astasia-abasia, as Prince comments in a footnote.

In this account we find a striking demonstration of the psychogenesis of a conversion symptom. Although it was the patient in her A state who, at the invitation of Dr. Putnam, observed his patient with astasia-abasia, both A and B were aware of what A saw. Unknown to A, as we have noted, the co-conscious B pursued her own train of thought about Dr. Putnam's patient, and as B was imagining "the girl with her toes curled up," her mental image was transformed into A's simultaneous ego-alien symptoms of muscular contractions in her feet, without A's being aware of their genesis in B's underlying co-conscious thought processes. An unconscious mental image rendered unconscious by the process of dissociation, in other words, provoked a consciously experienced, ego-alien, symptomatic motor dysfunction that directly and exactly reproduced the underlying unconscious thought content of which the patient had no conscious awareness.

## DISSOCIATION AS A PATHOGENIC PROCESS

Returning to our earlier observations of Martha G, we can see similarities to the patients described for us by Janet and Prince. Martha G had lost from consciousness both the awareness of sensation and the capacity for motor function (the anesthesia in her legs and her inability to walk), just as Janet's Marie had lost the vision in her left eye and the sensation in the left side of her face. Although both patients retained the capacity for these functions beneath their surface consciousness, their loss to conscious awareness through the process of dissociation resulted in specific, discrete, localized, clinical conversion symptoms. Furthermore, as with Prince's B.C.A., the dissociative process in Martha G had excluded from consciousness a rich complex of mental contents constituting a secondary personality, a process that set the stage in both for the development of a multiple personality disorder. But in both of them we find yet a further mechanism resulting in the production of conversion symptoms. When the dissociated, unconscious mental contents impinge on the patients' conscious awareness, they produce an active, ego-alien disturbance in sensorimotor function that represents the underlying unconscious mental elements. In B.C.A., for example, the transitory muscular spasm experienced by her A personality in her feet reflected the dissociated imagery of the secondary personality B as she co-consciously remembered the sight of Dr. Putnam's patient with a similar deformity. In Martha G, the hallucinated voice represented the dissociated Harriet's underlying commands.

In all of these patients, dissociation is the central pathogenic process from which their different, individual symptoms result. The variety of symptoms (and syndromes) merely reflects different aspects of the basic dissociative mechanism. Amnesia is the immediate experience of the dissociative exclusion of large complexes of mental contents from conscious awareness. Conversion symptoms result from the loss to voluntary control of specific, dissociated sensorimotor functions, or from the partial return to conscious awareness of disguised unconscious mental elements that produce dysfunctions experienced as being ego-alien. Multiple personality disorder represents the return to and the domination of consciousness by richly textured clusters of mental associations comprising a distinct personality previously rendered unconscious by dissociation. When viewed in this conceptual context, it is evident that however different they appear *phenomenologically*, conversion disorder and dissociative disorders are categorically inseparable.

It should be noted that this proposition is neither new nor original. Nearly 70 years ago, in a discussion of multiple personality disorder, Morton Prince wrote:

> As a result of . . . dissociation, systems of thoughts, ideas, memories, emotions and dispositions previously habitual in the individual may cease to take part in the affected person's mental processes. (p. 546) . . . Examination of recorded cases shows . . . that besides mental memories, physiological functions may be involved in dissociation. Thus, there may be a loss of sensation in its various forms, and of the special senses, or of the power of movement (paralysis), or of visceral functions (gastric, sexual, etc.). Dissociation may, then, involve quite large parts of the personality including very precise and definite physiological and psychological functions. (Prince 1924, p. 548)

Before pursuing the significance of these findings and concepts for late 20th century psychiatry, we must return briefly to the consideration of yet further clinical observations.

## SOMATIZATION

DSM-III-R (American Psychiatric Association 1987) assigns conversion disorder to the larger diagnostic category of somatoform disorders and distinguishes it on phenomenological grounds from another somatoform disorder: somatization disorder. It is interesting to observe, therefore, that, like conversion disorder, the symptoms of somatization disorder may also be found in a close and specific association with dissociative symptoms in individuals suffering from dissociative disorders.

### *Dissociation and Somatization Disorder*

One of the striking aspects of Martha G's illness was the fact that, as we have seen, in switching to her Harriet state, she not only became a different sort of person, but her conversion symptoms entirely disappeared. No longer an invalid, she "felt fine" until she reverted to Martha and was once again incapacitated. In fact, Martha had other debilitating symptoms of a vaguer, more diffuse sort. She was chronically tired and complained of persistent backache and headache and of being constantly cold. These symptoms, too, entirely disappeared when she became Harriet, only to recur in full force the moment Martha returned.

In this alternation between health and sickness, each state tied to one of the alternating personalities, Martha G resembles many of the patients with multiple personality disorder described in the clinical literature. Prince's (B.C.A. 1908–1909) patient, B.C.A., for example, in her A state was chronically fatigued; had multiple vague somatic pains; passed through periods of anorexia and loss of weight; often experienced difficulty in sleeping; was timid, fearful, anxious, and depressed; and at times "wished to die" (p. 243). As B she was asymptomatic, and, indeed, in "vigorous health" (p. 245). Prince's even more famous patient, Sally Beauchamp (who is perhaps the paradigm of multiple personality disorder) showed a similar alternation of states of health (Prince 1906). As Miss Beauchamp she consulted Prince for constant fatigue, palpitations, nausea, multiple somatic pains (especially in her abdomen), hot and cold feelings, anxiety, and depression. She was, as Prince said, "always ill, always suffering" (p. 14). This was in marked contrast to Sally, a secondary personality who emerged in the course of treatment. Sally was hale, hearty, vigorously active, and, as Prince phrased it, "did not know what illness meant" (p. 17).

At this distance in time, and without benefit of data derived from a modern structured clinical interview, it is not possible to make a definitive DSM-III-R diagnosis of these constellations of symptoms. In days gone by, they were often labeled "neurasthenia" (that was Prince's term for the somatic aspect of both B.C.A.'s and Miss Beauchamp's illnesses), but that diagnosis has, of course, been dropped from our current clinical vocabulary. Suffice it to say that the symptoms are not clearly those of a conversion disorder, that they are strongly suggestive of somatization disorder, and that they fit the criteria for undifferentiated somatoform disorder.

What is of particular interest in these clinical observations is the fact that diffuse somatic symptoms with the characteristics of those of somatization disorder appear, like conversion symptoms, to be associated with multiple personality disorder. It may, therefore, be legitimately asked whether the symptoms of somatization disorder are the surface manifestations of the same kind of dissociated, unconscious mental elements that have been shown to be pathogenic in conversion disorder—a question worthy of clinical investigation.

## MODERN STUDIES

In the light of these hints offered by the detailed study of individual case material, it is interesting to note that recent phenomenological investigations of several large series of patients with multiple personality disorder show the widespread presence of somatic complaints among the great variety of symptoms detected by systematically applied structured interviews (Bliss 1984; Coons et al. 1988; Putnam et al. 1986; Ross et al. 1989, 1990). Prominent among these symptom clusters are 1) classic conversion symptoms, which in one series (Putnam et al. 1986) were found in more than half of the patients; and 2) multiple somatic complaints, such as nausea and vomiting; headache; abdominal, back, and joint pain; palpitations and shortness of breath; and disturbances in menstrual and sexual functioning—all characteristic of somatization disorder. Indeed, in one recent study (Ross et al. 1990), nearly two-thirds of a large series of patients with multiple personality disorder also met the DSM-III-R criteria for somatization disorder.

In these studies, the analysis of the data does not indicate whether the somatic symptoms are associated with specific personalities in the repertoire of characters of each patient with multiple personality disorder—that is, whether (as suggested by the more detailed individual case studies) they are manifested only episodically when specific alternating personalities are dominating the patient's conscious awareness. Nor do these aggregate data allow us to observe directly the pathogenesis of the somatic symptoms, which, as we have seen, is often readily detectable when the psychological processes in a single patient are studied in depth. The data do, however, provide strong evidence that, however different the phenomenological characteristics of these disorders, both conversion disorder and somatization disorder are closely associated with multiple personality disorder.

## THEORETICAL CONSIDERATIONS

What, then, are the implications of these clinical observations concerning the psychological processes associated with dissociation and their role in symptom formation? In the first place, they have an important bearing on the diagnostic categorization and classification of clinical syndromes—a fact that should be kept in mind as we move from DSM-III-R to a possibly more definitive DSM-IV. But beyond that, they have important implications for the wider world of psychiatric treatment and research.

### Psychological Process and Diagnostic Classification

From the review of multiple personality disorder and its relation to conversion disorder and somatization disorder, it is evident that DSM-III-R is perhaps too restricted in its classification of these clinical phenomena. The sharp separation of conversion disorder and somatization disorder on the one hand from multiple personality disorder on the other into the two major and apparently unrelated diagnostic categories of somatoform and dissociative disorders overlooks important features shared in common. Although from a phenomenological point of view there may be justification for continuing their separation in DSM-IV, there could well be a cross-reference to the other in each category indicating the existence of important overlapping features. But beyond this specific change, an increased attention to the mechanisms of symptom formation is perhaps in order as we move forward to DSM-IV. Indeed, there appears to be a precedent in DSM-III-R itself for such an expansion beyond purely descriptive nosology.

It is to be remarked (as was done in DSM-III-R) that while the definition of diagnostic categories generally remains "atheoretical with regard to etiology or pathophysiologic process, [there is room for exceptions] with regard to disorders for which this is well established and therefore included in the definition of the disorder" (American Psychiatric Association 1987, p. xxiii). Indeed, such an exception appears to pertain to conversion disorder, of which the "essential feature . . . is an alteration or loss of physical functioning that suggests physical disorder, but that instead is apparently an expression of a psychological conflict or need" (p. 257).

It would appear from this definition that psychological processes are viewed within the framework of DSM-III-R as playing an essential role in the production of conversion disorder. Although the text does not specify the nature of these processes beyond its reference to "psychological conflict or need," we can readily supplement them with the specific mechanisms of symptom formation that result from dissociation as we have observed them earlier. These might easily be incorporated into future editions of the diagnostic manual to augment our understanding of the pathogenesis not only of conversion disorder but of the dissociative disorders as well, since dissociation is central to the latter. In so doing, we should increase the precision of our diagnostic classification since the understanding of the common pathogenic mechanisms underlying the symptoms of both conversion disorder and the dissociative disorders would enable us to appreciate their basic phenomenological unity despite their surface descriptive differences.

### Psychological Process and Treatment

Just as an understanding of psychological process can sharpen our diagnostic precision and accuracy, so too it can improve our ability to select appropriate treatment measures that are based on an informed diagnostic evaluation.

The modern treatment of dissociative disorders, especially multiple personality disorder (Braun 1986), emphasizes the necessity for raising the unconscious psychogenetic elements underlying the surface symptoms into the patient's conscious awareness to restore them to the control of a reunified ego. This therapeutic approach rests on the diagnostic recognition of the complex psychological structure and the psychodynamic processes that result in the presenting symptoms.

By way of contrast, it should be noted that patients with somatoform pain disorder are notoriously refractory to psychodynamic therapy (Barsky 1989). Their treatment usually requires techniques such as biofeedback, remodeling group therapy, and suppressive symptom control that are primarily supportive in nature. Therapy aimed at exploring unconscious factors and psychodynamic mechanisms is usually ineffective and a waste of time—a lack of therapeutic responsiveness in these patients that is a reflection of their psychological structure. Recent studies (Barsky 1989) suggest that many such patients are alexithymic; that is, they are unable to experience affect and to create fantasy (Nemiah and Sifneos 1970) and lack the psychological structure characteristic of persons with dissociative disorders and conversion disorder (Nemiah 1977). Indeed, instead of the complex array of unconscious mental elements and mechanisms seen in individuals with the latter disorders, one finds in those with somatoform pain disorder major *defects* in psychic structure and a poverty of psychological functioning that lead to quite different mechanisms of symptom formation and that require different therapeutic techniques. The presence or absence of these psychological functions and mechanisms provides important information for making the proper diagnosis and for selecting the appropriate treatment, and their clinical assessment should be part of the diagnostic evaluation.

## Psychological Process and Psychiatric Research

Finally, the concept of psychological process has important implications for the future direction of psychiatric research. I have noted earlier how a familiarity with the process of dissociation not only points to a possible connection between multiple personality disorder and somatization disorder that is not readily apparent in a purely descriptive approach, but suggests areas of clinical research concerning the psychogenic mechanisms underlying somatization.

Beyond such clinically oriented studies, moreover, the process of dissociation itself could be the focus of psychophysiologic investigation. As I have noted elsewhere (Nemiah 1989b), the modern biological investigation of psychiatric disorders has thus far been primarily concerned with the correlation of phenomenologically derived clinical syndromes and pathologic brain states as manifested by abnormalities in brain structure and neurotransmitter systems. However important and dramatic the findings of this modern research, its correlations are static; they provide us only with cross-sectional pictures of pathologic states frozen in time that ignore the knowledge of psychodynamic processes elaborated over the past century. The recent resurgence of interest in dissociative disorders (and in particular in multiple personality disorder) has once again focused our attention on the psychological processes in human beings as they respond to and deal with the horror of traumatic experiences (Putnam 1985; Spiegel 1986). As a consequence, we are rediscovering the psychological phenomena of dissociation, unconscious motivation, and the psychogenesis of symptoms first elucidated by

Janet, Freud, and their contemporaries a hundred years ago (Nemiah 1989a; van der Kolk and van der Hart 1989). The psychology of these earlier investigators, however, was far in advance of their knowledge of pathophysiology. As a result, their concepts remained mainly psychological in nature, and they were unable to achieve the vital correlation between psychopathology and neuropathology that informs modern clinical concepts and is the goal of modern psychiatric research.

With the recent advent of brain-imaging techniques that permit us to observe neurophysiologic processes, we appear to be in sight of attaining that goal—provided that we focus our research efforts on correlating brain function with psychodynamic processes rather than merely with static phenomenological diagnostic syndromes alone. The empirically observed process of dissociation is a sharply defined psychological mechanism that provides an ideal starting point for such correlations, and their elucidation could lead to an increased understanding of the psychobiological foundations of mental illness as we exploit the legacy of our psychological forebears.

## REFERENCES

American Psychiatric Association: Diagnostic and Statistical Manual of Mental Disorders, 3rd Edition. Washington, DC, American Psychiatric Association, 1980

American Psychiatric Association: Diagnostic and Statistical Manual of Mental Disorders, 3rd Edition, Revised. Washington, DC, American Psychiatric Association, 1987

"B": An introspective analysis of co-conscious life. J Abnorm Psychol 3:311–334, 1908–1909

"B.C.A.": My life as a dissociated personality. J Abnorm Psychol 3:240–260, 1908–1909

Barsky AJ: Somatoform disorders, in Comprehensive Textbook of Psychiatry, 5th Edition. Edited by Kaplan HI, Sadock BJ. Baltimore, MD, Williams & Wilkins, 1989, pp 1009–1027

Bliss E: A symptom profile of patients with multiple personalities, including MMPI results. J Nerv Ment Dis 172:197–202, 1984

Braun BG: Treatment of Multiple Personality Disorder. Washington, DC, American Psychiatric Press, 1986

Coons PM, Bowman ES, Milstein V: Multiple personality disorder: a clinical investigation of 50 cases. J Nerv Ment Dis 176:519–527, 1988

Frankel FH: Hypnosis: Trance as a Coping Mechanism. New York, Plenum, 1976

Hilgard ER: Divided Consciousness: Multiple Controls in Human Thought and Action. New York, Wiley-Interscience, 1977

Janet P: L'Automatisme Psychologique. Paris, Félix Alcan, 1889

Nemiah JC: Alexithymia: theoretical considerations. Psychother Psychosom 28:199–206, 1977

Nemiah JC: Dissociative amnesia: a clinical and theoretical reconsideration, in Functional Disorders of Memory. Edited by Kihlstrom JF, Evans FJ, Hillsdale, NJ, Lawrence Erlbaum, 1979, pp 303–323

Nemiah JC: Janet redivivus (editorial). Am J Psychiatry 146:1527–1529, 1989a

Nemiah JC: The varieties of human experience. Br J Psychiatry 154:459–466, 1989b

Nemiah JC, Sifneos PE: Affect and fantasy in patients with psychosomatic disorders, in Modern Trends in Psychosomatic Medicine-2. Edited by Hill O. London, Butterworths, 1970, pp 26–34

Prince M: The Dissociation of a Personality. New York, Longmans, Green, 1906

Prince M: The Unconscious. New York, Macmillan, 1924

Putnam FW Jr: Dissociation as response to extreme trauma, in Childhood Antecedents of Multiple Personality. Edited by Kluft RP. Washington, DC, American Psychiatric Press, 1985, pp 65–97

Putnam FW, Guroff JJ, Silberman EK, et al: The clinical phenomenology of multiple personality disorder: review of 100 recent cases. J Clin Psychiatry 47:285–293, 1986

Ross CA, Heber S, Norton GR, et al: Somatic symptoms in multiple personality disorder. Psychosomatics 30:154–160, 1989

Ross CA, Miller SD, Reagor P, et al: Multicenter structured interview data on 102 cases of multiple personality disorder. Am J Psychiatry 147:602–607, 1990

Schreiber FR: Sybil. New York, Warner Books, 1974

Spiegel D: Dissociation, double binds, and posttraumatic stress in multiple personality disorder, in Treatment of Multiple Personality Disorder. Edited by Braun BG. Washington, DC, American Psychiatric Press, 1986, pp 61–77

van der Kolk B, van der Hart O: Pierre Janet and the breakdown of adaptation in psychological trauma. Am J Psychiatry 146:1530–1540, 1989

# Chapter 6

# Dissociation and Trauma

*by David Spiegel, M.D.*

Trauma such as rape, natural disaster, or combat can be understood as a sudden extreme discontinuity in a person's experience. Physical threat and damage undermine many basic assumptions by which people live, including their sense of control over their bodies and physical environment and their myth of invulnerability (Yalom 1980). It is therefore not surprising that the psychological reaction to trauma should incorporate discontinuities of experience such as dissociation. Dissociative defenses, which allow individuals to compartmentalize perceptions and memories, seem to perform a dual function. They help victims separate themselves from the full impact of physical trauma while it is occurring, and, by the same token, they may delay the necessary working through and putting into perspective of these traumatic experiences after they have occurred. They help the trauma victim maintain a sense of control during an episode of physical helplessness, but then become a mechanism by which the individual feels psychologically helpless once he or she has regained physical control.

## DISSOCIATION DURING TRAUMA

Dissociation is a special form of consciousness in which events that would ordinarily be connected are divided from one another (Hilgard 1977). Dissociation is defined in DSM-III-R (American Psychiatric Association 1987, p. 269) as "a disturbance or alteration in the normally integrative functions of identity, memory, or consciousness." Dissociation has an intrinsically paradoxical element in that information is unavailable to consciousness and yet indicates its presence. For example, a hypnotized subject may have amnesia for an instruction to touch his ear when the word *red* is spoken, yet will in fact do so. He may be unaware of performing the behavior. Nonetheless, the response to the cue indicates that the instruction is remembered. A clinical parallel is psychogenic amnesia. A rape victim may report no conscious memory for the assault and yet show signs of depression, stimulus sensitivity, and numbing of responsiveness, indicating clearly that the traumatic memories are active. Thus a dissociated memory is distinctly different from one that is simply forgotten.

Dissociation has another unusual feature. It serves as a defense not only against warded-off memories, fears, and wishes, but against trauma while it is occurring. It is quite common for victims to report dissociative experiences during traumatic experiences (Rose 1986; Spiegel et al. 1988). These spontaneous experiences are often extremely helpful in allowing the person to defend against overwhelming fear, pain, and helplessness. Many rape victims report that they experienced the rape as if they were floating above their own body, feeling sorry for the person undergoing the sexual assault. It has been well demonstrated that hypnotizable individuals can employ dissociative mechanisms to provide partial or complete relief of physical pain (Hilgard and Hilgard 1975; Spiegel and Bloom 1983). This splitting of consciousness can be seen as a normal phenomenon—for example, the "hidden observer" who feels pain during hypnotic analgesia (Hilgard 1977). Dissociative phenomena may also be elicited during formal hypnotic inductions (Nemiah 1985), which intensify the focus of attention (Spiegel and Spiegel 1978), and enhance specific responsiveness to the environment or suggestibility (Orne 1959). It would be surprising indeed if people did not spontaneously use this capacity to reduce their perception of pain during acute trauma. Many victims report a strange kind of unreality to a traumatic experience, a discontinuity in their consciousness that mirrors the sudden discontinuity in their physical reality. This alteration may be transient and adaptive, or it may lead to an ongoing rupture in self-integration, ranging from transient depersonalization through psychogenic amnesia and fugue to multiple personality disorder. Although these dissociative disorders may seem unusual and strange, this may be due in part to the fact that we take for granted our ability to assemble a coherent and unified self-concept.

The essence of trauma is physical helplessness, the loss of control over one's body and environment at a time when pain and damage are being threatened or inflicted. One's will and desire is overridden by another's brutality, by accident, or by nature's indifference. When physical control is lost, mental control becomes paramount. One way to maintain such control is to distance oneself from one's body:

> A petite young woman, who experienced an accidental fall from a third story balcony which resulted in a broken pelvis, described the event in the following manner. She was at a party talking to a friend when a large man standing next to her turned around suddenly, knocking her over the railing. When asked how terrifying she had found the experience, she responded that it was "quite pleasant." This surprising statement led to further inquiry which revealed that she had experienced the fall as though she had been standing on a nearby balcony watching "a pink cloud float down to the ground. I felt no pain and tried to walk back upstairs."

Such extreme alterations of perception are not uncommon among individuals subjected to extreme trauma. The study of coping responses during and immediately after trauma is relatively new, and consequently there are comparatively few systematic studies. These coping responses will be examined from two perspectives: 1) the distinctive phenomenology of the stress response during and immediately after physical trauma and 2) symptoms that predict later posttraumatic symptomatology.[1]

The immediate response to trauma often involves an experience of unreality with distortions of perception, memory, temporal processing, and relating to the environment. Alterations of mental state are the rule rather than the exception during and after trauma. For example, Titchener and Kapp (1976) observed some 15 months after a dam collapsed, effectively destroying the Buffalo Creek community, that approximately 80% of the survivors presented traumatic neurotic reactions.

---

[1]This section is partly based on a manuscript prepared for and presented to the DSM-IV Work Group on Psychiatric System Interface Disorders, written by D. Spiegel, E. Cardena, and R. Spitzer.

# DETACHMENT

A predominant defense against physical trauma is a sense of psychological detachment from the physical environment. This may take the form of a general numbing of responsiveness to all stimuli, or a more specific detachment from one's body, personal experience, or certain somatic sensations, such as pain. In a careful review of the experience of 14 correctional officers held hostage during a violent prison riot, Hillman (1981) described the common use of dissociative perceptual alterations, including physical numbness during beatings, decrease in pain sensation, time distortion, feeling "dazed," and being in a "state of shock."

> One hostage was kicked in the head, back, ribs and testicles. Eventually he "saw" all these things happening to him, but he did not feel anything. Or he felt it, but it did not hurt. Another hostage said, "I could see my body moving so I knew that I had been kicked . . . but I didn't feel anything." (p. 1195)

Another example of dissociative experience is Hillman's description of a "pseudorational state in which the hostage responded unquestioningly to any command" (p. 1195), analogous to hypnotic suggestibility (Orne 1959; Spiegel and Spiegel 1978).

That such detachment is the rule rather than the exception is illustrated by Noyes and Kletti's (1977) survey of 101 survivors of life-threatening danger, such as automobile accidents and physical assault. Of these survivors, 72% had experienced feelings of unreality and an altered passage of time during the event, 57% automatic movement, and 52% a sense of detachment. Other symptoms of depersonalization during danger were lack of emotion (56%) and feeling detached from the body (34%); 30% experienced derealization. A dissociation between observing and participating selves was noted: "I knew what I was doing but was not in control of it" (p. 379). A factor analysis of a similar group of 189 accident victims yielded depersonalization and hyperalertness factors as the most prominent responses (Noyes and Slymen 1978–1979). Similarly, when Madakasira and O'Brien (1987) interviewed 116 survivors of a series of tornadoes in which 9 people were killed and more than 150 injured, they found frequent reports of detachment (57%), diminished interest (45%), diminished libido (35%), and concentration difficulties (66%) on the Hopkins Symptom Checklist-90 (Derogatis et al. 1974).

A systematic report on the extent of depersonalization and derealization symptoms in victims of disaster has been provided by Wilkinson (1983; Menninger and Wilkinson 1988). He began collecting data 1 week after the collapse of the Hyatt Regency Hotel skywalk in which 114 people died and 200 were injured. Out of 103 usable questionnaires, he found that 36.3% of survivors mentioned an inability to feel deeply about anything and 29.4% mentioned feelings of detachment.

Initial (i.e., 12 days after the incident) and long-term reactions to an airplane crash landing were investigated in a study of 30 young male survivors (Sloan 1988). Of the symptoms of posttraumatic stress disorder (PTSD) (Table 6-1), 93% of the sample initially reported four or more symptoms. Most frequent was hyperalertness (endorsed by 82%) and decreased concentration or memory (79%); 54% reported feeling detached or estranged. Sloan cautioned, however, that psychic numbing and detachment might have been overinflated because of the difficulties in assessing them.

A similar study by Feinstein (1989) assessed the effects of a bloody ambush in

Namibia, Africa, on 14 soldiers and 3 indirect participants. A checklist of symptoms based on DSM-III (American Psychiatric Association 1980) criteria administered 1 week after the ambush indicated that 66% of the victims experienced sudden reliving of the attack, 41% showed markedly diminished interest in usual activities, and 24% reported feelings of detachment or estrangement. Feinstein concluded that 1 week after the incident a PTSD diagnosis could have been given to the 14 men involved in the ambush and to 1 indirectly involved. Of those 15 men, 1 had to be evacuated because of the severity of his psychiatric symptoms and 14 had persisting symptoms for an average of 9 days (range, 2–24), although during the first week they "functioned efficiently" despite the tension.

Peritraumatic detachment has been described as a sense of being dazed or stunned, with an associated loss of any kind of emotion (Kleinman 1989). Using a

Table 6-1.　Diagnostic criteria for posttraumatic stress disorder

A. The person has experienced an event that is outside the range of usual human experience and that would be markedly distressing to almost anyone.
B. The traumatic event is persistently reexperienced in at least one of the following ways:
  (1) recurrent and intrusive distressing recollections of the event
  (2) recurrent distressing dreams of the event
  (3) sudden acting or feeling as if the traumatic event were recurring
  (4) intense psychological distress at exposure to events that symbolize or resemble an aspect of the traumatic event, including anniversaries of the trauma
C. Persistent avoidance of stimuli associated with the trauma or numbing or general responsiveness (not present before the trauma), as indicated by at least three of the following:
  (1) efforts to avoid thoughts or feelings associated with the trauma
  (2) efforts to avoid activities or situations that arouse recollections of the trauma
  (3) inability to recall an important aspect of the trauma (psychogenic amnesia)
  (4) markedly diminished interest in significant activities
  (5) feeling of detachment or estrangement from others
  (6) restricted range of affect
  (7) sense of a foreshortened future
D. Persistent symptoms of increased arousal (not present before the trauma), as indicated by at least two of the following:
  (1) difficulty falling or staying asleep
  (2) irritability or outbursts of anger
  (3) difficulty concentrating
  (4) hypervigilance
  (5) exaggerated startle response
  (6) physiologic reactivity upon exposure to events that symbolize or resemble an aspect of the traumatic event
E. Duration of the disturbance of at least one month.

*Note:* Reprinted from DSM-III-R (1987) with permission from American Psychiatric Association.

participant-observer methodology, Valent (1984) reported such reactions to the Ash Wednesday bushfires in Victoria, Australia, "one of the worst natural disasters in its history." He collected reports both while the fires were occurring and afterward. Some people described extraordinary physical feats (e.g., analgesia for burns, being able to carry very heavy loads), reminiscent of phenomena sometimes reported in association with hypnotic procedures (Hilgard 1977; Spiegel 1985). In a more clinical study of the bushfires disaster, McFarlane (1986) reported that those that had the most intense exposure to the disaster or those who had next of kin die showed emotional constriction. Solomon et al. (1988, 1989) interviewed 104 Israeli soldiers suffering combat stress reactions (CSR) 1 year after the Lebanon War. Seventeen common symptoms were reported by at least 10% of the soldiers. Factor analysis yielded six clusters of symptoms. The most prominent, accounting for 20% of the variance, was psychic numbing (PN):

> The first and most important CSR factor, PN, comprises various methods of "distancing" or dissociating, for example, detachment and thinking about civilian life. PN is a very common occurrence faced with extreme and prolonged stress and appears to reflect the individual's attempt to escape, at least mentally. (p. 42)

Other factors included anxiety reactions (11%), guilt (9%), loneliness/helplessness (8%), loss of control (7%), and confusion/disorientation (6.5%).

Detachment may take the extreme form of out-of-body experiences during trauma. In a thorough study of 31 people who had been hostages (e.g., kidnappings, terrorist situations), Siegel (1984) found that during the hostage episode, 12.9% had out-of-body experiences; 25.8% had lapses of concentration, disorientation, alterations in body imagery and sensations (e.g., "feeling numb"), and dissociation (including depersonalization).

In his classic paper on acute grief of disaster victims from the Coconut Grove fire in Boston, Lindemann (1944) observed that in addition to other symptoms, his patients showed "commonly a slight sense of unreality," along with emotional distance and estrangement from other people. He mentioned that individuals trying to avoid doing "grief work" and reacting as if no loss had occurred had a greater probability of having a more pathologic and long-term form of grief reaction. Conceivably, reactions such as derealization, depersonalization, and numbing are distancing mechanisms that defend the person from unbearable current distress. However, such procedures may have only a short-term positive effect and end up perpetuating psychological and social maladjustment. Another example of this association between an overly effective short-term defense and poor long-term outcome is provided by McFarlane (1988b), who found that the best predictor of an acute maladjustment reaction to the Victoria bushfires was avoidance of thinking through problems, not attending debriefing sessions, and sustaining great property loss. Avoidance of thinking through problems was also a good predictor of persistent chronic forms of PTSD.

Thus a number of studies provide evidence that one-quarter to more than half of trauma victims experience detachment, often accompanied by difficulty concentrating, conscious avoidance, and alteration in somatic function or perception. The mental mechanism involved is a compartmentalization of experience, creating the illusion that the event "did not happen to me." For example, one woman with a dissociative disorder responded to rape by creating a new dissociated personality with the name of "No One." She later reflected that "No one was raped" and was amnesic for the episode. When in the dissociated state the memories became available, and she said she was made to feel like "a nobody." The unreality of a sudden traumatic experience is mirrored in a mental structure that seems unreal and separate (dissociated) from ordinary experience. The mental discontinuity reflects the physical discontinuity of the trauma.

## ALTERATIONS IN MEMORY

Memory impairment may take the form described above of total amnesia for a period of time, usually that encompassing the trauma and immediate aftermath, or for discrete units of time during the trauma. Such phenomena are coherent with the theory of state-dependent memory (Bower 1982), which holds that content and affect are linked. To have best recall of mental content, one must be in a state of mind at the time of retrieval that is congruent with that in which the information was acquired. To remember painful events one must reexperience painful affect. Hence the way to avoid reexperiencing pain, fear, and helplessness is to dissociate the memories of events in which those emotions were experienced.

In a study of tornado victims (Madakasira and O'Brien 1987), 61% of the sample expressed some form of memory impairment, whereas Wilkinson (1983) found that 27.4% of the Hyatt Regency skywalk collapse survivors had some form of memory deficit. It is conceivable that the discrepancy in figures may reflect the sensitivity of the instruments to evaluate memory impairment, which may take different forms.

There is an on-off quality to dissociative experience (Spiegel et al. 1988), and the alternative form of memory impairment is intense reliving of the traumatic event as if it were occurring in the present. That is, the memory is not dissociated, but subsequent history is. The fact that one did indeed survive the catastrophe is not part of awareness when its memory is relived. This is analogous to hypnotic age regression, in which an individual relives the past as though it were the present (Spiegel and Rosenfeld 1984; Spiegel and Spiegel 1978).

Vivid memories or flashbacks are characteristic of PTSD (e.g., Horowitz 1986). Wilkinson (1983) reported that 88.2% of his sample had repeated recollections of disaster; Valent (1984) reported that attention to the fire disaster was so great that later memories of the event were very vivid, particularly when associated cues were present. Madakasira and O'Brien (1987) reported that 82% of their sample had intrusive thoughts, and 44% had recurrent dreams, presumably some of them about the disaster. Feinstein (1989) reported that two-thirds of the ambush victims he studied experienced sudden reliving of the attack.

Even though flashbacks are commonly found in association with psychopathology, they can also be found among well-adjusted individuals and are not per se signs of psychopathology, either organic or functional. Flashbacks may be a manifestation of normal attentional and memory processes (McGee 1984). McFarlane (1988a), for instance, reported that imagery alone is not an accurate predictor of the presence of PTSD. However, Meuser and Butler (1987) found a correlation between the intensity of imagery and severity of combat exposure among Vietnam veterans with PTSD. Thus it may well be that such dissociative defenses, which help individuals master trauma as it occurs, predispose them to later symptoms, such as those of PTSD.

## DISSOCIATIVE ALTERATIONS OF PERCEPTION

Hallucinatory experiences have been reported among concentration camp inmates (Jaffe 1968) and in 12% of a sample of 100 women interviewed immediately after childbirth (Farley et al. 1968). Further, 7% of the latter sample reported anesthesia to pain and 5% reported unconsciousness during the delivery. In her study of 23 children kidnapped in a school bus and held for several days in a truck, Terr (1979, 1988) found that 8 children had misperceived or hallucinated (e.g., sounds of footsteps) during the ordeal, and other children reported these phenomena later on. In addition, 8 children had a distorted sense of time in which events of the traumatic incident, or this in relation to other activities, were not arranged in the correct sequential order, which Terr has called "time skew."

Siegel (1984) found that approximately one-fourth of hostages he studied had hallucinatory experiences while captive. The first phenomena experienced were flashes of light and sometimes geometric patterns in the periphery of the visual field. More complex and realistic visual hallucinations appeared during later stages of the hostage experience. Interestingly, these visual experiences are remarkably similar to those of highly hypnotizable individuals in a hypnotic context with minimal suggestions (Cardena 1988). Further, highly hypnotizable individuals are capable of producing visual hallucinations so vivid that they result in alteration of event-related potentials to visual stimuli (Spiegel et al. 1985). Siegel speculated that the presence of hallucinations is elicited by the combination of both being isolated and facing the threat of death.

## BRIEF REACTIVE DISSOCIATIVE DISORDER

These and other observations have led to a proposal for the inclusion of a new-diagnostic category entitled brief reactive dissociative disorder[1] (Table 6-2). There

Table 6-2.    Brief reactive dissociative disorder

---

A. *Trauma*: The person has experienced an event that would be markedly distressing to almost anyone.
B. *Dissociation*: a disconnection of perception and memory from affect:
   (1) stupor
   (2) derealization
   (3) depersonalization
   (4) numbing or detachment
   (5) amnesia
C. *Disability*:
   (1) interferes with social or occupational functioning
   (2) prevents the individual from pursuing some necessary task
D. *Duration*: less than 4 weeks.

---

[1]This section is partly based on a manuscript prepared for and presented to the DSM-IV Work Group on Psychiatric System Interface Disorders, written by D. Spiegel, E. Cardena, and R. Spitzer.

was no place in DSM-III-R to describe symptoms of an acute as opposed to delayed (1 month or more) reaction to trauma. The current adjustment disorder with anxious mood category is inappropriate in that the nature of the stressor can be quite mild and the symptoms may also be mild and are limited to "nervousness, worry, and jitteriness." PTSD cannot by definition begin until 1 month after the trauma. Furthermore, there was little recognition in the psychiatric nosology of the prominence of dissociative features in the acute response to trauma.

## HYPNOSIS AND POSTTRAUMATIC STRESS DISORDER

Hypnosis can be understood as controlled and structured dissociation (Nemiah 1985; Spiegel and Spiegel 1978). There are three prominent components to the hypnotic experience. The first is absorption, or total involvement in one perception, idea, or memory at the expense of others (Frischholz et al. 1987; Spiegel 1988, 1990; Tellegen 1981; Tellegen and Atkinson 1974). The second component, dissociation, is compartmentalization of experience, which is a complementary attribute to the absorption. The more intensely a person focuses on one aspect of consciousness, the more other aspects are likely to be relegated to the periphery of awareness. Things that would ordinarily be conscious now come to seem unconscious. Thus a hypnotized individual may respond to a series of instructions without any conscious memory of having heard the instructions (Hilgard 1977; Spiegel and Spiegel 1978). The third main component of hypnotic experience, what has been called suggestibility, is a heightened responsiveness to social cues (Orne 1959; H Spiegel 1974). Because a person in the hypnotic state is fully absorbed in only one or two aspects of awareness, such a subject is less likely to judge or evaluate the meaning of the experience. Thus, if given an instruction in a hypnotic state, a subject is less likely to question the motivation of the person giving the instruction or think through the consequences of acting on it. It is not that hypnotized individuals are in any way deprived of their will, but they are less likely to act on it or be aware of it. Indeed, they may come to experience an instruction from someone else as if it were their own idea (Evans 1979). This source amnesia lends a sense of involuntariness to hypnotic experiences. Even though people choose to act in hypnotic and dissociative states, their actions may seem mysteriously imposed from outside. Even if they attribute the idea to themselves, they experience their action as relatively automatic. This sense of involuntariness associated with hypnotic phenomena fits naturally with the sense of involuntariness imposed on a victim of trauma, the essence of which is physical helplessness.

Indeed, the three major categories of symptomatology of PTSD in DSM-III-R are quite analogous to the extreme major components of hypnotic dissociation (Table 6-3). The sudden reliving of a traumatic event, not as a memory but as if it were recurring in the present tense, is very much like hypnotic absorption, in which the memories are so vivid they are not experienced as memories but rather as a reexperiencing of the trauma with the associated intense affect.

The second major category, the loss of pleasure or numbing of responsiveness, carries with it the flavor of dissociation. The dissociated traumatic memories tend to remove the PTSD patient from the full range of affective response. They are left feeling not quite whole and unable to respond fully to usually pleasurable activities. Thus the defense compartmentalization of traumatic memories has as its price a loss of the full range of affective responses.

Finally, the third category of PTSD symptoms includes startle responses and other exaggerated sensitivity to stimuli reminiscent of the traumatic experience. This can be viewed as analogous to suggestibility: heightened and uncritical response to social cues. The woman who is raped in an elevator finds the environment of an elevator enough to provoke a full-scale reenactment of the assault.

There is accumulating evidence of a link between trauma and latter dissociative symptoms. Two studies have now shown that Vietnam veterans with PTSD are more hypnotizable than normal controls. Stutman and Bliss (1985) compared the hypnotizability of nonpatient veterans who were high in PTSD symptoms with those who were low and found that the symptomatic group were more hypnotizable. Our group (Spiegel et al. 1988) compared the hypnotizability of 65 Vietnam veterans with PTSD to that of a normal comparison population and to patients with schizophrenia, affective disorders, and generalized anxiety disorders. The PTSD group had hypnotizability scores that were higher than those of all the other groups. Indeed, their scores were twice the mean scores obtained for schizophrenic patients (Spiegel et al. 1982). Hermann et al. (1989) studied traumatic histories in patients with borderline personality disorder. They found a high prevalence of such trauma but, in particular, noted that dissociative symptoms were strongly predicted by a traumatic history, even more so than a borderline diagnosis per se. These recent findings are congruent with Hilgard's (1970) early observations that highly hypnotizable students had a history with more frequent reports of punishment than low hypnotizable students. Indeed, she noted that it was possible that hypnotic or dissociative capacity might be useful in "escaping from an otherwise unpleasant reality."

## POSTTRAUMATIC MULTIPLE PERSONALITY DISORDER

Hypnotizability is a normal form of dissociative response, but it has recently been observed that patients with pathologic dissociation such as multiple personality disorder also report a very high prevalence of repeated childhood trauma, particularly physical and sexual abuse. Reports of the prevalence of such abuse in patients with multiple personality disorder range as high as 90% (Coons and Milstein 1986; Frischholz 1985; Putnam et al. 1986).

Clinically, these patients will often report that they first dissociated when the physical abuse began. A so-called protector personality emerges to take over for the patient, who is allowed to escape psychologically from the punishment. One such personality emerged during a first episode of sexual abuse by the patient's father.

Table 6-3. Analogies between hypnotic experience and PTSD

| Hypnosis | DSM-III-R PTSD |
| --- | --- |
| | Trauma |
| Absorption | Reexperiencing of traumatic event |
| Dissociation | Numbing of general responsiveness |
| Suggestibility | Increased arousal |

*Note.* PTSD = posttraumatic stress disorder.

The personality said, "You don't want to be with him. You come and be with me." It is interesting that often such protector personalities turn on the primary personality after the physical abuse stops. They cease to be defenders and become identified with the aggressor, thereby perpetuating the unconscious belief that the punishment inflicted on the child was deserved rather than unwarranted. Their very ability to absorb repeated abuse from parents comes to imply to such patients that they somehow deserved it, or even encouraged and participated in it. Very often these patients report having provoked assault as a way of protecting younger siblings from similar abuse; or it may be that such reports are their way of controlling in fantasy what they were helpless in fact to avoid. Clearly, again, dissociative capacity emerges as a means of coping with trauma and as a posttraumatic symptom. Indeed, multiple personality may be conceptualized as a chronic, severe PTSD (Spiegel 1984).

The highly prevalent history of physical and sexual abuse during the childhood of patients with multiple personality disorder (Coons and Milstein 1986; Frischholz 1985; Putnam et al. 1986), and the observation that a history of severe punishment in childhood is associated with higher hypnotizability (Hilgard 1970) provide further support for the concept of dissociation as a psychological defense against trauma (Braun 1984; Kluft 1984; Spiegel 1984, 1986). Bliss (1984) reported that patients with multiple personality disorder were significantly more hypnotizable than patients seeking treatment for cigarette smoking or college student controls. Although this finding is consistent with the above theory, the study is limited by the absence of controls for age and severity of psychiatric illness, and the examiners were not blind to the patient's diagnosis.

This dissociative understanding of multiple personality disorder suggests that psychotherapy must involve helping patients face and bear the traumatic experience while integrating it into a view of the self that is not overwhelmed by the trauma and yet does not dismiss its importance. The severity of dissociation in PTSD and multiple personality disorder implies a need for association. The sudden discontinuity of the traumatic experience and the patient's response to it needs to be smoothed by repeated access to and gradual integration of dissociated memories. Dissociation is at once an adaptive and yet problematic response to trauma. Controlled use of structured dissociation in therapy can help provide an effective means of mastering and working through traumatic memories.

## PSYCHOTHERAPY OF TRAUMATIC DISSOCIATION

Although dissociative defenses are effective in helping trauma victims manage fear, pain, and helplessness, they seem to carry a cost. The striking control they may provide the victim at the time of trauma may result in a failure to work through the experience, resulting in a loss of control over one's mental state, with intrusive reliving of the trauma, dissociative numbing of response, and hyperresponsiveness to stimuli reminiscent of the episode. Physical helplessness is translated into an inability to control memories of the event. The self-concept is fragmented, with dysjunctive views of the self stored separately. The degradation inflicted seems total and the outcome once again uncertain when the traumatic memories are relived. At other times, such individuals seek to act as though the trauma had never occurred. That such alterations of perception and concentration might lead to later symptomatology is suggested by McFarlane's (1988c) report that the best predictor of later PTSD symptomatology was an initial disturbance of attention and concentration.

Freud's two main topographies of the mind—unconscious, preconscious, and conscious; and ego, id, and superego—are top-down models. Theoretically, material can be moved from one place to another with little transformation. Dissociationist models, starting with Janet (1920; see also van der Kolk and van der Hart 1989) and since revived (Hilgard 1977) are more bottom-up in nature. The content of material as it is stored dictates patterns of interaction with other material (Spiegel 1990). Dissociated memories of the traumatized self are inconsistent with the normal and fully controlling self. Thus, memories reinforcing one self-image conflict with the other instrinsically, and so tend to exclude the other from consciousness, yielding dissociative symptoms. It may be that such symptoms are especially elicited by the sudden discontinuities in human experience induced by trauma. Effective treatment requires integrating these disparate self-schemas (Horowitz 1986). This is analogous to writing a path command in a DOS-type computer, allowing it to find information in a different directory no matter which directory it is in. This allows the patient to modulate the conflicting self-images and to integrate traumatic memories consciously (Spiegel 1981, 1990).

The psychotherapy of individuals suffering acute traumatic dissociative reactions can be summarized by eight "C" principles (Table 6-4).

1. Confrontation.  Trauma must be confronted. Such patients often present with a series of symptoms such as confusion, depression, and anxiety not clearly connected to traumatic experience in their mind, which is not surprising given the nature of the dissociative process. A careful history indicating acute onset of symptoms in conjunction with a traumatic experience can help clarify the diagnosis
2. Condensation.  A condensation of the traumatic experience, in the form of a memory, or series of memories that epitomize but may not exhaustively represent the trauma should be found. Techniques such as hypnosis may be quite helpful in allowing patients to relive the experiences and recover psychogenic amnesia. Patients with limited initial recall can also be helped by asking them about the time just prior to the trauma or by inquiring about the physical setting in which the event occurred.
3. Confession.  Confession is necessary. Patients often feel profoundly ashamed of their experience, either because of inappropriate guilt about the circumstances or simply because they felt humiliated by their own fear and the indignity of the episode. The guilt, if present, must be addressed, because it prevents them from facing and bearing the helplessness that is inevitable with trauma by giving them the fantasy that they could have controlled the situation.

Table 6-4.  Eight "C" principles of psychotherapy of acute traumatic dissociative reaction

| | |
|---|---|
| 1. Confrontation | 5. Consciousness |
| 2. Condensation | 6. Concentration |
| 3. Confession | 7. Control |
| 4. Consolation | 8. Congruence |

4. Consolation. Consolation is critical. Patients will expect rejection if not further traumatization from the therapist, so steps to comfort them actively are crucial. A simple "I'm sorry this happened" can go a long way. Professionally appropriate expressions of sympathy help the patient feel less alone with the new and upsetting image of self created by the trauma.

5. Consciousness. Patients may need help to make the material conscious. This implies to them that what happened is not so terrible that it cannot be faced. Furthermore, this provides the opportunity for restructuring the memories, allowing patients, for example, to face their helplessness while examining what they did to protect themselves. Their recollection is then   not totally demoralizing, but balanced by a review of their efforts at self-preservation or helping others.

6. Concentration. Focused concentration such as hypnosis may be used to facilitate this work. The rather explicit on-off quality of the hypnotic state is reassuring to patients in that it provides the promise of turning off the memories after they are turned on. This hypnotic work can be facilitated through the use of an imaginary screen on which patients visualize on one side what was done to them, and on the other what they did to protect themselves. An explicit self-hypnosis exercise can be used as a ceremony through which patients can work through their memories and feelings at certain times each day, and then set them aside.

7. Control. Control is crucial. Trauma victims have been made helpless by the situation (e.g., assault, earthquake, war), and they recapitulate that in a sense of helplessness over their mental state. Therapeutic sensitivity to their ability to manage memories and the associated affect is important. Patients must be made to feel in control of the memories, even as they use them to face their physical helplessness at the time of the trauma.

8. Congruence. Congruence is the goal of therapy. Patients can benefit from an approach that helps them to integrate traumatic memories in such a way that they do not overwhelmingly conflict with previous self-concepts. This means restructuring them so that they are bearable in consciousness because they are not unidimensional. They come to represent both trauma and the response to it, and are thus made suitable for integration.


## SUMMARY

There is considerable evidence that dissociative symptoms are prominent in the response of individuals undergoing physical trauma and in its immediate aftermath. They serve as a defense against pain, fear, helplessness, and panic, providing a welcome feeling of detachment from a terrifying physical reality and the emotions associated with it. This sense of detachment includes depersonalization, derealization, and other alterations in perception and memory. While less is known about those variables that predict good versus poor outcome, there is evidence that dissociative disturbances of concentration during the traumatic episode predict later PTSD symptomatology. It may be that such defenses are quite effective during trauma, but they may prevent working through the experience after it is over. This understanding of trauma offers opportunities for rapid and effective psychotherapeutic intervention.

# REFERENCES

American Psychiatric Association: Diagnostic and Statistical Manual of Mental Disorders, 3rd Edition. Washington, DC, American Psychiatric Association, 1980

American Psychiatric Association: Diagnostic and Statistical Manual of Mental Disorders, 3rd Edition, Revised. Washington, DC, American Psychiatric Association, 1987

Bliss EL: Spontaneous self-hypnosis in multiple personality disorder. Psychiatr Clin North Am 7:135–148, 1984

Bower G: Mood and memory. Am Psychol 36:129–148, 1982

Braun BG: Towards a theory of multiple personality and other dissociative phenomena. Psychiatr Clin North Am 7:171–194, 1984

Cardena E: The phenomenology of quiescent and physically active deep hypnosis. Paper presented at the 39th annual meeting of the Society for Clinical and Experimental Hypnosis, Asheville, NC, 1988

Coons PM, Milstein V: Psychosexual disturbances in multiple personality: characteristics, etiology, and treatment. J Clin Psychiatry 47:106–110, 1986

Derogatis LR, Lipman RS, Rickels K, et al: The Hopkins Symptom Checklist (HSCL): a self-report symptom inventory. Behav Sci 19:1–15, 1974

Evans FJ: Contextual forgetting: posthypnotic source amnesia. J Abnorm Psychol 88:556–563, 1979

Farley J, Woodruff R, Guze S: The prevalence of hysteria and conversion symptoms. Br J Psychiatry 114:1121–1125, 1968

Feinstein A: Posttraumatic stress disorder: a descriptive study supporting DSM-III-R criteria. Am J Psychiatry 146:665–666, 1989

Frischholz EJ: The relationship among dissociation, hypnosis and child abuse in the development of MPD, in Childhood Antecedents of Multiple Personality. Edited by Kluft RP. Washington, DC, American Psychiatric Press, 1985, pp 99–126

Frischholz EJ, Spiegel D, Trentalange MJ, et al: The Hypnotic Induction Profile and absorption. Am J Clin Hypn 30:87–93, 1987

Herman JL, Perry JC, van der Kolk BA: Childhood trauma in borderline personality disorder. Am J Psychiatry 146:490–495, 1989

Hilgard ER: Hypnotic Susceptibility. New York, Harcourt, Brace & World, 1965

Hilgard ER: Divided Consciousness: Multiple Controls in Human Thought and Action. New York, John Wiley, 1977

Hilgard ER, Hilgard JR: Hypnosis in the Relief of Pain. Los Altos, CA, William Kaufmann, 1975

Hilgard ER: Personality and Hypnosis: A Study of Imaginative Involvement. Chicago, IL, University of Chicago Press, 1970

Hillman RG: The psychopathology of being held hostage. Am J Psychiatry 138:1193–1197, 1981

Horowitz MJ: Stress Response Syndromes, 2nd Edition. Hillsdale, NJ, Jason Aronson, 1986

Jaffe R: Dissociative phenomena in former concentration camp inmates. Int J Psychoanal 49:310–312, 1968

Janet P: The Major Symptoms of Hysteria. New York, Macmillan, 1920

Kleinman SB: A terrorist hijacking: victims' experience initially and 9 years later. Journal of Traumatic Stress 2:49–58, 1989

Kluft RP: An introduction to multiple personality disorder. Psychiatr Clin North Am 14:21–24, 1984

Lindemann E: Symptomatology and management of acute grief. Am J Psychiatry 101:141–148, 1944

Madakasira S, O'Brien K: Acute posttraumatic stress disorder in victims of a natural disaster. J Nerv Ment Dis 175:286–290, 1987

McFarlane AC: Posttraumatic morbidity of a disaster. J Nerv Ment Dis 174:4–14, 1986

McFarlane AC: The aetiology of post-traumatic stress disorders following a natural disaster. Br J Psychiatry 152:116–121, 1988a

McFarlane AC: The longitudinal course of posttraumatic morbidity. J Nerv Ment Dis 176:30–39, 1988b

McFarlane AC: The phenomenology of posttraumatic stress disorders following a natural disaster. J Nerv Ment Dis 176:22–29, 1988c

McGee R: Flashbacks and memory phenomena. J Nerv Ment Dis 172:273–278, 1984

Menninger WW, Wilkinson CB: The aftermath of a catastrophe: the Hyatt Regency disaster. Bull Menninger Clin 52:65–74, 1988

Meuser KT, Butler RW: Auditory hallucination in combat-related chronic posttraumatic stress disorder. Am J Psychiatry 144:299–302, 1987

Nemiah JC: Dissociative disorders, in Comprehensive Textbook of Psychiatry, Vol 1, 4th Edition. Edited by Kaplan HI, Sadock BJ. Baltimore, MD, Williams & Wilkins, 1985, pp 942–957

Noyes R, Kletti R: Depersonalization in response to life-threatening danger. Compr Psychiatry 18:375–384, 1977

Noyes R, Slymen DJ: The subjective response to life-threatening danger. Omega 9:313–321, 1978-1979

Orne MT: The nature of hypnosis: artifact and essence. Journal of Abnormal and Social Psychology 58:277–299, 1959

Putnam FW, Guroff JJ, Silberman EK, et al: The clinical phenomenology of multiple personality disorder: review of 100 recent cases. J Clin Psychiatry 47:285–293, 1986

Rose DS: "Worse than death": psychodynamics of rape victims and the need for psychotherapy. Am J Psychiatry 143:817–824, 1986

Siegel RK: Hostage hallucinations. J Nerv Ment Dis 172:264–272, 1984

Sloan P: Post-traumatic stress in survivors of an airplane crash landing: a clinical and exploratory research intervention. Journal of Traumatic Stress 1:211–229, 1988

Solomon Z, Mikulincer M, Bleich A: Characteristic expressions of combat-related posttraumatic stress disorder Israeli soldiers in the 1982 Lebanon war. Behav Medicine Winter 1988, pp 171–178

Solomon Z, Mikulincer M, Benbenisty R: Combat stress reaction: clinical manifestations and correlates. Military Psychology 1:35–47, 1989

Spiegel D: Hypnotizability and psychoactive medication. Am J Clin Hypn 22:217–222, 1980

Spiegel D: Vietnam grief work using hypnosis. Am J Clin Hypn 24:33–40, 1981

Spiegel D: Multiple personality as a posttraumatic stress disorder. Psychiatr Clin North Am 7:101–110, 1984

Spiegel D: The use of hypnosis in controlling cancer pain. Cancer 35:221–231, 1985

Spiegel D: Dissociating damage. Am J Clin Hypn 29:123–131, 1986

Spiegel D: Hypnosis, in The American Psychiatric Press Textbook of Psychiatry. Edited by Talbott JA, Hales RE, Yudofsky SC. Washington, DC, American Psychiatric Press, 1988, pp 907–928

Spiegel D: Hypnosis, dissociation and trauma: hidden and overt observers, in Repression and Dissociation. Edited by Singer J. Chicago, IL, University of Chicago Press, 1990

Spiegel D, Bloom JR: Pain in metastatic breast cancer. Cancer 52:341–345, 1983

Spiegel D, Rosenfeld A: Spontaneous hypnotic age regression: case report. J Clin Psychiatry 45:522–524, 1984

Spiegel D, Detrick D, Frischholz EJ: Hypnotizability and psychopathology. Am J Psychiatry 136:777–781, 1982

Spiegel D, Cutcomb S, Ren C, et al: Hypnotic hallucination alters evoked potentials. J Abnorm Psychol 94:249–255, 1985

Spiegel D, Hunt T, Dondershine HE: Dissociation and hypnotizability in posttraumatic stress disorder. Am J Psychiatry 145:301–305, 1988

Spiegel H: The Grade 5 Syndrome: the highly hypnotizable person. Int J Clin Exp Hypn 22:303–319, 1974

Spiegel H, Spiegel D: Trance and Treatment: Clinical Uses of Hypnosis. New York, Basic Books, 1978 (Reprinted, Washington, DC, American Psychiatric Press, 1987)

Stutman RK, Bliss EL: Posttraumatic stress disorder, hypnotizability, and imagery. Am J Psychiatry 142:741–743, 1985

Tellegen A: Practicing the two disciplines for relaxation and enlightenment: comment on "Role of the Feedback Signal in Electromyograph Biofeedback: The Relevance of Attention" by Qualls and Sheehan. J Exp Psychol [Gen] 110:217–226, 1981

Tellegen A, Atkinson G: Openness to absorbing and self-altering experiences ("absorption"), a trait related to hypnotic susceptibility. J Abnorm Psychol 83:268–277, 1974

Terr LC: Children of Chowchilla: a study of psychic trauma, in The Psychoanalytic Study of the Child. Edited by Solnit AJ, Eissler R, Freud A, et al. New Haven, CT, Yale University Press, 1979, pp 547–623

Terr LC: What happens to early memories of trauma? A study of twenty children under age five at the time of documented traumatic events. J Am Acad Child Adolesc Psychiatry 27:96–104, 1988

Titchener JL, Kapp FT: Family and character change at Buffalo Creek. Am J Psychiatry 133:295–299, 1976

Valent P: The Ash Wednesday bushfires in Victoria. Med J Aust 141:291–300, 1984

van der Kolk B, van der Hart O: Pierre Janet and the breakdown of adaptation in psychological trauma. Am J Psychiatry 146:1530–1540, 1989

Wilkinson CB: Aftermath of a disaster: the collapse of the Hyatt Regency Hotel skywalks. Am J Psychiatry 140:1134–1139, 1983

Yalom ID: Existential Psychotherapy. New York, Basic Books, 1980

# Afterword

## by David Spiegel, M.D.

Recent research suggests that dissociation is more likely to happen during and in the aftermath of physical trauma. Depersonalization, derealization, and psychogenic amnesia are common symptoms during natural disasters, combat, and other forms of physical trauma. In turn, a history of trauma has been found to be an almost universal etiology of such extreme chronic dissociative disorders as multiple personality disorder. In these cases the failure of integration of memory and identity serves a defensive purpose—against painful affect, recognition of physical helplessness, and physical pain. While such defenses can be quite adaptive, they carry with them a risk of failure to work through traumatic events, leading to chronic and severe posttraumatic dissociative symptoms in some instances.

In his review of dissociative phenomena, Dr. Putnam emphasized the continuity between normal and abnormal failures of integration and noted physiological differences reflecting the variety of dissociative states. Dr. Loewenstein provided a comprehensive review of psychogenic amnesia and fugue, noting the frequent association of these disorders with sudden trauma. Dr. Steinberg observed that depersonalization disorder is an unusual dissociative symptom in that it co-occurs with a wide variety of other disorders, including anxiety and somatoform disorders. Dr. Kluft provided a concise and clear overview of the diagnosis and treatment of multiple personality disorder, emphasizing the structure necessary for effective psychotherapy, including recognition of transference problems elicited by early life trauma and the use of hypnosis. Dr. Nemiah provided a cogent argument for a reconciliation between the estranged conversion and dissociative disorders. In my chapter I reviewed the evidence linking trauma and dissociation.

Dissociation is an intrinsically interesting phenomenon. It seems to occur during experiences of physical trauma and to persist afterward, allowing individuals to ward off memories of abuse or trauma and the associated painful affects, but at the price of a sense of fragmentation, an inability to integrate and control memories, and a sense of demoralization. It is a disorder in which the part becomes the whole. The extremity of self as viewed during trauma comes to seem to be the real truth about a person, making for sudden and dizzying shifts in self-appraisal and mood. There are a variety of techniques, ranging from hypnosis to other kinds of psychotherapy that are clearly effective in helping patients manage dissociative disorders. Indeed, this is one of the hopeful areas in the domain of psychotherapy. Specific treatments have been shown to be efficacious, often more so than biologic treatments, which are generally adjunctive at best. It is hoped that in the future we will learn more about specific and effective psychotherapeutic techniques, new approaches to younger patients with dissociative disorders, and the psychophysiology of dissociation. As such, dissociation presents an unusual opportunity for advances in psychiatric research and treatment.

# Contributors

**Richard P. Kluft, M.D.**
Director, Dissociative Disorders Program, Institute of Pennsylvania Hospital, Philadelphia, PA

**Richard Loewenstein, M.D.**
Director of the Dissociative Disorders Program at Sheppard and Enoch Pratt Hospital, Baltimore, MD. Assistant Clinical Professor, Department of Psychiatry and Behavioral Sciences, University of Maryland School of Medicine, Baltimore, MD

**John C. Nemiah, M.D.**
Professor of Psychiatry, Dartmouth Medical School, Hanover, NH Emeritus Professor of Psychiatry, Harvard Medical School, Cambridge, MA

**Frank W. Putnam, M.D.**
Chief, Unit on Dissociative Disorders, Laboratory of Developmental Psychology, National Institute of Mental Health, Bethesda, MD

**David Spiegel, M.D.**
Professor of Psychiatry and Behavioral Sciences, Stanford University School of Medicine, Stanford, CA

**Marlene Steinberg, M.D.**
Associate Research Scientist, Yale University School of Medicine, New Haven, CT

# About The Sidran Foundation

The Sidran Foundation, Inc. is a national non-profit organization devoted to education, advocacy, and research on behalf of people with psychiatric disabilities, including individuals who have experienced mental health problems as a result of catastrophic trauma.

Currently available from the Sidran Press, the foundation's publishing division, is *Multiple Personality Disorder from the Inside Out* (1991), Cohen, Giller, and W., editors. In this acclaimed collection of personal writings, 146 people who have MPD and their significant others reveal the complex issues of diagnosis, therapy, and maintaining personal relationships. Forthcoming titles of related interest include *PTSD: A Survivor's Guide to Combat Trauma*, and *Knowing the Ropes: Advocacy for Consumers of Psychiatric Services*.

The foundation provides information for consumers, families, and professionals and maintains lists of therapists, support networks, publications and other resources specialized in the areas of trauma-induced emotional disabilities. The Sidran Foundation Bookshelf, a direct-mail book and tape distribution service, offers a carefully selected, annotated list of print and audio-visual materials about multiple personalities and dissociation.

For further information contact:

The Sidran Foundation and Press
2328 West Joppa Road, Suite 15
Lutherville, MD 21093
(410) 825-8888 phone; (410) 337-0747 fax